21st Century Keynesian Economics

International Papers in Political Economy Series
Series Editors: Philip Arestis and Malcolm Sawyer

This is the sixth volume of the new series of *International Papers in Political Economy (IPPE)*. The new series will consist of an annual volume with four to five papers on a single theme. The objective of the *IPPE* will continue to be the publication of papers dealing with important topics within the broad framework of Political Economy.

The original series of *International Papers in Political Economy* started in 1993 and has been published in the form of three issues a year with each issue containing a single extensive paper. Information on the old series and back copies can be obtained from Professor Malcolm Sawyer at the University of Leeds (e-mail: mcs@lubs.leeds.ac.uk)

Titles include:
Philip Arestis and Malcolm Sawyer (*editors*)

PATH DEPENDENCY AND MACROECONOMICS

CRITICAL ESSAYS ON THE PRIVATISATION EXPERIENCE

POLITICAL ECONOMY OF LATIN AMERICA
Recent Economic Performance

ALTERNATIVE PERSPECTIVES ON ECONOMIC POLICIES IN
THE EUROPEAN UNION

FINANCIAL LIBERALIZATION
Beyond Orthodox Concerns.

21st CENTURY KEYNESIAN ECONOMICS

International Papers in Political Economy
Series Standing Order ISBN 978–1–4039–9936–8

You can receive future titles in this series as they are published by placing a standing order. Please contact your bookseller or, in case of difficulty, write to us at the address below with your name and address, the title of the series and one of the ISBNs quoted above.

Customer Services Department, Macmillan Distribution Ltd, Houndmills, Basingstoke, Hampshire RG21 6XS, England

---

21st Century Keynesian Economics

Edited by

Philip Arestis

and

Malcolm Sawyer

First published 2010 by
PALGRAVE MACMILLAN

Palgrave Macmillan in the UK is an imprint of Macmillan Publishers Limited, registered in England, company number 785998, of Houndmills, Basingstoke, Hampshire RG21 6XS.

Palgrave Macmillan in the US is a division of St Martin's Press LLC, 175 Fifth Avenue, New York, NY 10010.

Palgrave Macmillan is the global academic imprint of the above companies and has companies and representatives throughout the world.

Palgrave® and Macmillan® are registered trademarks in the United States, the United Kingdom, Europe and other countries.

ISBN 978–0–230–23601–1   hardback

This book is printed on paper suitable for recycling and made from fully managed and sustained forest sources. Logging, pulping and manufacturing processes are expected to conform to the environmental regulations of the country of origin.

A catalogue record for this book is available from the British Library.

Library of Congress Cataloging-in-Publication Data

21st century Keynesian economics / edited by Philip Arestis and Malcolm Sawyer.
    p. cm. — (International papers in political economy series)
    ISBN 978–0–230–23601–1 (alk. paper)
    1. Keynesian economics. 2. Economic history—21st century. I. Arestis, Philip, 1941– II. Sawyer, Malcolm C. III. Title: Twenty-first century Keynesian economics.
    HB99.7.A14 2010
    330.15'6—dc22   2010002675

10 9 8 7 6 5 4 3 2 1
19 18 17 16 15 14 13 12 11 10

Printed and bound in Great Britain by
CPI Antony Rowe, Chippenham and Eastbourne

Contents

Preface

This is the sixth volume of the new series of *International Papers in Political Economy* (*IPPE*). This new series consists of an annual volume with five to six papers on a single theme. The objective of the *IPPE* continues to be the publication of papers dealing with important topics within the broad framework of Political Economy.

The original series of *International Papers in Political Economy* started in 1993 until the new series began in 2005 and was published in the form of three issues a year with each issue containing a single extensive paper. Information on the old series and back copies can be obtained from Professor Malcolm Sawyer at the University of Leeds (e-mail: mcs@lubs.leeds.ac.uk).

The theme of this sixth volume of six papers is 21st century Keynesian economics in terms of both theory and applications. The papers in this volume were initially presented at a one-day conference at the School of Oriental and African Studies (SOAS), University of London, London, UK, 8 May 2009; and subsequently at the 6th International Conference Developments in Economic Theory and Policy held at Universidad del Pais Vasco, Bilbao, Spain, 2–3 July 2009.

List of Figures and Tables

Figures

Tables

Notes on the Contributors

Philip Arestis is Honorary Senior Departmental Fellow, Cambridge Centre for Economics and Public Policy, Department of Land Economy, University of Cambridge, UK; Professor of Economics, Department of Applied Economics V, University of the Basque Country, Spain; Distinguished Adjunct Professor of Economics, Department of Economics, University of Utah, US; Senior Scholar, Levy Economics Institute, New York, US; Visiting Professor, Leeds Business School, University of Leeds, UK; Professorial Research Associate, Department of Finance and Management Studies, School of Oriental and African Studies (SOAS), University of London, UK; and current holder of the British Hispanic Foundation 'Queen Victoria Eugenia' British Hispanic Chair of Doctoral Studies. He is Chief Academic Adviser to the UK Government Economic Service (GES) on Professional Developments in Economics. He has published as sole author or editor, as well as co-author and co-editor, a number of books, contributed in the form of invited chapters to numerous books, produced research reports for research institutes, and has published widely in academic journals.

Terry Barker is the Director of the Cambridge Centre for Climate Change Mitigation Research (4CMR), Department of Land Economy, University of Cambridge, and Chairman, Cambridge Econometrics. He is also leading the theme of Integrated Modelling for the Tyndall Centre for Climate Change Research. His work on money stems from the wish to understand the financial crisis and its effect on the real economy, greenhouse gas emissions and climate-change mitigation. He was a Coordinating Lead Author (CLA) in the IPCC Third and Fourth Assessment Reports (2001 and 2007) for the chapters covering mitigation from a cross-sectoral perspective, including the macroeconomic costs to 2030 national, regional and global levels. He is now leading a team investigating the economics of decarbonising the global economy using a large-scale computable energy-environment-economy model E3MG. He has edited or authored some 12 books and over 100 articles and papers. See www.4cmr.org.

Amitava Krishna Dutt is Professor of Economics at the University of Notre Dame, Indiana, USA. His current research is on models of growth and distribution, uneven development and North–South interaction, consumption and happiness, and post-Keynesian macroeconomics. He is author or editor of a dozen books, and has published extensively in edited volumes and in journals such as *American Economic Review, Cambridge Journal of Economics, Journal of Development Studies, Journal of Post Keynesian Economics, Oxford Economic Papers* and *World Development.* He is a co-editor of *Metroeconomica.*

Ilene Grabel is a Professor at the Korbel School of International Studies at the University of Denver. Grabel has worked as a consultant to the UNDP/International Poverty Centre, UNCTAD/G24, and UNU-WIDER and various NGOs. She has published widely on financial policy and crises, international capital flows to the developing world, financial liberalisation and macroeconomic performance, central banking, and exchange rate regimes. Grabel is co-author (with Ha-Joon Chang) of *Reclaiming Development: An Alternative Policy Manual* (2004). She is currently researching the economic, political and social effects of remittances and the consequences of the global economic crisis for governance.

Eckhard Hein is a Professor of Economics at the Berlin School of Economics and Law. He is a member of the coordinating committee of the Research Network Macroeconomics and Macroeconomic Policies, a co-editor of the Series of the Research Network, Metropolis Publisher, Marburg, and a co-editor of *Intervention. European Journal of Economics and Economic Policies.* He has published in the *Cambridge Journal of Economics, European Journal of the History of Economic Thought, International Review of Applied Economics, Metroeconomica, Review of Political Economy and Structural Change* and *Economic Dynamics,* among others. His latest book with Palgrave Macmillan is *Money, Distribution Conflict and Capital Accumulation: Contributions to 'Monetary Analysis'* (2008).

Costas Lapavitsas is Professor of Economics at the School of Oriental and African Studies, University of London. He has worked on the political economy of money and finance, the Japanese economy, and the history of economic thought. He is currently researching the financialisation of contemporary capitalism, and his most recent book is the edited volume *Financialisation in Crisis* (forthcoming). He is also closely involved in the activities of the network Research on Money and Finance.

Malcolm Sawyer is Professor of Economics, University of Leeds, UK, and formerly Pro-Dean for Learning and Teaching for the Faculty of

Business. His research interests range over the analysis of the causes and consequences of the financial crises of 2008/09, fiscal and monetary policy, the political economy of the European Monetary Union, the nature of money, the causes and concepts of unemployment, the political economy of privatisation and the economics of Michal Kalecki. He is managing editor of *International Review of Applied Economics* and the editor of the series *New Directions in Modern Economics* published by Edward Elgar. He is the author of 11 books (the most recent being (with P. Arestis), *Re-examining Monetary and Fiscal Policies in the Twenty First Century* (Aldershot: Edward Elgar, 2004)), has edited 24 books (the most recent being (with J. Creel), *Current Thinking on Fiscal Policy* (Basingstoke: Palgrave Macmillan) and (with P. Arestis) *Critical Essays on the Privatisation Experience* (Basingstoke: Palgrave Macmillan)) and published 90 papers in refereed academic journals and contributed chapters to over 100 books.

1

Financial Systems and Economic Development in the 21st Century: Are We All Keynesians Yet?

Ilene Grabel*
Josef Korbel School of International Studies, University of Denver

Abstract

This paper explores the contribution of Keynesian economics to the matter of finance and development. It does so in several steps. First, the paper presents an account of the mainstream neoclassical approach to finance and development and traces through its historical evolution since the early 1970s. Second, the paper demonstrates that the failure of the neoclassical approach to finance and development stems from a variety of immutable theoretical and empirical problems with this approach. Third, the paper considers a range of Keynesian contributions to the debate over finance and development that have emerged in the wake of the repeated and consequential failures of the financial liberalization prescription and the related early warning models of financial crisis in developing countries that have been so important to neoclassical theorists. Fourth, the paper considers the kinds of commitments and broad approaches to financial policy in the developing world that are consonant with Keynesianism. Finally, the paper concludes with some speculations on the possibilities that the current global financial turmoil will create intellectual and policy space for Keynesianism to be taken more seriously as part of a sustained intellectual revival of the paradigm.

*Paper presented at University of London, School of Oriental and African Studies, May 8 2009 and at the "International Conference on Developments in Economic Theory and Policy," University of the Basque Country, Bilbao, Spain, July 2–3 2009. I thank Philip Arestis, Malcolm Sawyer and conference participants for their comments on this paper.

JEL Classification Codes: O16, O23, E12

Keywords: Keynesianism and financial development, financial policy and development, financial crisis and early warning systems

1. Introduction

The current global financial and economic crisis seems to have reminded the economics profession of Keynes's relevance. Even unreconstructed libertarians, most notably former Federal Reserve Chair, Alan Greenspan, have acknowledged the limitations of neoclassical theory and appear to be recalling some of the insights of Keynes. During the April 2009 Group of Twenty meeting in London, British Prime Minister Gordon Brown and US President Barack Obama seemed to be channeling the spirit of Keynes. This state of affairs is heartening to Keynesian economists, a group that has largely labored in the professional margins since the 1970s. Whether the rediscovery of Keynes will ultimately have a lasting effect on the profession and the policy world is unknown at this point. It is at least possible that Keynesianism may come to be seen (as it was from the vantage point of the 1970s) as the theory to be invoked only during each century's great economic crisis. Once the current turmoil subsides, it may be that the profession could return to its neoclassical center of gravity (as some have suggested, see Cohen, 2009).

A return to neoclassicism would be most unfortunate since Keynesianism is ever more relevant now as we seek to understand the economic challenges of the 21st century, challenges that neoclassical theory is ill-equipped to address. Moreover, in my view, Keynesianism has always had particular salience for the field of finance and economic development, a salience that the neoclassical theorists who dominate this area have been loath to acknowledge. Indeed, over the past several decades, neoclassical economic theorists and policy entrepreneurs have presented an unambiguous and even simplistic account of the means by which financial flows can be put in service of development. The general contours of this prescription, which entails a rather steadfast commitment to "financial liberalization," are fairly well known. But this prescription has met with repeated failures across the developing world, and among the post-Communist economies. As a consequence, the prescription has been amended repeatedly in order to account for these failures without sacrificing the economic science that founds the prescription, or its most central features.

In this paper I explore the contribution of Keynesian economics to the matter of finance and development. I will do this in a series of steps. First, I will present an account of the mainstream neoclassical approach to finance and trace through its historical development since the early 1970s. Relatedly, I examine efforts by neoclassical theorists to prevent financial crises in developing countries through the development of early warning models beginning in the 1990s. In the next two substantive sections of the paper I will attempt to demonstrate that the failure of these neoclassical projects stems from a variety of immutable theoretical and empirical problems with this approach. Among other things, I will argue that this approach fails to recognize the embeddedness of financial arrangements in broader political and social contexts, and that these contexts shape decisively the consequences that these arrangements have on economic outcomes. Moreover, I will argue that the refusal of this approach to recognize the interpenetration of the normative and the positive leaves its proponents in the grasp of ideological forces that they do not themselves recognize, which leaves them with no avenue but to reach for ad hoc adjustments to the theory to which they adhere rather than look beyond its confines for alternative explanations of events and sources of policy prescription.

The paper then considers a range of Keynesian contributions to the debate over finance and development that have emerged in the wake of the repeated and consequential failures of the financial liberalization prescription and the early warning models that have been so important to neoclassical theorists. I will focus on contributions that in some way or other draw on themes (and presumptions) that are central to Keynesian economics. The Keynesian approach is also consistent with ideas associated with other heterodox traditions, particularly institutional and socio-economics, both of which emphasize the connections between economic and non-economic institutions and practices, and foreground normative goals that reach far beyond (and often reject) the neoclassical commitment to efficiency. We will find in Keynesian (and other heterodox) accounts particular concern for those worst off, and the ways in which financial arrangements can either exacerbate or work to ameliorate economic inequality. We will also find in all of these approaches a concern with the effect of financial arrangements on political voice (in the sense of Albert Hirschman, 1986) and on national policy autonomy vis-à-vis external actors and domestic rentiers.

In concluding, I consider the kinds of commitments and broad approaches to financial policy in the developing world are consonant with Keynesianism. Finally, I offer some speculations on the possibilities that the current global financial turmoil will create intellectual and policy space for Keynesianism to be taken more seriously as part of a sustained intellectual revival of the paradigm.

2.   The evolution of the financial liberalization ideal in neoclassical economic theory[1]

For several decades the neoclassical approach to finance and development has predominated in the academy and policy circles. During that time advocates of this approach have offered significant amendments to the initial theory and prescription. These are viewed simply as marking the natural evolution of a maturing science that only began to explore the connections between finance and development in a systematic way in the early 1970s.[2]

2.1.   First-generation financial liberalization theory: the McKinnon–Shaw hypothesis

Following the publication of what became seminal works by Ronald McKinnon and Edward Shaw (published separately in 1973), neoclassical economists began to argue that the active regulation of financial systems in accordance with a state's development goals was counterproductive. This regulation – which they notably termed "financial repression" – was the norm under import-substitution industrialization strategies that were in place from the end of WWII until the mid-to-late 1970s. Financial systems were dominated by banks whose decisions were influenced by governments (rather than by capital markets) and were characterized by some combination of controls on interest and foreign exchange rates and credit allocation, the state imposition of non-interest-bearing reserve requirements, restrictions on the presence of foreign financial institutions and investors, and controls over international private capital inflows and outflows.

In the view of McKinnon and Shaw and their theoretical descendants, active state involvement in the financial sector has a number of adverse consequences. The maintenance of artificially low interest rates encourages domestic savers to hold funds abroad, and encourages current consumption rather than saving in domestic financial institutions. This aggravates inflationary pressures. Moreover, low savings rates also suppress bank lending activity. Thus, financial repression retards domestic investment and impedes employment and economic growth. In this account, then, economic stagnation and poverty are linked rather directly back to financial policy regimes that are ostensibly designed to promote development.

Neoclassical economists extended the critique of financial repression beyond these macroeconomic matters. They maintain that active state involvement in finance fragments domestic financial markets, with only a small segment of politically connected borrowers gaining access to scarce low-cost credit. Disenfranchised borrowers must resort to unregulated, "informal" lenders who often charge exorbitant interest rates, or otherwise have to manage in the face of unmet needs for capital. Entrepreneurship, employment creation, and growth thereby suffer. These negative effects are disproportionately experienced by the poor as the burden of scarce credit hits them hardest since they rarely have access to alternative, lower-cost sources of credit, such as the finance available on international capital markets or from international banks.

In view of the above, neoclassical economists from McKinnon and Shaw onward argued that developing countries must "liberalize" their domestic financial systems. A liberalized financial system with a competitive capital market is seen to be central to the promotion of high levels of savings, investment, employment, productivity, foreign capital inflows, and growth. From this perspective, liberalized systems serve the interests of the poor and the disenfranchised (as well as other groups) by increasing access to capital with attendant benefits for employment, investment and growth.

Neoclassical economists maintain that domestic financial liberalization not only increases the level of investment, but also increases its efficiency by allocating funds across investment projects according to rate-of-return criteria and via what are seen as objective or "arm's-length" practices. Domestic financial liberalization is seen to improve the overall efficiency of the financial system by eliminating the wasteful and corrupt practices that flourish under financial regulation, and by subjecting borrowers and firm managers to market discipline. Market discipline and a reduction in corruption are seen to improve the operating performance of financial institutions, and consequently enhance the prospects for financial stability.

In the neoclassical view, liberalization has other benefits. Not least, it encourages financial innovation, which reduces transactions costs while enhancing allocational efficiency. Investment and financial stability are promoted by new opportunities to diversify and disperse risk (through innovations such as securitization). By increasing the availability of finance, liberalization also eliminates the need for informal finance, and allows borrowers to utilize forms of finance that are most appropriate to their investment project.

Neoclassical economists see the finance provided through internationally integrated, liberal capital markets as preferable to bank loans because the former is understood to have a greater ability to disperse risk, is allocated according to efficiency and performance criteria, is cheaper than other forms of external finance (such as bank loans), and is highly liquid. The liquidity attribute is seen as especially desirable because it places firm managers under the threat of investor exit (or higher capital costs) if they under-perform. Internationally integrated capital markets are also seen to give the public and private sectors access to capital and other resources (such as technology) that are not being generated domestically. Thus, neoclassical economists maintain that an increase in private capital inflows will inaugurate a virtuous cycle by increasing the nation's capital stock, productivity, investment, growth and employment. All of these benefits redound to the benefit of society as a whole. But the poor may benefit particularly because higher levels of investment increase employment, especially in the technologically advanced firms that are financed by foreign investment. Sales of government bonds to foreign investors increase the resources available for public expenditure since these are rather scant thanks to problems with tax collection and the myriad demands on budgets.

Internationally integrated capital markets are also seen by neoclassical economists to increase efficiency and policy discipline. The need to attract private capital flows and the threat of capital flight are powerful incentives for the government and firms to maintain international standards for "good policy," macroeconomic performance, and corporate governance. Specifically, neoclassical economists maintain that governments seeking to attract international private capital flows are more likely to pursue anti-inflationary policies and anti-corruption measures because foreign investors value price stability, transparency, and the rule of law. The discipline that is enforced by financial integration is essential because of the commonly held view that public officials are inherently corrupt and/or incompetent (everywhere, but especially in developing countries). Note also that the poor are seen to benefit from stable prices and transparency since they are less able than the rich to hedge against inflation or extract benefits from corrupt regimes.

2.2.   Out of the laboratory and into the real world

What became known as the McKinnon–Shaw hypothesis proved to be immediately and immensely influential, not least because of the rhetorical power attached to the concepts of "repression" and "liberalization." By the early 1980s, the financial systems of many developing countries had been abruptly and radically liberalized in so-called "shock therapy" programs. Among the most ambitious and well studied efforts

to operationalize the McKinnon–Shaw hypothesis were the Southern
Cone countries of South America: Uruguay experimented with liberalization from 1973 to 1983, Chile from 1974/5 to 1983, and Argentina
from 1976/7 to 1983. With regard to the sequence of liberalization
implementation differed from country to country. For example, Chile
liberalized trade prior to finance, while Uruguay liberalized in the
reverse order. In each of these cases, however, full financial liberalization occurred swiftly, ranging from several months to less than two
years. Rarely are social scientists afforded a laboratory in which to
test their hypotheses. But in the space of ten years, McKinnon–Shaw
witnessed several thorough practical tests of their ideas.

Within five years of their initial liberalization, countries in the
Southern Cone experienced severe financial and macroeconomic difficulties. With soaring interest rates,[3] waves of bank failures and other
bankruptcies, extreme asset price volatility and extensive loan defaults,
the real sector entered deep and prolonged recessions. Widespread loan
defaults and bank distress necessitated massive bailouts of struggling
financial institutions. Moreover, the assumed benefits of financial liberalization (e.g., increases in savings and investment, reductions in capital
flight) failed to materialize.

2.3. Post hoc theoretical revisionism in the sequencing argument

While these events seemed to call into question the liberalization
prescription, neoclassical theorists remained committed to it. In what
I have elsewhere termed "neoclassical revisionism" (Grabel, 1996a),
these theorists modified the original thesis to take account of what they
now recognized as troublesome and previously overlooked attributes
of developing economies (cf., McKinnon 1973 with 1989 and 1991).
Through these post hoc theoretical extensions (including sequencing,
credibility and coherence, all of which are examined below), the liberalization prescription was repeatedly rescued from empirical refutation.

In self-critical assessments of the original prescription, neoclassical
economists (including McKinnon, 1989) concluded that sudden liberalization was not viable. A consensus emerged that a "second-best"
strategy had to be found, one that was more attuned to the features of
developing country economies. Neoclassical theorists began to incorporate new developments in macroeconomic theory – which focused
on the uniqueness of financial markets – into their ex-post assessments
of the early experiences with financial liberalization. For instance, neoclassical economists began to take seriously new theoretical work that

argued that high real interest rates could exacerbate moral hazard and adverse selection in lending. By the mid-1980s, neoclassical theory also reflected the insight that financial markets were unique in their ability to adjust instantaneously to changes in sentiments, information, etc. Goods markets, on the other hand, adjusted sluggishly. Thus, given these differences, financial markets could not be reformed in the same manner and in the same instance as other markets. Instead, a broad-based program of economic reform had to be sequenced. Successful reform of the real sector came to be seen as a prerequisite for financial reform: firewalls – in the form of temporary financial repression – had to be maintained during the first stage of liberalization in order to insulate the economy from financial disruptions.

But this insight about divergent adjustment speeds produced another; namely, that different aspects of reform programs may work at cross-purposes. This conflict has been termed the "competition of instruments." For present purposes the most important competition of instruments relates to the "Dutch disease effect" whereby the real currency appreciation generated by the opening of the capital account undermines the competitiveness of domestic goods, causing a deterioration of the current account. The second-best liberalization strategy requires that trade liberalization occur in the context of an appropriate degree of temporary financial repression. During a transition period following trade liberalization, the capital account is to be managed through the retention of capital controls (especially limiting inflows). Finally, the capital account is to be opened only after domestic financial markets have been liberalized.

Advocates of sequencing generally find their case strengthened following financial crises, as these are seen as a consequence of premature external financial liberalization. Indeed, had the East Asian financial crisis of 1997–98 not intervened, the IMF was poised to modify Article 6 of its Articles of Agreement to make the liberalization of international private capital flows a central purpose of the Fund and to extend its jurisdiction to capital movements. The Asian financial crisis did cause some neoclassical economists to step away from a blanket endorsement of external financial liberalization. Following the East Asian crisis, some studies, even by IMF staff, acknowledged that certain techniques to manage international capital flows can prevent undue financial volatility, *provided* that capital controls are temporary and that the rest of the economy is liberalized (Prasad, Rogoff, Wei, Kose, 2003; Kuczynski and Williamson, 2003). Even in these more nuanced and cautious minority views, however, there remains a strong commitment to the idea that liberalization is the *ultimate goal* for *all* developing countries – it is only a question of managing the timing appropriately.

Some neoclassical economists reject arguments for sequencing because of the problems introduced by this strategy (such as the possibility that it gives time for interest groups to mobilize to block liberalization). Neoclassical economists who nevertheless argue for sequencing today tend to add several non-economic factors to the menu of prerequisites, e.g., appropriate governance, institutions, the rule of law, and the protection of property rights.

2.4. Revisionism redux: the credibility and coherence arguments

The financial liberalization prescription was modified further in the mid- to late 1980s to take into account the policy environment in which liberalization is to occur. This new focus is manifested in discussions of the appropriate macroeconomic conditions for liberalization. Of particular importance is the determination whether the liberalization program is credible (see Grabel, 2000 on credibility). At issue are the perceptions of the economic actors in the affected economy concerning the viability of the proposed policies. An inconsistent liberalization program is one that the public believes is likely to be reversed. Such policies are likely to be sabotaged, as the public engages in behavior (such as capital flight) that undermines the success of the program.

How could economic policy be developed in this new, complex environment, in which the success of policy depends critically on agents' perceptions of its viability? There seemed to be two choices: one could shade policy toward existing popular sentiments; or, one could implement "correct" policy, one that respected the principles of neoclassical theory. The former option was ruled out of court on the simple grounds that incorrect policy could not possibly retain credibility in the wake of the disruptions that would inevitably attend it. The latter, on the other hand, would induce credibility as it proved itself uniquely capable of promoting development, even if it were unpopular in the short run. Hence, a correctly specified policy would impel rational agents to act "properly," at once achieving growth and the credibility necessary to sustain itself. On this account, financial liberalization could only be credibly implemented in an economy in which budget deficits are closed, inflation is tamed, and in which exchange rates reflect fundamentals (McKinnon, 1991: ch. 3).

In the last several years, neoclassical economists and members of the policy community have begun to raise the issue of policy coherence in explaining the success or failure of liberalization programs (see Grabel, 2007 on coherence). The intuition behind the concept of policy coherence is simple: any individual economic policy (such as financial liberalization) will only yield beneficial outcomes if it is nested in a broader policy environment that is consistent or coherent with its objectives. From this perspective, then, previous efforts to liberalize finance have failed to promote growth because of inconsistencies between financial and other economic and social policies. These new discussions of policy coherence seem to point neoclassical theory back toward McKinnon and Shaw's early work insofar as they provide a theoretical justification for across-the-board and abrupt liberalization in developing economies. It is impossible to say now if the new focus on policy coherence will have intellectual staying power, such that sequencing and gradualism will fall out of favor among neoclassical theorists.

3.   Neoclassical theory and the effort to prevent financial crises through information

Within the neoclassical model financial markets are presumed to be efficient in the sense that asset prices at any moment reflect fully and rationally all the available information. Prices adjust instantaneously to incorporate new information. From this perspective, in a well-functioning market, changes in prices result from the arrival of new information, and instability in prices stem from the instability of information and 'news'.

This model places heavy demands on the information available to market participants, of course, and it requires an absence of government interference in market processes. Unfortunately, the world we inhabit suffers from imperfect information (a problem exacerbated by the global spread of financial markets) and from obstreperous governments that refuse to behave just as neoclassical theory indicates that they should. Both problems are taken to be most acute in the developing world context, where dependable information is particularly difficult to ascertain (especially by foreign investors) and where governments are more apt to intervene in economic affairs in visible and obscure ways (such as through relationship-based lending, etc.). These problems were identified as among the chief culprits behind the recurring financial crises in the developing world throughout the 1980s and into the 1990s. To manage these problems, a theoretical strategy emerged within neoclassical theory to develop predictors, also known as "early warning systems," that are intended to identify the markers of looming financial instability or even crisis (especially in the developing world). During the 1990s prominent economists began to dedicate a good bit of energy to the attempt to design a workable, dependable early warning system. As with the 1990s, the 2000s were a fruitful time for those involved in the project of developing early warning systems of financial crisis in developing economies (not least because of the frequency, severity and contagious nature of financial crises in the era of financial liberalization and global financial integration). Indeed, the occurrence of a financial crisis in the previous eighteen months seems a rather reliable predictor of the development of new predictors. Neoclassical economists have sought to develop reliable predictors of currency, banking and generalized financial crises following the European currency crisis of 1992–3, the Mexican financial crisis of 1994–5, and the Asian financial crisis of 1997–8 (for example, Berg and Pattillo, 1998; Edison, 2000; Frankel and Rose, 1996; Goldstein, 1997a, 1997b; Goldstein, Kaminsky, Reinhart, 2000; Hardy and Pazarbasioglu, 1998; Kamin and Babson, 1999; Kaminsky, Lizondo, Reinhart, 1997; Kaminsky and Reinhart, 2000; Sachs, Tornell, Velasco, 1996).[4]

Unfortunately, the empirical record of crisis predictors is rather poor. Predictors developed after the European currency crisis failed to forecast the events in Mexico, those developed after the Mexican crisis failed to predict the Asian crisis, and those developed after the Asian crisis did not foresee the 2001 Turkish crisis (Corbett and Vines, 1998; Eichengreen, 1999; Sharma, 1999). The crisis in Argentina in the early 2000s was also not predicted by existing models. Additionally, counter-factual tests indicate that existing predictors would not have predicted the very crises that motivated their development (Berg and Patillo, 1998; Demirgüc-Kunt and Detragiache, 1999; Eichengreen and Portes, 1997; Goldfajn and Valdes, 1997; Hardy and Pazarbasioglu, 1998). However, undaunted by empirical failure, the effort to discover reliable crisis predictors/early warning systems (hereinafter, the neoclassical "predictors project") continued after the European and each developing country financial crisis. (See below for discussion of predictors and the current financial crisis.)

3.1. The neoclassical predictors project

The neoclassical predictors project begins from the premise that (many) financial crises can be prevented provided that economic actors know the extent of an economy's vulnerability (either in the aggregate, or in regards to weaknesses in the banking sector or the currency). Adequate provision of this knowledge in the form of individual predictors or a set of predictors packaged as an early warning system is a sufficient condition for crisis prevention. This is because rational economic agents are assumed to respond to information about crisis potentialities in ways that prevent realization of the predicted crisis. Participants in the neoclassical predictors project do not advocate any sort of regulatory or governmental response to the dangers revealed by predictors. The defensive postures adopted by private actors – themselves made possible only by unfettered markets – are a sufficient means to ward off the predicted crisis. Thus, microlevel reactions by market actors are stabilizing at the macrolevel.

The logic of the neoclassical approach to predictors is rather straightforward. There is an assumed independence between a predictor and an event. From this perspective, crisis prevention requires two things: good predictors that fill information gaps; and an open, liberalized regime in which agents are free to reallocate or liquidate their portfolios in response to problems made apparent by predictors. Hence, the self-regulating actions that rational agents take in response to predictors will prevent the predicted event from coming to fruition (or at least will mitigate its severity).

The neoclassical approach assumes that once a dangerous economic tendency is revealed, rational (private) economic actors will change their behaviors in a manner that ultimately stabilizes markets.

3.2. The predictors literature

Theoretical and empirical treatments of the etiology of currency crises is not a new area of research in neoclassical macroeconomics. The starting point for theoretical treatments of the subject is Krugman's seminal 1979 paper on the circumstances that lead to the collapse of fixed/pegged exchange rate regimes. Krugman maintains that such regimes collapse under the pressure of governmental distortion of economic fundamentals – to wit: excessively expansionary monetary and/or fiscal policies or persistent balance of payments deficits render fixed/pegged currencies untenable. Extensions of Krugman (1979) are legion; in these elaborations, weak fundamentals play a central role in triggering currency crises. The earliest extensions of Krugman (termed first-generation models) focus on the role of monetary and/or fiscal imbalances in speculative attacks against a multiplicity of exchange rate regimes; later extensions (termed second-generation models) center on the possibility for multiple equilibria and self-fulfilling attacks on a currency following the deterioration of fundamentals. The European currency crisis of 1992 reinvigorated efforts to understand the causes of currency crises; important works in this regard include Eichengreen and Wyplosz (1993), Eichengreen, Rose, and Wyplosz (1995), and Rose and Svensson (1994). Neither the work in the post-Krugman tradition nor the work of the Europeanists attempted to develop explicit predictors of financial crisis.

It was not until the Mexican crisis of 1994–5 that neoclassical economists moved beyond the project of uncovering the causes of crisis and attempted to elaborate predictors of financial crisis in developing economies. Official efforts to understand the Mexican crisis were very much guided by the view that crises could be prevented through the provision of accurate and timely information about conditions in developing economies. The central role of information in crisis prevention was indeed the main message of the June 1995 Group of Seven Summit held in Halifax in the wake of the Mexican crisis. At Halifax, the IMF was urged to encourage the prompt publication of economic and financial statistics and to identify regularly countries that did not comply with the institution's new information standards (standards that eventually became the International Monetary Fund's Special Data Dissemination Standard). The neoclassical predictors project builds directly on the International Monetary Fund's failed efforts to prevent crises in Asia through the provision of information through the Special Data Dissemination Standard.[5]

Participants in the neoclassical predictors project propose two broad types of predictors – the "regression" or "probit" approach associated with Frankel and Rose (1996) and the more frequently discussed early warning system (often termed the "signal extraction") approach associated with Goldstein, Kaminsky and Reinhart (2000).[6]

The regression approach estimates the probability of a currency or a banking crisis and identifies the variables that are statistically correlated with crisis. Econometric work by Frankel and Rose (1996) exemplifies this approach to crisis prediction (see also Sachs, Tornell and Velasco, 1996). For example, Frankel and Rose (1996) conclude that currency crashes in developing countries occur when foreign direct investment dries up, when currency reserves are low and falling, when domestic credit growth is high, when nominal interest rates in wealthy countries rise, and when the real exchange rate is overvalued by 10 percent (relative to the fundamental equilibrium exchange rate).

The early warning system approach compares the behavior of a variable before a crisis with its behavior during normal times. A variable is then taken to be useful if it displays anomalous behavior before a crisis but does not provide false signals of an impending crisis in normal times. When a variable exceeds or falls below a certain threshold, it is said to issue a signal that a crisis may occur.

Goldstein, Kaminsky and Reinhart (2000) is the point of departure for all efforts to develop early warning systems.[7] They find that there is a systemic pattern of empirical abnormalities leading up to most currency and banking crises in developing economies over a sample period ranging from 1970–95. For currency crises, they find that the best predictors using monthly data are appreciation of the real exchange rate (relative to trend), a banking crisis, a decline in stock prices, a fall in exports, a high ratio of broad money (M2) to international reserves, and a recession. Among the annual predictors of currency crises, the two most reliable predictors are a large current account deficit relative to both GDP and investment. For banking crises, they find that using monthly data the most reliable predictors of crisis (in descending order of importance) are appreciation of the real exchange rate (relative to trend), a decline in stock prices, a rise in the M2 money multiplier, a decline in real output, a fall in exports, and a rise in the real interest rate.[8] Among the annual predictors of banking crises, the most reliable are a high ratio of short-term capital inflows to GDP and a large current account deficit relative to investment. They find that in most banking and currency crises, a high proportion of the monthly leading indicators – on the order of 50–75 percent – reach their signaling threshold. In other words, when a developing economy is moving toward a financial crisis, many of the leading indicators signal a crisis.

Goldstein, Kaminsky and Reinhart (2000) show that there is a wide divergence in the performance across leading indicators; warnings usually appear 10–18 months prior to the onset of crisis. The authors remain firm in their view that the early warning system can make apparent an economy's vulnerability to crisis. They do make clear, however, that the system does not speak to the timing of a crisis.

3.3.   The empirical performance of predictors

The empirical performance of crisis predictors is rather dismal. Numerous empirical tests (many indeed conducted by proponents) conclude that predictors would not have provided ex-ante signals of the events in Mexico in 1994 or Asia in 1997/98 (on the current crisis, see below).

For example, Flood and Marion (1999), Hawkins and Klau (2000), and the International Monetary Fund (1998, ch. 4) all conclude that predictors, at best, have a mixed record of success. Goldfajn and Valdés (1997) are less ambiguous: the former study concludes that exchange rate crises are largely unpredictable events, a result they demonstrate in the case of the currency crises in Mexico and Thailand; the latter study concludes that the Asian banking crises would not have been predicted by the usual macroeconomic predictors. Eichengreen's (1999) survey of predictors concludes that they have remarkably poor power. His assessment is worth quoting at length: "If investors, with so much at stake, cannot reliably forecast crises, then it is hard to see why bureaucrats should do better...Their [predictors] track record is not good. Models built to explain the 1992–93 ERM crisis did not predict the 1994–95 Mexican crisis. Models built to explain the Mexican crisis did not predict the Asian crisis" (p. 84).

Several studies test a comprehensive battery of predictors; these studies, too, fail to offer empirical support to the neoclassical predictors project. In a test of nearly all existing predictors (both of the regression and the early warning variety), Berg and Patillo (1998) find that some models perform better than guesswork in predicting the Asian crisis. But they find that none of these models reliably predicts the timing of the crisis (that is, whether there would be a crisis in 1997). This is because false alarms, in almost all cases, always outnumber appropriate warnings. Edison (2000) also concludes that early warning systems issue many false alarms and miss important crises. Sharma's (1999) review of the empirical performance of early warning systems concludes that they would not have predicted the events in Asia (a conclusion echoed by Corbett and Vines 1998). Sharma sums up the matter definitively: "the holy grail of crisis prediction may be intrinsically unattainable" (p. 42).

The most prominent advocates of predictors remain unshaken by the weight of discouraging empirical evidence. Goldstein (1997a), for example, concludes that preliminary tests of the predictors he develops indicate that they would have predicted the Thai crisis. Goldstein, Kaminsky and Reinhart (2000) conclude that their system performs quite well, not only in tracking currency and banking crises in developing economies over the 1970–95 sample period, but also in anticipating most of the countries affected by the Asian crisis (particularly as regards currency crises in Asia).[9] To their credit, the authors clearly acknowledge that their early warning system is prone to many false alarms and would have missed some important crises: the best indicators send a significant share of false alarms on the order of one false alarm for every two to five true signals (see ch. 5).

The empirical shortcomings of the neoclassical predictors project are clear, even to some of its most ardent participants. What is not clear is why efforts to refine existing predictors and to develop new ones proceeded so steadily despite the empirical failings of the enterprise. At this time we simply do not know if the failure of models to predict the current global crisis will be the final death knell of this project.

4. The Keynesian response to the financial liberalization ideal

What neoclassical theorists view as a simple and altogether desirable evolution of financial liberalization theory, Keynesians recognize as something else: as a series of ad hoc theoretical adjustments designed to prevent the disconfirmation and even collapse of the financial liberalization agenda. The effect of these ad hoc adjustments is to repress this recognition, to block the realization that would otherwise emerge that the financial liberalization mission was flawed from the start, and has by now proven its deficiencies beyond the academy in the real world of development practice.

In what follows, I subject the neoclassical case for financial liberalization and early warning systems to critical scrutiny from the perspective of Keynesianism (and other heterodox traditions). From this vantage point, I identify two important failings with the liberalization prescription. First, the frequent resort to revisionism lends an ideological character to the neoclassical case for liberalization. Second, liberalization's advocates fail to appreciate the critical importance of national specificities, path dependence, the embeddedness of actors and institutions, the ineradicable nature of uncertainty in economic decision making, and the intrinsic volatility of liberalized, liquid and internationally integrated financial markets. This leads Keynesians (and other heterodox economists) to conclude that the failure of this prescription stems not from improper implementation, but rather from the inappropriateness of the model itself and from the futility of efforts to graft it onto diverse national contexts.

4.1. Ad hoc revisionism as ideology

The refusal of the neoclassical approach to recognize the interpenetration of the normative and the positive leaves its proponents in the grasp of ideological forces that they do not themselves recognize, which means that they have no avenue but to reach for ad hoc adjustments to the theory to which they adhere rather than look beyond its confines for alternative explanations of events and sources of policy prescription. For this reason, the neoclassical case for financial liberalization has been subject to several bouts of revisionism, without ever challenging the basic myth underlying all of this that liberalized finance is the ideal to which developing countries must aspire, no matter the cost. Insofar as it can always be asserted ex-post that the environment in which financial liberalization failed was not credible (e.g., in the sense of lacking sufficient political support) or that financial liberalization policy was not consistent (i.e., coherent) with other policies, it is possible to insulate financial liberalization from critique. Thus, for neoclassical economics, the failure of financial liberalization to achieve its chief goals does not stem from the inappropriateness of the policy or from the underlying theoretical framework that gives rise to it. Rather, policy failure is explained by the presence of all manner of distortions that characterize the economy, by political uncertainty, by the public's lack of confidence in the capacity of policymakers.

Polanyi (1944) wrote precisely of this phenomenon when discussing the propensity of advocates of free markets (in general) to explain their failure as stemming from insufficient liberalization rather than from the failure of markets themselves:

> Its apologists [i.e., defenders of market liberalization] are repeating in endless variations that but for the policies advocated by its critics, liberalism would have delivered the goods; that not the competitive system and the self-regulating market, but interference with that system and interventions with that market are responsible for our ills. (p. 143)

This strategy leaves the neoclassical argument for financial liberalization immune to any substantive empirical refutation. It is the impossibility of testing (and therefore rejecting) its central propositions, combined with its self-understanding as the uniquely adequate and objective positive economic science, that imparts to this approach its ideological content.

The ideological content of the neoclassical case for financial liberalization emerges even more directly in the credibility argument. A proposition stating that credible policies are more likely to succeed is, on its face, innocuous. But upon closer examination we see that this proposition carries with it a particularly ideological and troubling claim about the unique truthfulness of the neoclassical case.

The credibility thesis can be reduced to a simple set of propositions: (1) An economic policy will garner credibility only to the degree that it is likely to survive; (2) An economic policy is likely to survive only to the degree that it attains its stated objectives; (3) An economic policy is likely to attain its stated objectives only to the degree that it reflects and operationalizes the true theory of market economies; (4) A policy reflects the true theory of market economies only to the degree that it is neoclassical. The exclusionary, dissent-suppressing maneuver that has been undertaken here is captured in propositions (3) and (4). Non-neoclassical economic theories are ruled out of court on the grounds that they could not possibly meet the unforgiving "credibility" test, because they could not possibly be true. Hence, policy regimes founded upon non-neoclassical theories must collapse, with deleterious social and economic consequences.

The recent effort to incorporate coherence into examinations of policy regimes shares with the credibility literature a strong ideological content. In principle, the concept of coherence (like credibility) is empty of substantive content; that is, coherence does not in and of itself entail a commitment to any particular kind of policy regime. Hence, deployment of this concept can be entirely benign. But if the concept is intrinsically open-ended, in practice it has come to be understood by neoclassical economists and by the key multilateral institutions/organizations (namely, the International Monetary Fund, World Bank and World Trade Organization) in a way that biases policy prescription in a very particular direction. The concept of policy coherence has been invoked to legitimize ambitious and comprehensive liberalization schemes. It is used to validate the common, dangerous and incorrect view that neoliberal policies represent the only viable path to development for all countries. Like credibility, then, it serves to close off consideration of any and all other paths to development.

That policy coherence must entail liberalization has been contradicted by historical and cross-country experience (see Chang 2002). Chang and Grabel (2004) and Rodrik (2007) (among others) demonstrate that there exist multiple paths to development, and that high levels of economic growth that are feasible, sustainable and stable can be achieved via an array of heterogeneous strategies. While any one country's policies must exhibit a degree of internal coherence in order to succeed, the evidence is clear that the alternative policy regimes need not cohere around liberalization.

4.2. Embeddedness, resilience, path dependence and the failure of financial liberalization

From the perspective of Keynesian (and other heterodox approaches to) economics, there are a number of related factors that help to explain the failures of financial liberalization in the developing world. The neoclassical approach refuses the idea that financial arrangements and financial actors are embedded in a constellation of historically-contingent political and social relationships that may enable development along all sorts of non-neoliberal paths. This view explains why neoclassical economists approach the task of financial reform as if it merely involves grafting the liberalized financial model that predominates in the USA and the UK onto the economies of the developing world. But the matter of financial reform is not nearly as uncomplicated as neoclassical theory suggests.

From the perspective of Keynesian economics and other heterodox traditions, it is critically important to foreground the concepts of social embeddedness, institutional resilience/stickiness and path dependence as key attributes of all economies, and hence as critical factors that must be taken account of by those considering structural reform programs. These understandings suggest that any one program of financial reform cannot be expected to perform uniformly across diverse national contexts, and that any effort to transplant financial arrangements will be fraught with all manner of unintended and undesirable consequences. In particular, institutional stickiness helps to account for the fact that new market-oriented financial institutions tend to function eerily like their *dirigiste* predecessors following liberalization, and that old, dysfunctional behaviors (such as corruption) re-appear in new forms in a reformed environment. Finally, the recognition of specificity and embeddedness in Keynesian and especially socio-economics implies that a uniform set of financial arrangements could not possibly be viable, let alone suitable, for all countries at all times.

4.3. The faulty premises of neoclassical financial liberalization theory[10]

On the most abstract theoretical level, Keynesian economists argue that liberalized markets are not efficient in the ways that neoclassical theory claims. Keynesians argue that there is no demonstrated empirical or historical relationship between a market-based allocation of capital and satisfaction of growth and social objectives. This is not surprising since the allocation of capital in market-based systems relies on private financial returns as the singular yardstick of investment success. The private financial return on an investment can be quite different from its social return, where the latter refers to the promotion of important social goals (such as poverty reduction, equality and economic security) not reducible to economic efficiency narrowly defined.

Despite the claims of neoclassical economists, a market-based allocation of capital is not a magic cure for inefficiency, waste, and corruption.

Liberalization frequently changes the form, but not the level, of corruption or inefficiency. The situation of Russia after financial liberalization exemplifies this point, but the country is by no means exceptional in this regard (Kotz, 1997). For instance, research on Nigeria, South Korea, and South America describes quite persuasively the corruption that so often flourishes following financial liberalization (Crotty and Lee, 2004; Lewis and Stein, 1997). Thus, financial liberalization does not resolve the problems of corruption and the lack of transparency that frequently operate to the detriment of the poor.

Liberalized financial markets are at least as apt as governments to allocate capital in an inefficient, wasteful or developmentally unproductive manner. In many developing countries, market-based allocations of domestic capital and increased access to international private flows following liberalization financed speculation in commercial real estate and the stock market, the creation of excess capacity in certain sectors, and allowed domestic banks and investors to take on positions of excessive leverage, often involving currency and locational mismatches that culminate in crises.

Neoclassical economists often herald the disciplining effects of capital markets, arguing that the threat of investor exit and corporate takeovers creates pressure to improve corporate governance. We know that the exit and takeover mechanisms are well developed in the markets of the USA and UK. But there is simply no evidence to support the case that these mechanisms have, on balance, been beneficial. Indeed, numerous studies find that the threat of investor exit shortens the time horizon of managers, and takeovers have increased concentration and induced job losses (e.g., see Cosh and Hughes, 2008). The case that developing country firms and consumers benefit from enhancing possibilities for exit and takeover by liberalizing financial markets is therefore without merit.

There is a large body of empirical evidence demonstrating that domestic financial liberalization has unambiguously failed to deliver most of the rewards claimed by its proponents (see Grabel, 2003b, and references therein). For instance, domestic savings have not responded positively to domestic financial liberalization. Moreover, the liberalization of domestic and international financial flows has not promoted long-term investment in the types of projects or sectors that are central to development and to the amelioration of social ills, such as unemployment, poverty, and inequality. Financial liberalization has created the climate, opportunity and incentives for investment in speculative activities and a focus on short-term financial as opposed to long-term developmental returns. Granted, the creation of a speculative bubble may temporarily result in an increase in investment and overall economic activity. But an unsustainable and financially fragile environment or what Grabel (1995) terms "speculation-led development" is hardly in the long-term interest of developing countries. Such an environment certainly does not improve the situation of the poor – indeed it worsens their conditions of life, as we will see.

One channel by which the speculation-led development induced by financial liberalization worsens the situation of the poor is by increasing income and wealth inequality and by aggravating existing disparities in political and economic power. This is because only a very small proportion of the population is situated to exploit the opportunities for speculative gain available in a liberalized financial environment. Speculation-led development often creates a small class of rentiers who maintain greater ties to financial markets abroad than to those in their own country, and it is also associated with a shift in political and economic power from non-financial to financial actors. In such an environment, the financial community and powerful external actors such as the International Monetary Fund become the anointed arbiters of the "national interest" and the judges of precisely what constitutes sound, sustainable economic and social policies. This means that macroeconomic policies that advance the interests of the financial community (such as those that promote low inflation, high interest rates, and fiscal restraint) are justified on the basis that they serve the broader public interest when this is simply not the case.

The range of acceptable policy options is further constrained by the threat or actuality of capital flight, itself made possible by the liberalization of international capital flows. This dynamic of "constrained policy autonomy" (Grabel, 1996b) means that the political voice of rentiers and the International Monetary Fund are empowered over those of other social actors (such as the poor and middle-class, export-oriented industrialists, and agricultural producers) in discussions of macroeconomic policy. In practice, this means that macroeconomic policies exhibit a restrictive bias that favors rentiers and the International Monetary Fund. Research by Braunstein and Heintz (2006) shows that such policies have a negative effect on the poor and women.

The speculation-led development induced by financial liberalization also worsens the situation of the poor through its effect on financial fragility, and ultimately on the prevalence of currency, banking and generalized financial crises. There is now a large body of unambiguous empirical evidence that shows that the liberalization of domestic and international financial flows is strongly associated with banking, currency and financial crises (see Grabel 2003b, and references therein;

Weller 2001). Since the Southern Cone crises of the mid-1970s, we have seen financial crises on the heels of liberalization in a great many developing countries, such as Russia, Nigeria, Jamaica, Korea, Thailand, Indonesia, Mexico and Turkey. Of course, the recent collapse of the Icelandic economy, the serious financial instability that is being witnessed in so many post-Communist and developing countries, and the global spread of the US's financial crisis collectively illustrate the rather profound link between financial liberalization, financial innovation, international financial integration and financial instability.

Contrary to the neoclassical view, the increase in liquidity that is associated with liberalization, financial innovation (such as securitization), and the creation of internationally integrated capital markets increases the level of financial and economic volatility.[11] In addition, the removal of restrictions on international private capital inflows and outflows introduces the possibility of the Dutch disease or, alternatively, of sudden, large capital outflows (i.e., capital flight) that place the domestic currency under pressure to depreciate. Capital flight often induces a vicious cycle of additional flight and currency depreciation, debt-service difficulties and reductions in stock (or other asset) values. In this manner, capital flight introduces or aggravates existing macroeconomic vulnerabilities and financial instability. These can culminate in a financial crisis which, as we have seen, impairs economic performance and living standards (particularly for the poor and the politically weak) and often provides a channel for increased external and rentier influence over domestic decisionmaking.

Numerous recent cross-country and historical studies demonstrate conclusively that there is no reliable empirical relationship between the liberalization of international capital flows and performance in terms of inflation, growth or investment in developing countries (Eichengreen, 2001). Moreover, studies also show that the liberalization of international capital flows is associated with increases in poverty and inequality, though the authors of these studies take care to point out that it is difficult to isolate the negative effects of financial liberalization from those associated with broader programs of economic liberalization (involving, for instance, the simultaneous adoption of trade and labor market liberalization). With this caveat in mind, it is worth noting that Weller and Hersh (2004) find that capital and current account liberalization hurt the poor in developing countries in the short run (see Epstein and Grabel, 2006, for further discussion). The poor are harmed by international financial liberalization through a chain of related effects that have been established in several studies. Increased short-term international financial flows (especially portfolio flows) are often associated with a greater chance of financial crisis (Weller, 2001), especially in more liberalized environments (Demirgüc-Kunt and Detragiache, 1999); financial crises have disproportionately negative consequences for a country's poor (Baldacci et al., 2002), not least through labor market effects (Eichengreen, et al., 1996); and the poor are the first to lose under the fiscal contractions and the last to gain when crises subside and fiscal spending expands (Ravallion, 2002).

Cornia (2003) argues that of the six components of what he terms the "liberal package," liberalization of international private capital flows appears to have the strongest impact on widening within-country inequality. He finds that the next most important negative effects on the poor derive from domestic financial liberalization, followed by labor market deregulation and tax reform. Weisbrot et al. (2001) concludes that there is a strong *prima facie* case that structural and policy changes implemented during the last two decades, such as financial liberalization, are at least partly responsible for worsening growth and health and other social indicators.

Inequality among countries has also increased during liberalization, partly as a result of the high degree of concentration of international private capital flows. The United Nations Development Programme (UNDP) finds that in 1960 the countries with the richest 20 percent of the world's population had aggregate income 30 times that of those countries with the poorest 20 percent of the world's population. By 1980, that ratio had risen to 45 to one; by 1989, it stood at 59 to one; in 1997, it rose to 70 to one (UNDP, 2001, 1999). In the era of intensified commitment to liberalization, there was a near doubling of inequality between the richest and the poorest countries.

The theoretical insights and empirical findings summarized above have prompted Keynesian economists to articulate a range of alternatives to financial liberalization that are consistent with the theoretical precepts and value commitments associated with Keynesianism. The task now must be not to give it new life through some new theoretical amendment, but to find and advocate for genuine alternatives that promise human and economic development of a sort that has been frustrated by financial liberalization.

5. A Keynesian critique of neoclassical efforts to prevent crises through information

In the wake of the current global financial crisis, even steadfast advocates of the neoclassical model have come to recognize the failures of early warning models. Most notably, the former Federal Reserve Chair Alan Greenspan acknowledged in a Congressional hearing in October 2008 that he had made an 'error' in assuming that the markets would regulate themselves, and added that he had no idea a financial disaster was in the making. More to the point he acknowledged that the Fed's own computer models and economic experts simply 'did not forecast' the current financial crisis (Shiller, 2008). Indeed, many analysts have now noted with apparent surprise that a variety of models used by governments, multilateral organizations and financial institutions had not predicted the current global financial crisis. However, it must be remembered that there were a few models that highlighted systemic risks (see Lohr, 2008; Shiller, 2008). More importantly, there were a number of prominent analysts, most especially, Dean Baker, Paul Krugman and Stephen Roach, who warned frequently, consistently and loudly of dangers ahead. These warnings were roundly dismissed and, in some cases, ignored insofar as they were seen as the predictions of Cassandra-like figures who failed to understand that things had changed fundamentally during the boom of the 1990s and early 2000s. This would not have surprised Keynes since it is a classic illustration of the hold of conventional wisdom, herd behavior, and the endogeneity of expectations. At this time we cannot say whether current events will ultimately mean that analysts go back to the drawing board with the aim of refining their models (as they have in the recent past), or whether the entire enterprise will be abandoned.

From a Keynesian perspective, the failure of even the most highly regarded early warning models to predict the current crisis (let alone crises in developing countries over the past decade) is unsurprising. Keynesians have long viewed these models with suspicion. For instance, John Kenneth Galbraith said years ago that "the only function of economic forecasting is to make astrology look respectable" (Bajaj, 2009).

Keynesians understand that the neoclassical predictors project is based on several misguided initial assumptions. First, that in the context of a neoliberal policy environment, financial markets will self-regulate in a stabilizing manner provided that agents have access to information that reveals the economy's vulnerability to crisis and are free to take the defensive actions that they deem warranted. In this view, the neoliberal financial regime is entirely inculpable in the financial instability and recurrent crises that have proliferated during the era of neoliberal reform. Second, that the information on which the success of these predictors is predicated can reasonably be expected to be accurate. Third, that the interpretation of predictors is exogenous to the economic environment and the state of expectations. The collective weight of these logical problems (coupled with the empirical failure of predictive exercises) frustrates the neoclassical enterprise of crisis prediction. From a Keynesian perspective advanced notably by Minsky (among others), there is no reason to expect that the mere provision of accurate and timely information about the changing state of "market fundamentals" in developing economies will prevent crisis by changing agents' behaviors.

In addition, these indicators themselves do not represent a sufficient means to prevent financial crisis in developing economies. Ironically, as agents develop confidence in the predictive capacity of crisis indicators, they may be more likely to engage in actions that increase the economy's vulnerability to crisis. Moreover, the dissemination of information about the economy's vulnerability to a crisis may in fact accelerate investor exit, thereby bringing about precisely the crisis that the indicators are designed to predict. Far more important to the project of preventing financial crisis in developing economies is the implementation of constraints on those investor behaviors that render them prone to currency, banking and financial crises. Hence, the intellectual capital of the economics profession could be more productively expended devising appropriate changes in the overall regime in which investors operate (such as measures that compel changes in financing strategies and that control international movements of capital) rather than searching for the correct set of crisis predictors.

Recall that the neoclassical predictors project begins from the presumption that the provision of accurate and timely information about an economy's vulnerability is ultimately market stabilizing, provided that agents are able to adopt appropriate defensive postures in response to this information. Keynesians reject this view for a number of reasons.

5.1. Agents can respond to new information in a manner that is either market stabilizing or destabilizing

In the Keynesian view, the idea that predictors and events are independent of one another does not make sense. By making agents aware of fragilities in the economy, predictors may induce market-stabilizing or destabilizing changes in behavior. This is because, from a Keynesian perspective, predictors and crises (as events) are entirely dependent on one another. Given endogenous expectations and the inherent instability of liquid, liberalized, internationally integrated financial markets, rational economic actors are just as likely to engage in destabilizing herd behavior in response to new information as they are to engage in market-stabilizing behavior. In the game of musical chairs, no one wants to be the last one left standing, as Keynes noted long ago. We simply cannot predict with certainty whether agents will respond to the information provided by predictors in a market-destabilizing or -stabilizing manner. In light of recent events (e.g., the collapse of the firm, Lehman Brothers), investor panic seems a likely response to warnings of dire circumstances ahead.

In the context of a neoliberal financial regime (in which agents are free to take defensive actions in response to new information, changes in market sentiment, etc.), predictors have indeterminate effects on macroeconomic stability.

From the Keynesian perspective, we discover what I will call the "predictor credibility paradox." In short, the enhanced credibility of a predictor may subvert it. To the degree that a predictor induces a heightened level of confidence among economic actors, it may introduce and validate risky behaviors that bring about a crisis. Thus, the degree of confidence with which predictors are held influences the way that predictors themselves will move markets. Crises result from the behavior of agents, and the behavior of agents is predicated on expectations which are, in turn, a function of their "knowledge." So a predictor becomes yet another piece of information that can change the behavior of agents for better or worse. Predictors, then, do not report on the future in a neutral way – they can induce changes in investor behavior that can be market stabilizing or destabilizing.

5.2. The informational prerequisites for early warning systems are simply unreasonable in the developing economy context

The success of neoclassical predictors depends very much on the accuracy and availability of information about a range of economic conditions. But these informational prerequisites cannot be accommodated in the developing economy context where problems of data inaccuracy are to be expected. Indeed, the identification of precisely this problem motivated the IMF's creation of the SDSS. But identification of the problem has not solved it. For instance, the IMF has acknowledged that important data have been mis-reported by authorities in Ukraine. (And, of course, mis-reporting of data was an important component of the US's current financial difficulties.) False and missed alarms are likely as long as the integrity of data are compromised. And false alarms are obviously no small matter insofar as they can trigger real crises by causing an investor panic. Moreover, governments have a strong incentive to mis-report data once a "predictors regime" is in place, and this incentive deepens as a country enters crisis territory. Paradoxically, then, the introduction of predictors is likely to reduce the quality of reported data.

5.3. The interpretation of predictors is endogenous to the economic environment

The neoclassical predictors project presumes that the interpretation of predictors is a science rather than an art. The former implies that the determination as to what constitutes a "dangerous reading" is independent of the economic climate and the state of expectations. In contrast, Keynesians view the interpretation of predictors as far more art than science. (through this hardly implies the economic performance is determined exclusively by interpretation). The determination as to what constitutes a dangerous level for some set of predictive variables is endogenous to the economic environment.

5.4. Neoclassical predictors are predicated on the false notion that there exists a consistent set of knowable macroeconomic fundamentals (embodied in predictors) and that economic agents make decisions based on a rational assessment of these fundamentals

At its base, the predictors developed by neoclassical economists begin from the assumption that there exists a set of objective fundamentals, that these fundamentals are knowable, and that rational agents make decisions based on the state of fundamentals. From a Keynesian perspective, of course, there is no set of static, knowable fundamentals in the domain of investment decisions. As Keynes's (1964) beauty contest and musical chairs analogies make clear, investment decisions are made in an environment of fundamental uncertainty, are driven by expectations and conventional wisdom, and are characterized by herd effects. Hence, when agents believe they are making rational investment decisions based on objective fundamentals, they fail to recognize that the identification of fundamentals is itself largely an interpretative exercise. For example, a rising current account deficit may be taken as a sign of an impending crisis and a reflection of underlying economic fragility, or may be taken as a reflection of a country's strength, ability to run a rising capital account surplus and desirability to investors.

Moreover, if the etiology of every crisis is at least slightly different, then we have no reason to expect that a standard early warning system based on a static set of fundamentals would be appropriate for the job. For example, the root causes of the European, Mexican, and Asian crises remain distinct. Therefore, it comes as no surprise that predictors developed after each crisis failed to predict the next one.

5.5.   Refining existing neoclassical predictors will not end the pattern of recurrent crisis in developing economies. The problem lies with the regime: regimes of neoliberal finance are inherently prone to crisis, particularly in the developing economy context

The search for predictors by neoclassical economists assumes that crises are a consequence of informational inadequacy rather than a fundamental, structural feature of the economic environment of regimes of neoliberal finance. Economies with internationally integrated, liquid, liberalized financial systems are inherently crisis prone, as Keynes long argued and recent events have shown clearly. (Arestis and Demetriades (1997), Arestis and Glickman (2002), papers in Chang, Palma, and Whittaker (2001), Crotty and Lee (2001), Grabel (2003a, 1995), Nissanke and Stein (2003), Palma (1998), Singh and Weisse (1998) and Weller (2001) treat this issue in the context of developing economies; numerous Keynesians, such as Davidson (1972) and Minsky (1986) treat this issue in the context of wealthy countries.)

Neoclassical economists fail to appreciate that the neoliberal financial regime that they promote in developing countries plays a critical role in the promulgation of the very financial crises that they seek to predict. In particular, the promotion of highly liquid, internationally integrated capital markets in these countries – in the context of insufficient financial and regulatory architecture – plays an important role in explaining many recent crises. Consistent with the assumptions of Keynesian theory, several empirical studies show that financial liberalization in developing countries is a strong (and, in some cases, the best) predictor of banking, currency and/or generalized financial crises (Demirgüç-Kunt and Detragiache, 1998; Weller, 2001). (Empirical evidence that links financial liberalization and financial crisis is also reviewed in Arestis and Demetriades, 1997; Williamson and Mahar, 1998.)

5.6.   Economists have never succeeded in predicting economic turning points

Finally, it bears mentioning that efforts at divining market swings have never met with much success. The spectacular failure of the hedge fund, Long Term Capital Management, a fund managed by Nobel laureates and other distinguished economists, demonstrates that even pioneers of elaborate risk management models cannot anticipate market shifts with great accuracy. Developing economies simply cannot afford to bear the costs of failed efforts at crisis prediction (namely, false signals that trigger investor panics, or missed signals).

Keynesian theory and current events collectively provide us with a basis to reject new efforts to refine early warning models. From this perspective, the crises that occur under a neoliberal regime don't result from inadequate information; they result from the inherent dynamics that necessarily infuse the neoliberal model itself. To put it plainly, appending an early warning system to the neoliberal model to prevent crisis is akin to trying to prevent a collision by installing a more sophisticated speedometer into a car with no steering wheel or brakes.

6. New directions for future research on post-financial liberalization regimes

Keynesian economists have in the last few years begun to move beyond the task of explaining the failures of financial liberalization to thinking seriously about the nature of post-liberalization regimes. Three pertinent questions confront advocates of a post-financial liberalization agenda. (1) What are the principal objectives of financial systems in developing countries? (2) What types of financial arrangements might best serve the goals of substantive equality and human development, while also engaging private actors? And (3) How can global financial rules and national financial arrangements provide space for local financial institutions and practices that meet local needs? In what follows, I offer some thoughts on these questions with the hope of stimulating research and debate on these critical issues within Keynesian economics.

6.1. Performance objectives for financial systems in developing countries

Keynesian economists have attempted to articulate goals for financial systems in developing countries. I now summarize three such contributions.

With regard to the goals of the domestic financial system, Chang and Grabel (2004) submit that regulation should be guided by one fundamental consideration, to wit: the domestic financial system should operate in the service of sustainable, stable and equitable economic development. The chief function of the financial sector in developing countries is to provide finance in adequate quantities and at appropriate prices for those investment projects that are central to this kind of development. Chang and Grabel argue that all financial reforms should be evaluated against the extent to which they achieve this aim. Domestic financial reforms that improve the functioning of the financial system along other dimensions (such as liquidity, international integration, etc.) should be seen as secondary to its primary developmental goal.

The most important way in which the financial system can serve appropriate economic development is through the provision of long-term finance. Long-term finance is necessary to the success and viability of most projects that are central to economic development (e.g., investment in infrastructure and the promotion of infant industries). In his research on the US financial system, Nobel laureate James Tobin (1984) used the term functional efficiency to refer to the ability of the financial system to provide finance for long-term investment. The concept of functional efficiency contrasts with the more conventional (neoclassical) notion of efficiency that focuses on the pricing mechanism. Any proposed financial reform in the developing world should be evaluated based on its ability to contribute to the critical objective of functional efficiency.

Grabel (2003b) argues that capital controls should maximize the net developmental benefits of international private capital flows by focusing on three objectives. First, a program of well-designed capital controls should promote financial stability, and thereby prevent the economic and social devastation that is associated with financial crises. Second, policies should promote desirable types of investment and financing arrangements (i.e., those that are long-term, stable and sustainable, and that create employment opportunities, improve living standards, promote income equality, technology transfer and learning-by-doing) and discourage less desirable types of investment/financing strategies. Finally, capital controls should enhance democracy and national policy autonomy by reducing the potential for speculators and various external actors to exercise undue influence (and even veto power) over domestic decision making and/or control over national resources.[12]

Epstein and Grabel (2006) argue that financial systems in developing countries should be restructured so that they directly promote "pro-poor economic growth" rather than hope, as does neoclassical theory with its decidedly unjust "trickle-down" approach, that reforms that target the wealthy will eventually redound to the benefit of the poor. Pro-poor economic growth would involve designing a far-reaching program of institutional and financial policy reform that is guided by a very particular set of goals. In this view, the financial system should mobilize savings that can be used for productive investment and employment creation; create credit for employment generation and poverty reduction at modest and stable real interest rates; allocate credit for employment generation and help the poor to build assets, including in agriculture and in small and medium-sized enterprises and in housing; provide long-term credit for productivity-enhancing innovation and investment and provide financing for public investment; help to allocate risks to those who can most easily and efficiently bear those risks; contribute to the economy's stabilization by reducing vulnerability to financial crises, pro-cyclical movements in finance, and by helping to maintain moderate rates of inflation; and aid the poor by providing basic financial and banking services.

6.2. Towards a post-financial liberalization policy agenda

In the last few years, Keynesian economists have begun to articulate a post-financial liberalization agenda. This emerging body of work is wide ranging, and space constraints preclude anything more than a brief treatment of this literature. This research is founded on the following four propositions. (1) There is no single, correct template for financial policy in developing countries. (2) It is the task of national policymakers to design and implement those financial policies that are consistent with human and economic development objectives, reflect the priorities of diverse social groups, and take account of the needs of the disenfranchised. (3) Policymakers in developing countries have the right to engage in policy and institutional experimentation on the national and regional level. (4) The rights and priorities of members of the financial community and external actors are no more important than those of other domestic social actors.

Beyond the general themes articulated above, we see in the Keynesian literature presentation of a diverse array of policies toward internal and external financial flows. Discussion of the specifics of these policies is beyond the scope of this paper, but for the sake of illustration I highlight below a few policies that have been proposed. I direct interested readers to the original sources for specific discussions of policy (for example, Chang and Grabel, 2004; Epstein and Grabel, 2006; Epstein, Grabel and Jomo KS, 2004; Grabel 2003a, 2003b, 2004, and references therein).

For instance, in Grabel (2004) I make a case for what I term a "trip wire–speed bump" regime. This regime is essentially a system of graduated, transparent capital controls that are activated whenever information about the economy indicates that controls are necessary to prevent nascent macroeconomic fragilities from culminating in serious difficulties or even in a crisis. In this view, measures that reduce financial instability and the likelihood of crises can protect living standards and economic growth, while also protecting policy autonomy by making it less likely that external actors can trade influence over policy for financial assistance. The trip wires that I develop are consistent with post-Keynesian theory, but I acknowledge that these, too, are insufficient policy tools to avert crisis. I argue that trip wires can contribute to crisis prevention only if they operate in the context of an overall policy regime in which investor options and market volatility are constrained by governmental action (such as through speed bumps). As such, a trip wire–speed bump regime reaches far beyond dissemination of information, the hallmark of the neoclassical predictors project.

Many heterodox (and even some mainstream) economists have written favorably of the controls over international private capital inflow utilized in both Chile and Colombia during much of the 1990s (for example, Eichengreen, 1999; Grabel, 2003a; Prasad, Rogoff, Wei, and Kose, 2003). These Chilean-style capital controls, as they have come to be known, had the effect of lengthening the time horizons of foreign investors and of shifting the composition of international capital flows towards foreign direct and away from debt and portfolio investment. Many heterodox economists have also noted that Malaysia's use of far more stringent (though shorter-lived) capital controls following the East Asian crisis of 1997–98 (and also in 1994) demonstrates the positive role that capital controls can play in promoting financial stability and economic stabilization and in protecting policy autonomy.

Other studies have argued that restrictions on currency convertibility and ceilings or surcharges on foreign debt levels can enhance financial stability and policy autonomy (Grabel, 2003a); that "developmentalist" central banks have a central role to play in the achievement of pro-poor economic growth; that variable asset-based reserve requirements can promote stability and facilitate the flow of funds to projects of the highest developmental and social priority; and that programs that forge linkages between informal and formal financial institutions, support microfinance institutions, and establish specialized lending institutions can enhance the ability of the financial system to serve diverse constituencies (Epstein and Grabel, 2006).

The foregoing has demonstrated that the neoclassical financial liberalization prescription has been marked by false starts and is now at a dead end. As a consequence, the opportunity now exists for Keynesian economists to make substantial contributions to post-liberalization development policy for the 21st century. Progressive and feasible financial

institutions and practices must be founded on the theoretical and normative commitments of the Keynesian tradition.

7.   Are we all Keynesians yet?

It may well be that the current global financial crisis and the significant
shifts in national power that will likely follow it create intellectual and
political space for the policy diversity and the right to policy experimentation with which a commitment to Keynesianism has been long
associated. As at the time of writing, the IMF is being pressed by member countries to increase the representation and voice of countries such
as China that have long rejected the idea that neoclassical economic
theory is the appropriate intellectual foundation for economic policy in
developing countries. Moreover, the momentum behind the movement
to enforce conformance with policies that derive from neoclassical theory may have been dealt a fatal blow by the failures of this regime in its
home. This may especially be the case because one consequence of the
crisis (and of the change in the US administration) is a diminution in US
hubris about economic policy. We may also take heart from the fact that
policymakers in some countries (including Bolivia, Ecuador, Venezuela,
Argentina, Turkey, China, India, Brazil, and many European countries)
are taking pains to indict the neoliberal model with which the USA, the
IMF–World Bank–WTO and the economics profession have been so long
associated. While such sentiments, especially in the developing world
are not new, the current conjuncture may weaken the case for neoliberalism to the point that critics can finally be heard. This takes us back
to the work of Keynes, whose ideas are ever more relevant as we seek to
understand the economic challenges of the 21st century.

It is obviously too early to say whether current circumstances will leave
a lasting intellectual imprint on the economics profession. Were these
matters to be decided by an unbiased community of scholars with no
reputational or professional stake in the outcome – were the community
to deliberate about these matters behind a veil of ignorance – we
would have good reason to expect a rapid and dramatic restoration of
Keynesianism in the field of finance and development. But intellectual
controversies of this sort are not resolved in that way. And so, the
greater hope must lie in the openness of graduate students and emerging scholars to the value of Keynesian insights. One wonders how many
more crises the world will have to suffer before these "new Keynesians"
are in a position to influence economic policy choices in the North
and in the South. It may be that these cohorts of economists will take

some confidence from the actions and statements of contemporary political leaders (such as those in Latin America, China, and India) who rightly see in the current crisis proof of the bankruptcy of neoliberalism and support for the case that the challenges of these times demand new strategies that build on and extend the key tenets of Keynesianism.

Notes

1 This section draws heavily on Grabel (1995, 1996a,b, 2000, 2003a,b, 2004, 2007, 2008), Epstein and Grabel (2006) and Chang and Grabel (2004). See these works for further discussion and citations to relevant literature.

2 Writing in finance and development certainly predates the 1970s, but serious study in this area only began in the early 1970s with the publication of McKinnon and Shaw's work.

3 Ramos (1986) reports that real deposit rates peaked at 9, 29, and 27 percent in Chile, Argentina, and Uruguay, respectively, while real lending rates in these countries peaked at 27, 127, and 40 percent.

4 The voluminous predictors literature is usefully reviewed in several works – e.g., Berg and Patillo (1998), Edison (2000), Eichengreen (1999: ch. 6), Flood and Marion (1999), Goldfajn and Valdés (1997), Gonzalez-Hermillosa (1999), Hardy (1998), Hawkins and Klau (2000), IMF (1998, ch. 4), and Sharma (1999). It bears noting that not all neoclassical development economists view efforts to create predictors as viable or sufficient to prevent crisis.

5 See Eichengreen and Portes (1997) and the papers collected in Kenen (1996) for a summary and evaluation of the decisions taken at the Halifax Summit. These works also discuss the recommendations of the Rey Committee (formed at Halifax) and the decisions taken at the 1996 Group of Seven Summit (in Lyons) on crisis prevention and the need for information dissemination.

6 General descriptions of these approaches draw on Goldstein, Kaminsky and Reinhart (2000).

7 Goldstein, Kaminsky and Reinhart (2000) deploy the "signals methodology" elaborated in Kaminsky and Reinhart (1999) and other related work by these authors, e.g., Goldstein (1997a), Kaminsky, Lizondo and Reinhart (1997), and Kaminsky and Reinhart (2000). The description of the authors' empirical findings is taken from Goldstein, Kaminsky and Reinhart (2000: ch. 8).

8 Note that they find that banking crises in developing economies are harder to predict using monthly data than are currency crises.

9 They acknowledge that their early warning system would neither have predicted difficulties in Indonesia during the Asian crisis, nor Argentina's difficulties following the Mexican crisis.

10 Discussion in this subsection draws heavily on work cited in note 1.

11 It is worth recalling Minsky's 1987 observations about the macroeconomic costs incurred by acting on the view that "that which can be securitized, will be securitized" (cited in Minsky, 2008, p. 2).

12 See Epstein, Grabel and Jomo KS (2004) for discussion of the extent and means by which financial arrangements in Chile, Colombia, Taiwan, India, China, Singapore and Malaysia achieved these three objectives during the 1990s.

References

Arestis, P. and Demetriades, P. (1997), 'Financial development and economic growth: Assessing the evidence', *Economic Journal*, May, pp. 783–99.
Arestis, P. and Glickman, M. (2002), 'Financial crisis in Southeast Asia: Dispelling illusion the Minskyian way', *Cambridge Journal of Economics*, pp. 237–60.
Bajaj, Vikas. (2009), 'Has the economy hit bottom yet?', *New York Times*, March 15, p. WK1.
Baldacci, E., de Mello, L. and Inchauste, G. (2002), *Financial Crisis, Poverty and Income Distribution*, paper presented at the IMF conference on Macroeconomic Policies and Poverty Reduction, Washington DC.
Berg, A. and Pattillo, C. (1998), 'Are currency crises predictable? A test', IMF Working Paper, November.
Braunstein, E. and Heintz, J. (2006), 'Gender bias and central bank policy: Employment and inflation reduction', PERI Working Paper www.peri.umass.edu.
Chang, H.-J. (2002), *Kicking Away the Ladder*, London: Anthem.
Chang, H.-J. and Grabel, I. (2004), *Reclaiming Development: An Alternative Economic Policy Manual*, London: Zed Books.
Chang, H.-J., Palma, G. and Whittaker, H. (2001), *Financial Liberalization and the Asian Financial Crisis*. Basingstoke: Palgrave.
Cohen, P. (2009), 'Ivory tower unswayed by crashing economy', *New York Times*, March 4, p. C1.
Corbett, J. and Vines, D. (1998), *The Asian Crisis: Competing Explanations*, Center for Economic Policy Analysis. Working Paper Series III, July.
Cornia, G.A. (2003), 'Globalization and the distribution of income between and within countries', in Ha-Joon Chang (ed.), *Rethinking Development Economics*, London: Anthem Press, pp. 325–45.
Cosh, A. and Hughes, A. (2008), 'Takeovers after takeovers', in Philip Arestis and John Eatwell (eds), *Issues in Finance and Industry: Essays in Honour of Ajit Singh*, Basingstoke, Hampshire: Palgrave Macmillan, pp. 215–36.
Crotty, J. and Kang-kook Lee (2004), 'From East Asian miracle to neoliberal mediocrity: The effects of liberalization and financial opening on the post-crisis Korean economy', unpublished paper, University of Massachusetts, Political Economy Research Institute, www.peri.umass.edu.
Davidson, P. (1972), *Money and the Real World*, New York: Halsted Press.
Demirgüç-Kunt, A. and Detragiache, E. 1999. 'Financial liberalization and financial fragility', in B. Pleskovic and J. Stiglitz (eds), *Annual World Bank Conference on Development Economics*, Washington, DC: World Bank, pp. 303–31.
Demirgüç-Kunt, A. and Detragiache, E. (1998), 'Financial liberalization and financial fragility', International Monetary Fund Working Paper, No. 83.
Edison, H. (2000), 'Do indicators of financial crises work? An evaluation of an early warning system', Board of Governors of the Federal Reserve System. International Finance DiscussionPapers, July.

Eichengreen, B. (1999), *Toward a New International Financial Architecture*, Washington, DC: Institute for International Economics.

Eichengreen, B. (2001), 'Capital account liberalization: what do cross-country studies tell us?', *World Bank Economic Review* 15(3), 341–65.

Eichengreen, B. and Portes, R. (1997), 'Managing financial crises in emerging market', in Maintaining Financial Stability in a Global Economy. A symposium sponsored by the Federal Reserve Bank of Kansas City, August, pp. 193–225.

Eichengreen, B., Rose, A. and Wyplosz, C. (1996), 'Exchange rate mayhem: the antecedents and aftermath of speculative attacks', *Economic Policy*, 21(21), 249–312.

Eichengreen, B. and Wyplosz, C. (1993), 'The Unstable EMS', *Brookings Papers on Economic Activity*, pp. 51–124.

Epstein, G. and Grabel, I. (2006), *Financial Policies for Pro-Poor Growth*, study prepared for the United Nations Development Programme (UNDP), International Poverty Centre, Global Training Programme on Economic Policies for Growth, Employment and Poverty Reduction.

Epstein, G., Grabel, I. and Jomo, K.S. (2004), 'Capital management techniques in developing countries: An assessment of experiences from the 1990's and lessons for the future', G24 Discussion Paper No. 27, New York and Geneva: United Nations.

Flood, R. and Marion, N. (1999), 'Perspectives on the recent currency crisis literature', *International Journal of Finance and Economics*, pp. 1–26.

Frankel, J. and Rose, A. (1996), 'Currency crashes in emerging markets: An empirical treatment', *Journal of International Economics*, November, pp. 351–68.

Goldfajn, I. and Valdés, R. (1997), *Are Currency Crises Predictable?*, Working paper of the International Monetary Fund, Number 159, December.

Goldstein, M. (1997a), 'Presumptive indicators of vulnerability to financial crises in emerging economies', in P. Basu (ed.), *Creating Resilient Financial Regimes in Asia: Challenges and Policy Options*, Oxford: Oxford University Press, pp. 79–132.

Goldstein, M. (1997b), 'Commentary: The causes and propagation of financial instability: lessons for policymakers', in 'Maintaining Financial Stability in a Global Economy', A symposium sponsored by the Federal Reserve Bank of Kansas City, August, pp. 96–117.

Goldstein, M., Kaminsky, G. and Reinhart, C. (2000), *Assessing Financial Vulnerability: An Early Warning System for Emerging Markets*, Washington, DC: Institute for International Economics.

Gonzalez-Hermillosa, B. (1999), 'Developing indicators to provide early warnings of banking crises', *Finance and Development*, June, pp. 36–9.

Grabel, I. (1995), 'Speculation-led economic development: A post-Keynesian interpretation of financial liberalization in the Third World', *International Review of Applied Economics*, 9(2), 127–49.

Grabel, I. (1996a), 'Financial markets, the state and economic development: Controversies within theory and policy', *International Papers in Political Economy*, 3(1), pp. 1–42.

Grabel, I. (1996b), 'Marketing the Third World: The contradictions of portfolio investment in the global Economy', *World Development*, 24(11), pp. 1761–76.

Grabel, I. (2000), 'The political economy of "policy credibility": The new-classical macroeconomics and the remaking of emerging economies', *Cambridge Journal of Economics*, 24(1), pp. 1–19.

Grabel, I. (2003a), 'Averting crisis: Assessing measures to manage financial integration in emerging economies', *Cambridge Journal of Economics*, 27(3), pp. 317–36.

Grabel, I. (2003b), 'International private capital flows and developing countries', in Ha-Joon Chang (ed.), *Rethinking Development Economics*, London: Anthem Press, pp. 325–45.

Grabel, I. (2004), 'Trip wires and speed bumps: Managing financial risks and reducing the potential for financial crises in developing economies', G-24 Discussion Paper No. 33, New York and Geneva: United Nations.

Grabel, I. (2007), 'Policy coherence or conformance? The new World Bank–IMF–WTO rhetoric on trade and investment in developing countries', *Review of Radical Political Economics*, 39(3), 335–41.

Grabel, I. (2008b), 'Global Finance and Development: False Starts, Dead Ends, and Socio-Economic Alternatives', in John B. Davis and Wilfred Dolfsma (eds), *The Elgar Companion to Social Economics*, Cheltenham, UK and Northampton, USA: Edward Elgar, pp. 496–518.

Hardy, D. 1998. 'Are banking crises predictable?', *Finance and Development*, December, pp. 32–5.

Hardy, D. and Pazarbasioglu, C. (1998), 'Leading indicators of banking crises: Was Asia different?', *International Monetary Fund Working Paper*, June.

Hawkins, J. and Klau, M. (2000), 'Measuring potential vulnerabilities in emerging market economies', Bank for International Settlements. Working Papers, October.

Hirschmann, Albert. (1986), *Rival Views of Market Society*, New York: Viking.

International Monetary Fund (IMF) (1998), 'Financial crises: Characteristics and indicators of vulnerability', *World Economic Outlook*, May, pp. 74–97.

Kamin, S. and Babson, O. (1999), 'The contributions of domestic and external factors to Latin American devaluation crisis: an early warning systems approach', Board of Governors of the Federal Reserve System. International Finance Discussion Papers, September.

Kaminsky, G., Lizondo, S. and Reinhart, C. (1997), 'Leading indicators of currency crises', Working paper of the International Monetary Fund, Number 79, July.

Kaminsky, G. and Reinhart, C. (2000), 'On crises, contagion, and confusion', *Journal of International Economics*, pp. 145–68.

Kaminsky, G. and Reinhart, C. (1999), 'The twin crises: the causes of banking and balance-of-payments problems', *American Economic Review*, June, pp. 473–500.

Kenen, P. (ed.). (1996), From Halifax to Lyons: What has been done about crisis management? Essays in International Finance. Princeton University: Department of Economics, October.

Keynes, J.M. (1964), *The General Theory of Employment, Interest and Prices*. New York: Harcourt Brace Jovanovich.

Kotz, D. (1997), *Revolution from Above*. London: Routledge.

Krugman, P. (1979), 'A model of balance-of-payments crises', *Journal of Money, Credit, and Banking*, pp. 311–25.

Kuczynski, P.-P. and Williamson, J. (eds) (2003), *After the Washington Consensus*, Washington, DC: Institute for International Economics.

Lewis, P. and Stein, H. (1997), 'Shifting fortunes: The political economy of financial liberalization in Nigeria', *World Development*, 25(1), pp. 5–22.

Lohr, S. (2008), 'Wall Street's Extreme Sport', *New York Times*, November 5, p. B8.

McKinnon, R. (1973), *Money and Capital in Economic Development*, Washington, DC: Brookings Institution.

McKinnon, R. (1989), 'Macroeconomic instability and moral hazard in banking in a liberalizing economy', in P. Brock, M. Connolly and C. Gonzalez-Vega (eds), *Latin American Debt and Adjustment*, New York: Praeger, pp. 99–111.

McKinnon, R. (1991), *The Order of Economic Liberalization: Financial Control in the Transition to a Market Economy*, Baltimore: Johns Hopkins University Press.

Minsky, H.P. (2008), 'Securitization', issued as Policy Note No. 2, The Levy Economics Institute of Bard College.

Minsky, H. (1986), *Stabilizing an Unstable Economy*. New Haven: Yale University Press.

Nissanke, M. and Stein, H. (2003), 'Financial globalisation and economic development: Toward an institutional foundation', *Eastern Economics Journal*, 29(3).

Palma, G. (1998), 'Three and a half cycles of "mania, panic and [asymmetric] crash"', *Cambridge Journal of Economics*.

Polanyi, K. (1944), *The Great Transformation*. Boston: Beacon Press.

Prasad, E., Rogoff, K., Wei, S.-J. and Ayhan Kose, M. (2003), 'Effects of financial globalization on developing countries: Some empirical evidence'. http://www.imf.org/external/np/res/docs/2003/031703.htm.

Ramos, J. (1986), *Neoconservative Economics in the Southern Cone of Latin America, 1973–1983*, Baltimore: Johns Hopkins University Press.

Ravallion, M. (2002), 'Who is protected? On the incidence of fiscal adjustment', paper presented at the International Monetary Fund conference on Macroeconomic Policies and Poverty Reduction, Washington, DC, March 14–15.

Rodrik, D. (2007), *One Economics Many Recipes*, Princeton: Princeton University Press.

Rose, A. and Svensson, L.E.O. (1994), 'European exchange rate credibility before the fall', *European Economic Review*, May, pp. 1185–216.

Sachs, J., Tornell, A. and Velasco, A. (1996), 'Financial crises in emerging markets: the lessons from 1995', *Brookings Papers on Economic Activity*, pp. 147–215.

Sharma, S. (1999), 'The challenge of predicting economic crises', *Finance and Development*, June, pp. 40–2.

Shaw, E. (1973), *Financial Deepening in Economic Development*, New York: Oxford University Press.

Shiller, R. (2008), 'Challenging the crowd in whispers, not shouts', *New York Times*, November 2, p. B5.

Singh, A. and Weisse, B. (1998), 'Emerging stock markets, portfolio capital flows and long-term economic growth: micro and macroeconomic perspectives', *World Development*, 26(4), pp. 607–22.

Tobin, J. (1984), 'On the efficiency of the financial system', *Lloyds Bank Review*, 153, pp. 1–15.

United Nations Development Program (UNDP) (various years) *Human Development Report*, Oxford: Oxford University Press.

Weisbrot, M., Baker, D., Kraev, E. and Chen, J. (2001), 'The scorecard on globalization 1980–2000', Center for Economic Policy Research, September, www.cepr.net/globalization/scorecard_on_globalization.htm.

Weller, C. (2001), 'Financial crises after financial liberalisation: Exceptional circumstances or structural weakness?', *Journal of Development Studies*, 38(1), pp. 98–127.

Weller, C. and Hersh, A. (2004), 'The long and short of it: Global liberalization, poverty and inequality', *Journal of Post Keynesian Economics*, 26(3), pp. 471–504.

Williamson, J. and Mahar, M. (1998), 'A survey of financial liberalization', *Essays in International Finance*. Princeton University: Department of Economics, November.

2
Keynesian Growth Theory in the 21st Century

Amitava Krishna Dutt
Department of Economics and Policy Studies, University of Notre Dame

Abstract

This paper examines the future of Keynesian growth theory in terms of its relevance, prospects and likely characteristics. To do so, it first defines what it means by Keynesian growth theory, by focusing on the long-run role of aggregate demand, and briefly reviews short- and long-term changes in the world economy to argue that the relevance of Keynesian growth theory will increase in the 21st century. The paper then examines three specific models as examples of possible relevant Keynesian growth models. One of these features endogenous technological change and government investment, a second analyzes the interaction of animal spirits and financial fragility, and a third examines the determinants of growth and distribution in a growth context in which education converts low-skilled workers into high-skilled workers. The paper concludes by summarizing its main implications and by commenting on related methodological and policy issues.

JEL Classification: O41, E12

Keywords: Economic growth, aggregate demand, Keynesian growth models, technological change, government investment, business cycles, financialization, education, labor skills

1. Introduction[1]

What can be called Keynesian growth theory emerged in the 20th century after the publication of Keynes's *General Theory*, with early major contributions including those of Harrod (1939), Kahn (1959) and Robinson (1962). However, it is not quite accurate to say that it emerged anew, out of nowhere or, indeed, that it ever really 'emerged'. The theory was anticipated in the writings of earlier economists including, most notably, Malthus and Marx, who recognized that there could be general overproduction and deficient aggregate demand, although Marx seemed to think that such problems were of a temporary, and perhaps not long-run, nature. Moreover, the emergence of the theory after Keynes proved to be limited and short-lived since mainstream growth theory went in a pre-Keynesian direction by ignoring the possibility of deficient aggregate demand from the start by assuming that all saving is automatically invested and resources are always fully employed, as in the Solovian neoclassical model and in new or endogenous neoclassical growth theory.[2] Mainstream macroeconomic theory does take into consideration the Keynesian problem of aggregate demand, but only in short-run analysis; in the long run the problem is solved either by the invisible hand of the market working through labor and asset market adjustments, or by the visible hand of government macroeconomic policy. Keynesian growth theory lives on only in the heterodox underworld of the economics profession.

The purpose of this paper is to examine the possible fate and likely nature of Keynesian growth theory in the 21st century. Is it likely to continue to exist in the underworld of economic heterodoxy or will it finally emerge as the new dominant theory of growth or at least a strong alternative to the (old and new) neoclassical theory of growth? If it does emerge, what form will it take? These questions are impossible to answer if one takes Keynesian growth theory at all seriously, since the future is unpredictable and we simply do not know. Instead, this paper will examine whether, given the conditions of the 21st century, there are stronger reasons (both in the sense that it is more necessary and more likely) for it to emerge than those that existed in the previous century, and if so, in what form or forms.

These questions still remain very difficult to answer, partly because they are open to different interpretations depending on our answers to the following further questions. What do we mean by Keynesian growth theory? What are the conditions of the 21st century that make it different – at least in degree – from the previous century? The next two brief sections discuss what is meant by Keynesian growth theory and the 21st century. Sections 4 through 6 examine three sets of issues which make Keynesian growth theory relevant for the 21st century and suggests directions in which it is likely to, and should, go. Section 7 offers some remarks on methodology and concludes.

2. What is Keynesian growth theory?

This section defines what is meant by Keynesian growth theory for the purposes of this paper. It does so by discussing some general meanings of Keynesian growth theory and by reviewing some simple growth models that can be justifiably called Keynesian and contrasting them with those that cannot be given that epithet.

As the name suggests, Keynesian growth theory can be defined as the theory of growth which grew out of Keynes's (1936) macroeconomics, as developed in *The General Theory*. There is a sense in which this is true, since Keynesian growth theory was based on Keynes's macroeconomics of *The General Theory* which examined the determination of short-run equilibrium unemployment, abstracting from longer-run dynamics due to capital accumulation, technological change and population growth, and since it was developed by Keynesian economists such as Harrod (1939), Kahn (1959) and Robinson (1962), as mentioned earlier. However, as also mentioned earlier, Keynes's theory had much in common with the earlier dynamic theories of economists like Malthus and Marx, and, indeed, with some of his contemporaries, most notably Kalecki. Moreover, defining Keynesian growth theory in terms of its historical lineage from Keynes has the problem that we are not clear on what precisely is meant by Keynes's economics. As developments in short-run macroeconomics suggest, Keynesian economics has been characterized variously (and not necessarily equivalently) as the economics in which: aggregate demand plays a major role in determining output and employment; involuntary unemployment can persist; the economy is subject to economic fluctuations and instability; uncertainty and psychological factors have an important role in affecting the behavior of economic decision-makers; and fiscal and monetary policy can affect the level of output and employment. It therefore seems preferable to define Keynesian growth theory in terms of its analytical characteristics.

All of these features of Keynesian economics in general have some claim to capturing some key characteristics of Keynesian growth theory. The focus on aggregate demand – which depends on determinants of consumption and investment demand – distinguishes it from theories – both classical and neoclassical – which stress the role of aggregate supply, that is, determinants of the supply of factors of production like capital and labor, and their productivity. The existence of unemployment distinguishes it from neoclassical theories of growth in which growth occurs with full employment. Aggregate demand fluctuations and instability have been emphasized in it, as compared to growth models with stable growth. The importance of animal spirits in an uncertain environment is stressed in Keynesian growth models in which greater business optimism results in higher growth, while uncertainty is replaced by calculable risk in the form of white-noise error terms and rational expectations in other models. Finally, macroeconomic policy changes have long-run effects in such models, while policy seems to be ineffective in other models where, for instance, money is superneutral and fiscal policy either has no effects – due to Ricardian equivalence – or negative effects due to the crowding out of investment by fiscal expansion. However, not all of these characteristics are unique to Keynesian growth models. Classical and Marxian models of growth allow for unemployment in a growing economy, real-business cycles with aggregate supply shocks imply economic fluctuations, "new" neoclassical growth theory models imply that the growth rate is determined by the saving rate, which depends on psychological factors like the rate of time preference, and economic policy – in the form of fiscal incentives or government spending promoting research and development – can have positive growth effects in new endogenous growth models. Moreover, some models that can be called Keynesian models of growth do not exhibit all these characteristics: for instance, Robinson's model of growth does not imply instability or fluctuations, but rather seems to imply a stable growth path in which the desired rate of accumulation (determined by investment demand) becomes equal to the actual rate of accumulation (determined by saving), and some models along Kaleckian lines do not seem to explicitly introduce uncertainty, although they are not necessarily inconsistent with it. The feature that is uniquely Keynesian in growth models, and is found in all such models, however, is the role of aggregate demand as a determinant of growth.

The simplest Keynesian model (of a closed economy without government fiscal activity) in which aggregate demand has a central role to play assumes that I, real investment, is exogenously given, and real saving is given by

$$S = sY, \tag{1}$$

where Y is real income and output. Output increases (decreases) when there is excess demand (supply) in the goods market so that, in equilibrium, we have

$$Y = C + I. \tag{2}$$

where C is real consumption, and, by definition, $S = Y - C$. The equilibrium level of output is given by

$$Y = \frac{I}{s}.$$

Only a slight modification of the assumptions of this model generates a Keynesian endogenous growth model. We maintain equations (1) and (2) but, rather than assuming that investment is exogenously given, we assume that

$$I = \gamma_0 K + \gamma_1 Y \tag{3}$$

where $\gamma_i > 0$ are positive investment parameters and K is the stock of real capital. Investment, being the addition to capital stock (abstracting from depreciation, for simplicity), is assumed to be higher when the stock of capital is higher (representing a scale effect). It is also assumed to increase with the level of Y, as is usual in macroeconomic models, to show that more buoyant markets make firms increase investment. The equilibrium level of capacity utilization, $u = Y/K$, is now given by

$$u = \frac{\gamma_0}{s - \gamma_1} \tag{4}$$

where, we assume, for a positive level of output and capacity utilization and for the stability of equilibrium, that $s > \gamma_1$. Substituting this equilibrium value of capacity utilization into the saving equation (1) or the investment equation (3) we can solve for the equilibrium level of growth of capital, $g = I/K$, that is,

$$g = \frac{s\gamma_0}{s - \gamma_1} \tag{5}$$

The determination of equilibrium in this model can be shown graphically as shown in Figure 2.1. The g^S curve shows the relation between saving as a ratio of capital stock and the level of capacity utilization, that is,

$$g^S = s\,u \tag{1'}$$

and the g^I shows the relation between investment as a ratio of capital stock and capacity utilization, that is,

$$g^I = \gamma_0 + \gamma_1 u. \tag{3'}$$

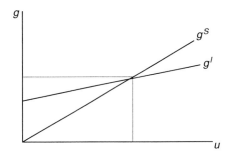

Figure 2.1   The simplest Keynesian growth model

The goods market is in equilibrium when the two curves intersect, so that saving and investment are equal, that is, $g^S = g^I$.

What makes this simple model a Keynesian model? Two properties of the model are worth emphasizing. First, capacity utilization adjusts to bring the goods market to equilibrium, as in the standard Keynesian macroeconomic model, where output adjusts to bring saving and investment to equilibrium. Second, the equilibrium level of growth of capital, and hence output, which grows at the same rate as capital since u does not change in equilibrium, is determined by the aggregate demand parameters, s and γ_i. A rise in s implies a lower rate of growth, illustrating the paradox of thrift for the growing economy, and a rise in say γ_0, autonomous investment, increases growth. We will call growth models Keynesian if they satisfy these two properties, although the first is not necessary.[3] The essential characteristic of a Keynesian growth model is therefore one in which the rate of growth of the economy is affected by parameters that represent the aggregate demand side of the economy, that is, saving, investment and other parameters (for instance, government expenditure or tax parameters in a more general model).

The model discussed so far is a very simple Keynesian growth model. What more complicated models can be called Keynesian ones? To examine this question in a general way, we extend it by introducing two sets of parameters into the model, **x** and **κ**, where the elements of vector **x** are given at a point in time and the elements of vector **κ** are always given.[4] Assume that we can solve for equilibrium values of u and g (denoting, as before, the rate of capacity utilization and the rate of growth of capital stock), given **x** and **κ**, given by

$$u = u(\mathbf{x}, \boldsymbol{\kappa}) \tag{6}$$

and

$$g = g(\mathbf{x}, \boldsymbol{\kappa}). \tag{7}$$

The elements of vector x can vary over time according to some dynamic equations of the form

$$\frac{d\mathbf{x}}{dt} = F(u, g, \mathbf{x}, \boldsymbol{\kappa}), \tag{8}$$

where the elements of vector $\boldsymbol{\kappa}$ are given. Substituting equations (6) and (7) into (8) we obtain a dynamic system for x. This system may exhibit a wide range of dynamic behaviors: it can converge to a unique stable equilibrium, have a finite number of stable equilibria, a continuum of equilibria, imply limit cycles, or be globally unstable. Let there be a subset of the parameters in the vectors x and $\boldsymbol{\kappa}$ that can represent aggregate demand parameters, which can be represented by the vectors $\mathbf{x}^d$ and $\boldsymbol{\kappa}^d$. Then we can define a growth model represented by these equations to be a Keynesian one if (a) in equations (6) and (7) u and g change when the values of some element of $\mathbf{x}^d$ or $\boldsymbol{\kappa}^d$ change (to represent an increase in aggregate demand) holding all other elements of x and $\boldsymbol{\kappa}$ constant and (b) if equation (8) has a solution, $\mathbf{x}^*$ which satisfies F( ) = 0, g in equation (7) after substituting the value $\mathbf{x}^*$ into it, changes when some elements of $\boldsymbol{\kappa}^d$ change to represent an increase in aggregate demand.

Keynesian models of growth that are more complicated than the simple one discussed earlier can introduce variables or parameters representing the distribution of income between different classes, and allow different classes to have different saving propensities. Some models with these features are well known among heterodox growth theorists.

In the model that has its origins in the writings of Kalecki (1971) and Steindl (1952), firms are assumed to fix their price and adjust their output level in response to demand. Firms are assumed to have a given labor–output ratio a_0. Given the money wage and the price, the real wage, ω is given, so that the rate of profit is given by

$$r = (1 - a_0 \, \omega) \, u.$$

Assuming that workers who receive wage income do not save, but capitalists who receive profits save a fraction s_c of their profits, we obtain

$$S = s_c \, r \, K. \tag{9}$$

Using the same investment function as before, we find that the equilibrium levels of capacity utilization and growth are given by

$$u = \frac{\gamma_0}{s_c(1 - a_0\varpi) - \gamma_1}.$$ (4')

and

$$g = \frac{s_c(1 - a_0\varpi)\gamma_0}{s_c(1 - a_0\varpi) - \gamma_1}$$ (5')

where we assume that $s_c(1 - a_0\omega) > \gamma_1$. This condition is the standard stability condition of Keynesian models and states that the responsiveness of savings to changes in the capacity utilization rate exceeds the responsiveness of investment. In this model, there is only one run, since all of the parameters of the model, including ω, are given throughout. The model is obviously a Keynesian one by our definition, since both u and g are affected by our aggregate demand parameters. Moreover, it implies wage-led growth: an increase in the real wage, as equation (5') shows, increases the rate of growth of capital stock and output.[5]

There are also models that end up with u converging to an exogenously given rate of capacity utilization. If such a model implies that the growth rate of the economy still depends positively on aggregate demand parameters, it can still be called a Keynesian growth model. Assume that the investment and saving functions are given by equations (3') and (9). In the short run ω is given and u changes in response to excess demand in the goods market, so that in short-run equilibrium, with $g^S = g^I$, capacity utilization and the rate of growth of capital are determined, as in the previous model, by equations (4') and (5'). In the long run, assume that if firms have excess capacity, so that u is lower than u_d, they reduce their price-cost markup in order to increase the demand for their product. Since the markup and the real wage are inversely related, as shown by the equation

$$\varpi = \frac{1}{(1 + z)a_0},$$

where z is the markup rate, in the long run we have a dynamic equation of the form

$$\dot{\varpi} = -\psi[u - u_d]$$ (10)

where the overdot denotes a time derivative, and where $\psi > 0$ is a speed of adjustment constant. If there is excess capacity in the short run, so that $u < u_d$, the markup will fall and the real wage will rise, which will increase capacity utilization by increasing consumption demand, making u adjust towards u_d. In long-run equilibrium ω attains its stationary value and $u = u_d$. The long-run equilibrium values of the real wage and the growth rate of capital and output can be determined by substituting $u = u_d$ into equations (4') and (5'), which imply

$$\omega = \frac{(s_c - \gamma_1)u_d - \gamma_0}{s_c a_0 u_d}$$

and

$$g = \gamma_0 + \gamma_1 u_d.$$

When the aggregate demand parameter denoting autonomous investment, γ_0, increases the long-run rate of capacity utilization remains at u_d but the rate of growth of capital, g, increases. This model, which is basically Robinson's (1962) model of growth, and which Marglin (1984) calls the neo-Keynesian growth model, is therefore a Keynesian growth model.[6] The increase in autonomous investment increases capacity utilization in the short run and therefore increases short-run growth, but in the long run increases growth by reducing ω. In the long run, the increase in autonomous demand increases the price relative to the money wage, reducing the real wage, and by redistributing income from wage recipients to profit recipients, who have a higher propensity to save, increases saving, investment and the rate of capital accumulation.

However, if economic growth is constrained by an exogenously fixed rate of growth of labor supply and given or exogenously growing technology, or, if growth is constrained by saving, and saving in equilibrium is identically equal to investment, then an increase in aggregate demand parameters will have no growth-enhancing effect and models with these features are not Keynesian. The neoclassical model assumes that at least in the long run, growth occurs with full employment. If the rate of growth of labor supply is given, say at the rate n, since the labor–output ratio, a_0 is given, and if output is always at desired capacity utilization (or even full capacity utilization), full employment growth requires that $g = n$, which determines g. With $u = u_d$ and $g = n$, we can no longer ensure that the investment function given by equation (3') will be satisfied in its present form. So we may drop the investment function, assuming that all saving is automatically invested, there being no autonomous investment function.[7] Therefore, the saving function, equation (9), will determine the rate of profit, which is given by

$$r = \frac{n}{s_c u_d},$$

which, in turn, will determine the real wage, ω. The growth rate of output depends on the growth rate of labor supply and is unaffected by any investment parameters (because there are none in the model).[8] If we allow for technological change, with labor augmenting technological change at a given rate a, the rate of growth of capital and output will be given by $g = n + a$, the rate of growth of effective labor supply. The neo-Marxian model assumes that the real wage, ω, is given exogenously by the state of class struggle, and there is full or desired capacity utilization, so that $u = u_d$, so that the saving function again determines the rate of growth of capital, given by $g = s_c(1 - a_0 \omega)u_d$. Again, there is no room for the investment function, which we can drop, under the assumption is that excess investment demand will not be realized (or will be choked off by increases in the interest rate which will reduce investment demand). Again, an increase in autonomous investment has no effect on growth, which is determined by saving. Growth depends on the saving rate and on the exogenously given wage rate: an increase in the saving rate will increase the growth rate, while a fall in the real wage (which increases profits) will also increase the growth rate. In this case, we have profit-led growth.[9]

The Keynesian growth models that we have discussed here can be, and indeed have been, criticized on several counts. First, it is argued that they seem to conflate short-run and long-run issues. According to this view, aggregate demand considerations are relevant in the short run, but are irrelevant for the long run, in which aggregate supply determines growth. Keynesian growth models, unwarrantedly bring in short-run considerations into the analysis of the long run. The problem with this criticism is that it makes an a priori judgment about what is relevant for the short run and the long run, arbitrarily relegating aggregate demand issues to the short run. It would be more appropriate to deduce what happens in the short and long runs given the assumptions of the model based on important relevant features of real economies, and show whether aggregate demand has a role in the long run or not. Second, it is argued that they have some undesirable long-run properties. All of them imply that rate of growth of labor demand (which presumably depends on the rates of growth of capital and output and on the rate of technological change) can be different from the rate of growth of labor supply, so that the unemployment rate can increase or decrease indefinitely. Such an outcome is neither realistic nor consistent with the notion of a long-run equilibrium. Additionally, some of the Keynesian growth models imply that the rate of capacity utilization, which is endogenously determined, does not have to be equal to some exogenously given planned or desired rate of capacity utilization. This, again, can be argued to be inconsistent with the notion of long-run equilibrium at which, one would suppose, all plans would be realized.[10] Third, the models allegedly lack proper micro-foundations. In particular, the firms and consumers are not "rational" optimizing agents. A distinctive feature of many neoclassical and new growth theory models is that they involve optimizing agents – an important exception being Solow's (1956) pioneering neoclassical growth model! – usually maximizing utility or profits over infinite horizons.

3.   Characteristics of the 21st century

One way of defining the term 21st century is simply as whatever comes in the future. A more useful way is to interpret it as a future with some specific characteristics. Any list of such characteristics will be contentious. To avoid unnecessary controversy I will simply list, without any defense, some characteristics and discuss their implications both for the likelihood of the emergence of Keynesian growth theory and for the forms it is likely to take. By characteristics I refer to both those of the real world and of growth theory.

Regarding the real world, there are both short-term and longer-term issues. For the short term the most obvious issues relate to the financial and economic troubles in which the world economy, including the economies of the economically advanced nations, finds itself at the time of this writing. In fact, the crisis has its origins in the housing and financial markets of the United States. Unemployment levels are high, capacity utilization low, growth rates reduced, and the need for activist government macroeconomic policy and even government regulation of the financial system, and limited direct intervention of the government in the economy, are more widely accepted. However, these acceptances are sometimes grudging, and by no means unanimous. There is also the sense that many have that these issues are only of a short-term nature, and will disappear in the longer term, even if the longer term comes less soon than in past downturns since World War II. However, it is also possible that the effects of the recession may last for a long time, perhaps through the imposition of financial regulations which prevent high levels of debt-financed consumption spending, and there is likely to be greater reliance on government fiscal activity, including government investment, for promoting growth.

Longer-term considerations refer to interrelated changes that have come about as a result of government policies, technological change and the spread of economic development, even if uneven, to less-developed regions of the world. The major policy changes involve liberalization and increasing openness due to neoliberal reforms. Liberalization has deregulated product, labor and financial markets within countries, privatized government enterprises, and cut back the role of the government in general by reducing taxes and government expenditures. Fears of inflation have also made countries adopt restrictive monetary policies and inflation targeting. Countries have also become more open to trade, foreign investment, and financial capital flows with reduction of trade barriers and capital market restrictions. International labor mobility has not increased correspondingly, but even on this front an upward trend is detectable, as shown by the increasing number of foreign-born people living in countries, and by increases in international remittances. Several aspects of these changes have been collectively referred to as globalization, and others as financialization. Technological change has increased production capacity and reduced the costs of transport, communications and transactions. Economic development has been made possible by government policies of a relatively dirigiste and inward-looking type, and has in turn made neoliberal policies possible, and consequently – by expanding trade and capital flows – fueled development unevenly over regions and people. Also as a result of technological changes, the distinction between skilled and unskilled workers has become sharper, so much so that many think that overall income distributional changes reflect mainly changes in the relative wages of skilled and unskilled workers and the extent to which unskilled labor can acquire skills, rather than changes in the relative position of capitalists and workers.

These changes have implications both for the relevance and the nature of Keynesian growth theory.

Regarding relevance, contractionary monetary policies, and the smaller size of governments, obviously imply lower levels of aggregate demand. The spread of development to more countries, thereby increasing the importance of external financing of productive units and the increase in capital movements, which sometimes relaxes foreign exchange constraints and occasionally makes it bind strongly with a vengeance, increases the relevance of aggregate demand management and makes growth depend more strongly on aggregate demand. Labor migration, capital flows and technological change make labor less of a constraint on growth in most countries, if ever it was a constraint except sporadically. Even at the world level, the shift in production to sections of the less-developed world with more unequal income distribution and huge supplies of labor, the transfer of technology to these countries, and the pursuit of generally contractionary policies, results in aggregate demand being outstripped by aggregate supply. All of this makes Keynesian models more relevant.

Regarding the nature of Keynesian growth models, we may confine our attention to a few obvious examples. First, there is the need to model the implications of increasing government expenditure, especially government investment to prop up growth in the face of recession but possibly in the future as well, as borrowing-led consumption becomes a less trustworthy engine of growth, and as environmental concerns and the role of government investment aimed at developing cleaner technology grows. Second, there is the need to analyze the implications of greater uncertainty and financialization to understand better how problems that produce crises like the current one can come about. Third, there is the need to analyze the implications of changes in the distribution of income between skilled and unskilled workers and the role of education.

Regarding growth theory, mainstream growth theory has examined the causes and consequences of technological change with renewed interest. Growth is no longer viewed as being determined by the growth of primary factors of production and limited by diminishing returns to produced factors of production, and increasingly seen as being affected by factors which endogenously determine technological change. Meanwhile, heterodox growth theory has – at least in the underworld – developed rich models of growth which stress the roles of class divisions and aggregate demand (see, for instance, Taylor, 2004). The stage seems set for the emergence of Keynesian growth theory.

4.   Government policy and endogenous technological change

Recent macroeconomic debates concern the role of government policy in mitigating crises and in affecting long-run growth. While there seems to be general agreement about the need for government fiscal expansion to deal with recessions in view of the problems related to the efficacy of monetary policy, debates surround the long-run implications of fiscal expansion. This section develops a simple Keynesian growth model which incorporates government fiscal policy and technological change to address the long-run consequences of certain kinds of expansionary fiscal policy.

We use a variant of a simple Keynesian growth model that assumes that the government raises revenue through an income tax at rate τ, and spends on government consumption expenditure, denoted by G, and government investment expenditure, denoted by I_G. We also assume for now, for simplicity, that the government balances its budget and does not carry a debt, so that

$$\tau Y = G + I_G. \tag{11}$$

The level of government investment as a ratio of real income is assumed to be given by θ, so that

$$I_G = \theta\, Y. \tag{12}$$

The government fixes the tax rate and adjusts G to satisfy equation (11). We will examine fiscal policy changes mainly in terms of a change in the parameter θ, which implies substituting between government investment and government consumption expenditures.

Private saving is assumed to be a fraction, s, of disposable income (we do not distinguish between different classes of income recipients), so that the level of real consumption is given by

$$C = (1-s)\,(1-\tau)\, Y. \tag{13}$$

Private investment depends on the level of capacity utilization and on the ratio of the level of government investment to the capital stock. We assume here that private investment is complementary to government investment because of what has been called "crowding in", that is, government investment in infrastructure and technology provides a boost to private investment (see Taylor, 1991, and Aschauer, 1989, for empirical evidence).[11] We write the private investment function in the simple linear form

$$I/K = \gamma + \gamma_1\, u + \gamma_2\, (I_G/K), \tag{14}$$

where K is the stock of privately owned capital.

In the short run we assume that stocks of both private and government capital are fixed, as are levels of technology, and the level of "autonomous" private investment, given by γ, and that, as usual, the goods market clears through variations in the level of output and capacity utilization, which depend on the level of excess demand for goods. Assuming that the economy is closed, goods market equilibrium requires that

$$Y = (1-s)(1-\tau)Y + I + G + I_G. \tag{15}$$

Substituting from equations (11) through (14) into (15) we obtain the short-run equilibrium value of the level of capacity utilization,

$$u = \frac{\gamma}{s(1-\tau) - \gamma_1 - \gamma_2 \theta} \tag{16}$$

The equilibrium level of u increases with the level of "autonomous" investment, γ, falls with the saving rate (the paradox of thrift), rises with the tax rate, τ, and rises with the share of output invested by the government, θ. While the first two are standard results of Keynesian short-run macroeconomics, the last two deserve comment. The rise in the tax rate has an expansionary effect because of the balanced-budget assumption: a higher tax rate reduces consumption only partially because some of the disposable is saved, while the entire tax revenue is spent by the government, resulting in an increase in aggregate demand. The government investment–output ratio has a positive effect because although it represents a switch from government consumption to government investment expenditure, and therefore does not increase the level of aggregate demand directly, the indirect effect of the increase in government investment on private investment through the crowding-in effect expands aggregate demand and output.

In the long run we assume that stocks of capital, and γ and technology can change over time. The changes in the stocks of private and public capital are equal to the levels of private and government investment, respectively, assuming away depreciation, for simplicity. The growth rate of private capital stock, g, is therefore given by the equation

$$g = I/K. \tag{17}$$

There is no need to track changes in the public capital stock because it does not affect the levels of any of the variables of the model. It may be noted that the rate of (private) capital accumulation in the short run, substituting equations (14) and (16) into (17), is given by

$$g = \frac{s(1-\tau)\gamma}{s(1-\tau) - \gamma_1 - \gamma_2\theta} \tag{17'}$$

The productivity of labor at a point in time is given at the level A, so that we have

$$Y = AL, \tag{18}$$

where L is the level of employment. Denoting the rates of growth for variables with their level given by upper-case letter with corresponding lower-case letters, this implies that

$$y = a + l, \tag{19}$$

where, for instance, a is the rate of labor productivity growth. We assume that the rate of growth of labor productivity growth, a, depends on labor market conditions, that is, increasing tightness of the labor market results in a higher rate of labor productivity growth, and on the government investment–output ratio, θ. We represent technological change with the equation

$$\hat{a} = \mu(\theta)[l - n] \tag{20}$$

where μ, the rate at which labor productivity growth adjusts to the difference between the rate of growth of employment, l, and the rate of growth of the exogenously given level of labor supply, n, depends positively on θ. Firms increase labor productivity growth when the labor market becomes tighter, or the employment rate rises: necessity is the mother of invention. However, the rate at which labor productivity growth increases depends on the share of output invested by the government, investment which represents infrastructural and technology investment.

The first term of the investment function is given in the short run, but we assume that investment changes over the long run because of financial conditions and government policy responses. If the unemployment rate falls, γ is assumed to fall. A fall in the unemployment rate is assumed to exert an upward pressure on wages and prices, which reduces real money balances, which increases the interest rate and increases investment. Moreover, as the unemployment rate falls the Central Bank is assumed to slow down the economy by increasing the interest rate, thereby reducing inflation. In the long run, therefore, we assume that

$$\hat{\gamma} = -\lambda\,[l-n] \tag{21}$$

where $\lambda > 0$ is a speed of adjustment constant.[12]

The long-run dynamics of the model can be examined by using equations (20) and (21) after substituting from the other equations of the model. Using equations (16) and (19), and the definition $u = Y/K$, we obtain

$$l = \hat{\gamma} + g - a. \tag{22}$$

Substituting this into equations (20) and (21), and using equation (17′), we obtain

$$\hat{\gamma} = \frac{\lambda}{1+\lambda}\left[n + a - \frac{s(1-\tau)\gamma}{s(1-\tau)-\gamma_1-\gamma_2\theta} \right] \tag{23}$$

and

$$\hat{a} = \frac{\mu(\theta)}{1+\lambda}\left[\frac{s(1-\tau)\gamma}{s(1-\tau)-\gamma_1-\gamma_2\theta} - (n+a) \right]. \tag{24}$$

These two equations are the dynamic equations of the model which provide us with the relationships between γ and a and their rates of growth. We may examine the dynamics of the model using these equations and examine the nature of long-run equilibrium in it, at which γ and a become stationary.

It can be seen that if the equation

$$a = \frac{s(1-\tau)}{s(1-\tau)-\gamma_1-\gamma_2\theta}\gamma - n \tag{25}$$

is satisfied, equations (23) and (24) imply that $\hat{\gamma} = 0$ and $\hat{a} = 0$, so that the economy is in long-run equilibrium. The locus of long-run equilibrium levels of γ and a are as shown by the line marked $\hat{\gamma} = \hat{a} = 0$, the equation of which is given by (25). The model is therefore a zero-root model in which, rather than there being a unique long-run equilibrium, we have a continuum of equilibria on the $\hat{\gamma} = \hat{a} = 0$ line marked LR_1. The out-of-equilibrium dynamics of γ and a are shown by the horizontal and vertical arrows. The long-run equilibria are stable. This property of multiple long-run equilibria has some interesting implications for the long-run dynamics of the economy.

First, the long-run equilibrium position of the economy is path dependent in the sense that it depends on the initial position and hence, subsequent path, of the economy. If the economy starts from any given pair of γ and a that is not at a long-run equilibrium, say B_1, it will end up at the long-run equilibrium position shown by E_1. If, instead, the economy starts at B_2, it will end up at E_2. The move from B_1 to B_2 could be the result of an increase in the level of animal spirits or greater optimism on the part of firms, that is, an instantaneous increase in γ. This increase implies an increase in the rates of capacity utilization and growth in the short run, as shown by equations (16) and (17'). In the long run, γ falls, but the higher rate of accumulation and employment growth increases the rate of growth of labor productivity, and implies a higher rate of long-run equilibrium productivity growth and hence per-capita income growth at the long-run equilibrium compared to what it would have been had the initial level of γ not increased.

Second, when the economy is in long-run equilibrium, the unemployment rate becomes constant, since labor supply and labor demand grow at the same rate. This happens because if the unemployment rate is increasing (decreasing) there are induced adjustments in both aggregate demand (changes in γ) and in labor productivity growth (changes in a) which make the growth rate of labor demand adjust to that of labor supply. This result weakens the force of the criticism of basic Keynesian models of growth that disapproves of the fact that their long-run equilibrium positions in general imply continuous changes in the unemployment rate.[13]

Third, changes in government fiscal policy can have long-run effects on the growth rate of the economy. This can be illustrated by examining the effects of a change in the main parameter of interest in our model, that is, θ, the ratio of government investment to output. Suppose we are initially at the long-run equilibrium at E_1. An increase in θ will increase the rate of capacity utilization as discussed earlier and the rate of private capital accumulation in the short run, for the given levels of γ and a. To examine the long-run impact, we note that, as can be seen from equation (25), the $\hat{\gamma} = \hat{a} = 0$ line becomes steeper when θ increases, rotating from LR_1 to LR_2. Moreover, since the increase in θ increases μ, the rate of change of a increases, as seen from equation (24). Since the rate of change of a is higher relative to that of that of γ, it follows that the economy will move along a steeper path from E_1 to the new long-run equilibrium, E_3, than the one on which it moved from B_1 to E_1.

Fourth, the kind of fiscal policy used will affect the magnitude of the long-run impact of the policy change. This can be seen by examining the effects of a change in the tax rate, τ, without a change in θ, with the effects of the change in θ just discussed. It should be remembered that an increase in θ implies a change in the composition of government spending favoring government investment to government current consumption, without changes in the tax rate, while an increase in τ implies an increase in taxes as well as an increase in government expenditures leaving unchanged the government investment–GDP ratio, that is, a tax-financed increase in government current expenditure. The increase in τ, as discussed earlier, increases the short-run rate of capacity utilization, and equation (17′) shows that it also increases the rate of capital accumulation: the increase in capacity utilization results in an increase in investment directly, and indirectly by increasing the government investment–capital stock ratio due to the increase in the rate of capacity utilization with a given government investment–output ratio. For the long run the increase in τ rotates the LR curve up, from LR₁ to say LR₂, but does not alter the relative rates of change of a and γ, so that the economy ends up at a point like E₄.

To compare the effects of increases in θ and τ, consider increases in the two that increase capacity capacity utilization by the same amount. The effect on g will be greater for the rise in θ. It can also be seen that the LR locus will rotate up more in the case of the increase in θ than for the case of the increase in τ. Moreover, for the increase in θ the economy will move along a steeper path. Therefore, as shown in Figure 2.2, the effect on the rate of growth of labor productivity will be greater for the increase in θ.

Two further comments on this model are in order. One, we have assumed that the government budget is balanced and that there is no debt. This is a simplification that we have adopted to avoid increasing the dimensionality of the model through the introduction of an additional long-run variable, the government debt to capital ratio. If we were

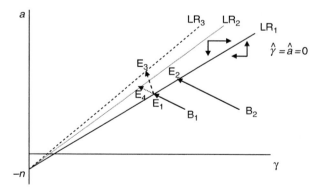

Figure 2.2 Growth model with endogenous technological change and government fiscal policy

to introduce government debt into the analysis, and assume that the interest rate is constant, the expansionary effects of increased government investment spending on capacity utilization and growth could still remain (see, for instance, You and Dutt, 1996). In fact, with households receiving interest payments, which add to their disposable income, the expansionary effects of debt-financed government spending may be greater than in the model without debt. If the interest rate is very high, the model may become unstable and government debt will explode. However, since the growth rate depends positively on the level of government spending, the chances of instability are lower than in standard models in which the growth rate of output is exogenously given at the natural rate of growth. If the interest rate increases with the debt–capital ratio then the dynamics may change and increase the possibility of instability, but this requires an examination on whether, in fact, increases in the debt–capital ratio have such an effect of financial markets.

Two, the model is able to address a number of reasons why government investment spending can increase growth. The increase occurs for three reasons. First, it raises aggregate demand and employment through the standard multiplier effect. In this it is no different from government consumption expenditure. Second, it crowds in private investment. Third, it speeds up technological change. In choosing which kinds of investment the government should focus on for increasing the long-run performance of the economy, it is necessary to look at all three types of effects of different kinds of investment. While some recent debates on the appropriateness of sectors worthy of receiving public investment have focused on the direct employment creating effects of such investment, the other two aspects should also be taken into account. We have not taken into account a fourth factor, which deals with the environmental effects of such investment, directly by how much pollution such investments will create, but also indirectly by how much pollution such investment will help to reduce in the future by adopted greener methods of production.

5. Financial issues and uncertainty

Two major aspects of Keynesian macroeconomics, over and above the role of effective demand, are financial factors and uncertainty. In this section we return to the simple model of aggregate-demand determined growth discussed in section 3, eschewing aggregate supply considerations discussed in the previous section. We introduce financial factors with a variable, δ, which captures the notion of financial fragility as measured by a variable such as the debt to asset ratio of firms and households. We model decision-making under uncertainty by introducing another variable, α, which captures what can be called animal spirits or confidence.[14]

Our investment function is given by

$$I/K = g^I (u, \alpha, \delta). \tag{26}$$

As before, we assume that $g^I_u > 0$, where the subscript denotes the partial derivative with respect to the variable u. We assume that $g^I_\alpha > 0$, since greater confidence and more buoyant animal spirits on the part of both firms and financiers implies higher levels of investment. Finally, $g^I_\delta < 0$, since a more leveraged position will imply that firms and financiers will cut back on investment and lending, although at low levels of δ, this effect is likely to be negligible.

Saving is assumed to depend positively on output and capacity utilization. However, it is also possible, and increasingly more the case, that confidence and financial fragility also have an effect on consumption and saving. As consumer debt becomes more important, the effect of financial fragility on consumption is likely to become stronger, at least when δ is high, and consumption becomes more strongly related to confidence, for instance, about future employment and income prospects of consumers. Thus we assume that the saving function is given by

$$S/K = g^S (u, \alpha, \delta). \tag{27}$$

where $g^S_u > 0$, $g^S_\alpha < 0$, and $g^S_\delta > 0$. Saving falls with confidence and rises with financial fragility since consumption rises with confidence and falls with fragility. As households become less confident about the future, they start saving more, and they also cut down on consumption when their debt position worsens.

For the short run we assume that α and δ are given, and that u adjusts to clear the goods market. The short-run equilibrium value of u, which satisfies the condition (2), can be written as

$$u = u(\alpha, \delta) \tag{28}$$

where our assumptions imply $u_\alpha > 0$ and $u_\delta < 0$. These derivatives will be larger in absolute value if saving and investment responds to α and δ than if only investment responds to them. At low levels of δ, u_δ is likely to be small in absolute value, since investment and consumption will not be deterred much by increases in financial fragility when financial fragility is low. It will become larger in absolute value at higher levels of δ.

In the long run we assume that

$$d\alpha/dt = X(u, \alpha, \delta) \tag{29}$$

and

$$d\delta/dt = F(u, \alpha, \delta). \tag{30}$$

The partial derivatives are assumed to have the following signs. For the animal spirits function we assume that $X_u > 0$, $X_\alpha > 0$, and $X_\delta < 0$. Animal spirits are excited when the economy, measured by its rate of capacity utilization, does better. Animal spirits are further excited when animal spirits are high, due to what Akerlof and Shiller (2009) call the confidence multiplier. Finally, confidence declines when the economy becomes more financially fragile. This can occur because the level of confidence of firms, financiers and households declines when their debt level rises, but also because higher debt may imply a fall in asset prices which shakes confidence. For the financial fragility function we assume that $F_u > 0$, $F_\alpha > 0$, and $F_\delta < 0$, although for low levels of δ, $F_\delta \geq 0$ is possible. Increases in economic activity will imply that households and firms are willing and able to borrow more (by being deemed more creditworthy). Increases in confidence will also increase borrowing and hence debt. Increases in indebtedness can increase indebtedness further by increasing debt service obligations including interest payments; this may be exacerbated by increasing interest rates which increase interest payments. However, beyond a point, further increases in δ will reduce the net income of borrowers, thereby reducing their willingness and ability to borrow, especially because financiers find themselves overextended and do not wish to lend more. Greater financial fragility implies more lender's and borrower's risk, so that credit constraints bind more strongly and borrowers are loath to further increase their indebtedness. Moreover, increases in fragility may imply a fall in asset prices which can result in a further reduction in lending.

Substituting equation (28) into equations (29) and (30) we obtain the dynamic equations

$$d\alpha/dt = x(\alpha, \delta) \tag{29'}$$

and

$$d\delta/dt = f(\alpha, \delta). \qquad (30')$$

where our assumptions imply that $x_\alpha > 0$, and $x_\delta < 0$, and $f_\alpha > 0$, and $f_\delta < 0$, although $f_\delta > 0$, is possible at low levels of δ. The dynamics of the system can be examined using the phase diagrams shown in Figure 2.3. The slope of the $d\alpha/dt = 0$ isocline is $-(x_\delta/x_\alpha)$, and that of $d\delta/dt = 0$ is $-(f_\delta/f_\alpha)$; the vertical and horizontal arrows, showing movements in α and δ are determined by the signs of x_α and f_δ.

Long-run equilibrium is given at the intersection of the two isoclines. The stability of long-run equilibrium depends on the signs of the trace, given by $x_\alpha + f_\delta$, and the determinant, given by $x_\alpha f_\delta - x_\delta f_\alpha$, of the Jacobian of the dynamic system given by equations (29') and (30'). If the trace is negative and the determinant is positive at the long-run equilibrium, it will be stable. The confidence multiplier and the positive effect of α on short-run capacity utilization, which imply that $x_\alpha > 0$, contribute to instability in the system. A negative f_δ which is large in absolute value can contribute towards making the trace negative, but it also makes it more likely that the determinant condition is violated.

Two possible configurations of the curves are shown in Figure 2.3. In (a) there are two long-run equilibria, the lower one of which is unstable and the upper one is saddlepoint unstable. If the economy starts below the dashed separatrix it can experience increases in α and δ as in the dynamic path shown by the curved arrow, but once it passes the $d\alpha/dt = 0$ isocline animal spirits will start to falter and then financial fragility may be able to correct itself, although not by enough to reverse

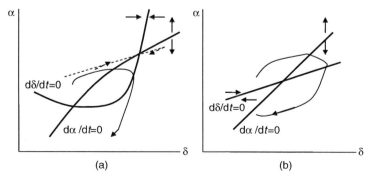

Figure 2.3 Model with finance and uncertainty

the decline in capacity utilization and growth (both of which depend positively on α and inversely on δ). In (b) there is one equilibrium which implies cycles which may be stable or unstable, depending on the sizes of x_α and f_δ.

Though rather crudely reduced-form in nature, the simple model has enough structure to allow us to examine reasons for increases in financial fragility and cyclical instability. Two examples of such an analysis may be briefly presented. One, financial innovation can be represented by a reduction in the absolute value of f_δ, which, as shown in the figure, makes cyclical instability more likely. It can also imply a fall in the absolute value of x_δ, which also destabilizes the system. Two, an increase in the importance of confidence and debt in consumption spending decisions implies, by increasing u_α and increasing the absolute value of u_δ, that it increases x_α and f_α and makes the values of x_δ and f_δ more strongly negative, which has an ambiguous effect on stability, but is likely to increase the amplitude of the system by making the booms and recessions stronger. A combination of these two tendencies, however, is likely to destabilize the system.

We have discussed these financial issues using a simple reduced-form model of growth and finance. If this type of analysis is found useful, it can be enriched in a number of ways. First, it can be extended to deal with specific types of assets, such as bonds, stocks and real estate. Second, in so doing, one can introduce additional short-run variables into the model, such as the stock price and the interest rate, which change quickly in the short run (see Taylor, 2004, for examples of both types of models). Third, it may be instructive to analyze explicitly the relation between flows and stocks concerning not only physical capital (as done in the model), but also financial assets and liabilities, by using what are called stock-flow-consistent models. However, these models become extremely complicated very quickly since they require the explicit analysis of a large number of stock variables, and therefore necessitate the use of simulation techniques (see Godley and Lavoie, 2007).

6. Distributional issues

The Keynesian models discussed in sections 4 and 5 have not distinguished between different classes of people. However, Keynesian growth models have at least since the time of Robinson's (1962) model stressed the importance of the distribution of income between different classes of people, such as workers and capitalists. This has happened because Keynesian economists are often interested in the question of income distribution and the ability of capitalist economies not only to produce with high levels of output and employment, but to distribute income in a fair and equitable manner. Moreover, Keynesian economists have concerned themselves with the way in which the distribution of income affects the rate of growth of the economy, thereby, examining income distribution from an instrumentalist point of view. Keynes (1936) had pointed out that wage reductions need not increase aggregate demand, contradicting the prevailing orthodoxy that wage reductions increase employment and output. Subsequently, post-Keynesian economists have been influenced in particular by the writings of the classical economists, Marx and Kalecki, in seeing the distribution of income between classes as a fundamental determinant of the dynamics of accumulation and technological change in capitalist economies, and some have argued that wage reductions are contractionary.

As was seen in section 2, distributional issues have for long been incorporated into Keynesian growth models by distinguishing between workers and capitalists, and by assuming that workers have a higher propensity to consume than capitalists. The implication of this assumption is that if the distribution of income changes to favor workers, aggregate consumption increases, increasing aggregate demand and output, and if investment depends positively on capacity utilization, this results in an increase in capital accumulation and growth. The positive relation between the wage share and the rate of growth of output may or may not hold if the investment function is altered to make investment, for instance, depend on the profit share and capacity utilization, in which case we may have wage-led or profit-led growth (see Bhaduri and Marglin, 1990). Thus, the relationship between growth and distribution is a complex one, even for closed economies.[15]

The distribution of income between capitalists and workers continues to be of interest and relevance. However, other aspects of income distribution are beginning to attract widespread attention. The distribution between industrial and financial capitalists has been extensively studied in post-Keynesian growth models.[16] Changes in income distribution favoring financial capitalists and rentiers, who receive interest income as opposed to net profits which are received by industrial capitalists, can reduce the rate of growth of the economy by reducing investment and reducing the wage share (if firms pass on higher interest costs by raising price), but may also increase growth by increasing aggregate demand if rentiers have a higher propensity to consume than industrial capitalists and firms (see Dutt, 1992). Thus, increasing financialization may have implications for fluctuations, as discussed in the previous section, as well as for long-run growth trends for capitalist economies. Less studied is the implication of income distributional changes between high-skilled and low-skilled workers, which many argue to be an important aspect of recent overall income distributional changes in many parts of the world.

A simple model, which examines the implications of changes in this distribution, proceeds by assuming that there are two kinds of workers, high- and low-skilled (see Dutt, 2008). The quantities employed of these two kinds of workers are given by H and L, and they receive money wages W_H and W_L. We define the ratio of skilled to unskilled wage as

$$\Phi = W_H/W_L, \tag{31}$$

which represents the skill premium. It is assumed that the low-skilled worker wage serves as a reference level of wages, and given the premium, an increase low-skilled wages increase the high-skilled wage proportionately. We assume that a single good is produced with low-skilled labor and capital, with the productivity of this labor being given by A. Firms are assumed to have at least enough capital to produce output to meet the aggregate demand for goods at a given price which is set as a markup on prime or variable costs. High-skilled labor is treated as overhead labor, and not taken into account into these costs. Thus,

$$P = (1+z)\, W_L/A, \tag{32}$$

where z, the markup, represents what Kalecki (1971) called the degree of monopoly, which depends, among other things, on the level of industrial concentration, W_L the money wage of low-skilled workers, and P the price level. The markup is taken as given in the standard Kaleckian manner. The real wage of low-skilled workers is thus given by

$$w_L = A/(1+z) \tag{33}$$

and the income share of low-skilled workers by

$$\Lambda = 1/(1+z) \tag{34}$$

We assume that the supply of low-skilled workers is large enough to produce all the output demanded.

The amount of high-skilled labor demanded depends positively on the amount of capital installed and negatively on the relative wage of high-skilled and low-skilled workers. For simplicity, we assume that firms have a desired effective amount of high-skilled labor to capital ratio of b so that the demand for high skilled labor is

$$H^d = b(\Phi) \, K/A, \quad b' < 0 \qquad (35)$$

where A is also the productivity of high-skilled workers (or, the productivity of high-skilled workers is proportional to that of low-skilled workers). High-skilled labor does not participate in the direct production process, but performs activity which improves labor productivity (of both high- and low-skilled labor). It is assumed that when Φ rises, firms reduce b.

We formalize the relationship between the use of high-skilled labor and labor productivity growth by assuming that the rate of growth of labor productivity (of both high-skilled and low-skilled workers)[17] depends positively and linearly on the amount of high skilled labor in efficiency units as a ratio of the stock of capital, that is,

$$a = \tau_0 + \tau_1 \, (AH/K) \qquad (36)$$

where, as before, a denotes the rate of growth of A. We measure high-skilled labor input as a ratio of capital stock as a scaling factor representing the size of the productive economy. We assume that all firms are identical, so that, for instance, A can be thought of as representing aggregate average productivity or the individual firm's productivity. Thus, although there may be externalities involved here, they are not required for our analysis.

Low-skilled labor is converted into high-skilled labor through the process of education. The dynamics of H is formalized with the equation

$$dH/dt = \Theta \, g(\Phi) \, H, \quad g' > 0 \qquad (37)$$

We also assume that $g(\Phi) = 0$ for all $\Phi \le \Phi_{min} \ge 1$. This will ensure that no one will seek education if the wage premium falls below a certain level. The change in the stock of high-skilled workers depends on: the demand for education which, in turn, depends positively on the skill premium, which increases the 'return' to education; on the size of the stock of high-skilled workers, both by increasing the availability of mentors and educators, and by increasing the support for, and access to, education (for instance, a higher stock results in higher number added from high-skilled worker families); and on a parameter, Θ, which captures the openness of the education system, either through government policy or through the degree of exclusivity of the education system. Easier access to low-cost public education and greater access to student loans and grants, and a more open private education system which is less elitist on the basis of class and income increases Θ. We assume that workers – whether high or low skilled – do not save, but consume their entire income. Profit recipients or capitalists save a fraction, s_c, of their income, which is given by

$$rK = Y - w_L L - w_H H \tag{38}$$

where r is the rate of profit received by capitalists, and w_i is the real wage of labor of type i. Total consumption expenditure in the economy is therefore given by

$$C = (1 - s_c)rK + w_L L + w_H H$$

This implies that saving is given by the standard saving function given by equation (10).

Firms, having excess capacity, are assumed to make investment plans based on profitability, capacity utilization and the rate of technological change. We assume a simple linear investment function given by

$$I/K = \gamma_0 + \gamma_\pi \pi + \gamma_u u + \gamma_a a \tag{39}$$

where γ_i are positive parameters and where π is the profit share given by rK/Y. Profitability enters because profits affect investment both by increasing profit expectations and by increasing internal saving and finance. Profitability depends on both the profit share and the rate of capacity utilization. The profit share is included following Bhaduri and Marglin (1990) and is measured net of payments to high-skilled workers. A higher rate of capacity utilization not only represents higher profits, but also more buoyant markets, so that more excess capacity deters investment, as argued by Steindl (1952). Faster technological change speeds up investment to install new machines, use new methods and produce new products.

In the short run, A, K and H are given, implying that $h = AH/K$ is given. Short-run equilibrium requires that the markets for high-skilled workers and for goods clear. Equilibrium in the market for high-skilled workers requires that the demand for high-skilled workers equals its available supply, so that

$$H^d = H. \tag{40}$$

Substituting from equation (35) this determines the short-run equilibrium skill premium, given by

$$\Phi = b^{-1}(h) \tag{41}$$

where an increase in h implies an excess supply of high-skilled labor and, hence, a reduction in the wage premium, Φ. Using equations (2), (32) through (34), and (38), we can write the equilibrium condition for the goods market as the saving-investment equality condition,

$$s_c\, r = \gamma_0 + \gamma_\pi\, (r/u) + \gamma_u\, u + \gamma_a\, a \tag{42}$$

where the rate of profit is given by

$$r = (1 - \Lambda)u - \Lambda h\Phi(h), \tag{43}$$

where the function $\Phi(.)$ denotes the function $b^{-1}(.)$. Using equations (36), (41) and (42) we obtain

$$[s_s(1-\Lambda)-\gamma_u]u^2 =[\gamma_0 + \gamma_a(\tau_0 + \tau_1 h) + s_c\Lambda\Omega(h)]u - \gamma_\pi\Lambda\Omega(h)] \tag{44}$$

where $\Omega(h) = h\Phi(h)$. This quadratic equation can be solved for u to obtain the short-run equilibrium level of capacity utilization. The determination of equilibrium can be shown in Figure 2.4, where the line *LS* shows the left-hand side of equation (44) and the line *RS* the right-hand side.

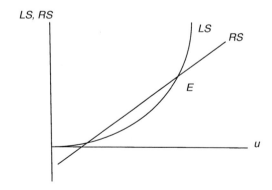

Figure 2.4 Short-run equilibrium in model with education

There are two equilibria, but it can be shown that only the upper one, at E, is the stable equilibrium, given that an excess demand for goods results in an increase in u. We will denote the stable short-run equilibrium value of u by $u(h)$. An increase in h does not shift the LS line, since for a given u it leaves the left-hand side of equation (44) unchanged. The effect of an increase in h on the right-hand side depends on the sign of $d\Omega/dh$. Suppose that $d\Omega/dh < 0$, which happens when a rise in h reduces the skill premium, ϕ, and results in a fall in the total cost of high-skilled workers because the elasticity of h with respect to ϕ is small. Then the rise in h, by reducing Ω, will push the intercept of the RS line upwards (making it less negative), and tend to increase u by increasing profitability and, hence, investment. However, the increase in h has an ambiguous effect on the slope of the RS line: it tends to increase it by inducing a higher rate of technological change, thereby increasing investment, but to reduce it by redistributing income from high-skilled workers who do not save to profit recipients who do save, thereby reducing aggregate demand. If we assume that the investment responses are weak, the slope of the RS line will be reduced sufficiently so that the result will be to reduce the short-run equilibrium level of u. If, however, $d\Omega/dh > 0$ (because the fall in the skill premium induces firms to hire so much more high-skilled labor so as to increase their high-skilled labor costs), the effect of an increase in h is to shift the RS curve down but to increase its slope. With relatively weak investment responses, u increases with h.

From now we will assume that the first case prevails, that is, that the elasticity of demand for high-skilled workers is low, which is consistent with the plausible consequence that a fall in the skill premium (despite adjustments in the use of low- and high-skilled labor) reduces costs for firms.

Once we know the equilibrium value of u, we can solve for the equilibrium rate of investment, I/K, from equation (39) after substituting from equation (36) and by noting from equation (43) and the definition of Ω that the profit share is given by

$$\pi = r/u = (1-\Lambda) - \Lambda\Omega(h)/u. \tag{45}$$

The effect of an increase in h on I/K may be positive or negative. If u falls due to an increase in h, because of the negative aggregate demand effects, investment will tend to fall because of the effect of capacity utilization on investment, as captured by the strength of the term γ_u. But the effect through the profit share, due to the term involving γ_π is ambiguous, since the rise in h will increase the profit share directly and reduce it indirectly by reducing u (which reduces the profit share by increasing the relative cost of overhead high-skilled workers), and the effect of a higher rate of technological change, a, on investment, captured by the term involving γ_a, is positive. The net effect on the investment rate of the increase in h is more likely to be negative if the profitability effect is weak (due to a small value of γ_π), and more likely to be positive if the technology effect is strong (due to a large γ_a).

In the long run we can examine the dynamics of the economy by analyzing the dynamics of h, which are given by the equation

$$\hat{h} = \hat{A} + \hat{H} - \hat{K} \tag{46}$$

Substituting equations (36), (37), (39), (42) and (43) into equation (46) we get

$$\hat{h} = \tau_0 + \tau_1 h + \Theta g(\phi(h)) - s_c[(1 - \Lambda)u(h) - \Lambda \Omega(h)] \tag{47}$$

where the first two terms on the right-hand side show the growth rate of A, that is, a, the next term shows the growth rate of H, and the last term the growth rate of K, determined by the left- or right-hand side of equation (42). The dynamics of h are shown graphically in Figures 2.5 and 2.6. The effect of an increase of h on a is positive, explaining the positively-sloped $\hat{A}$ curve in the figures: higher h speeds up technological

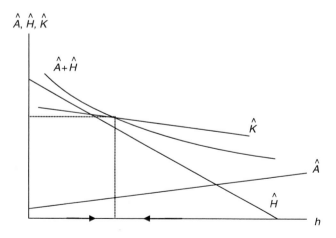

Figure 2.5 Long-run dynamics in model with education with weak profitability effect

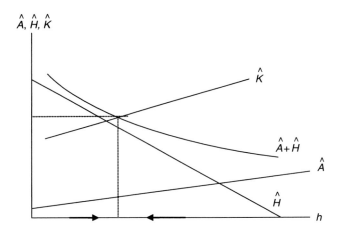

Figure 2.6   Long-run dynamics in model with education with strong profitability effect

change. Since ϕ falls with h and $g' > 0$, $\hat{H}$ rises with h, explaining the negatively-sloped $\hat{H}$ curve: an increase in h reduces the skill differential and slows down the growth of high-skilled workers.

The effect of an increase in h on $\hat{K}$ can be positive or negative, as discussed earlier. If the profitability effect (captured by a small γ_π) is weak, the increase in h will reduce aggregate demand and therefore capacity utilization and the rate of accumulation. This case is shown with the negatively sloped $\hat{K}$ curve of Figure 2.6. With this curve negatively sloped, it is possible for the long-run equilibrium to be unstable, which happens if the $\hat{A} + \hat{H}$ curve is flatter than the $\hat{K}$ curve. In this case, an increase (decrease in h) will result in increases (decreases) in $\hat{h}$ resulting in an explosive growth (implosive fall) in h and reduction (increase) in the rate of growth of capital accumulation. Thus, we may either have increasing growth with less education expansion, or decreasing growth with more education expansion. The stable case, in which h attains a stable long-run equilibrium level at the intersection of the $\hat{A} + \hat{H}$ and $\hat{K}$ curves, is shown in the figure. In this case, greater openness in education, by increasing Θ, will shift up the $\hat{H}$ and $\hat{A} + \hat{H}$ curves and increase the long-run equilibrium level of h, but reduce the long-run equilibrium rate of capital accumulation. Increasing access to education implies that more workers upgrade their skills, but since the skill premium falls, aggregate consumption demand, and hence aggregate demand, falls, reducing growth.

If the profitability effect (captured by a large γ_π) is strong, the increase in h will increase investment and aggregate demand by increasing profitability sufficiently to overwhelm the negative effect of u on investment. This case is shown in Figure 2.6, where the $\hat{K}$ curve is positively sloped, and in which the long-run equilibrium is necessarily stable. An increase in Θ will now shift up the $\hat{H}$ and $\hat{A} + \hat{H}$ curves as in the case of Figure 2.5. This will increase the long-run equilibrium level of h, but this time it will increase the long-run equilibrium rate of capital accumulation. More access to education reduces the skill premium and makes high-skilled workers less expensive, which increases profitability and speeds up accumulation.

It follows that in this Keynesian model of growth with education which converts low-skilled workers into high-skilled workers, greater access to education may not necessarily increase the rate of growth of the economy as measured by the growth rates of capital and output (since, in long-run equilibrium, in which u attains its long-run equilibrium value, output and capital grow at the same rate), although it will speed up the rate of labor productivity growth. Whether or not it does, depends on the strength of the profitability effect on investment (as opposed to the technological change and capacity utilization effects on investment). Thus, increasing skill accumulation may go hand in hand with lower growth in the long run, unlike in standard neoclassical models in which full employment growth ensures that greater human capital accumulation increases technological change and growth.[18]

The model also focuses on the distribution of income between high-skilled and low-skilled workers, which depends on the skill differential ϕ, which depends negatively on h. An increase in Θ is found to reduce the skill differential by opening up access to education, and benefits low-skilled workers relative to high-skilled workers both by reducing the skill differential and by allowing relatively more low-skilled workers to become high-skilled workers. However, whether or not this is beneficial for low-skilled workers or workers as a whole depends on the effect on the rate of growth of output, and the rate of growth of employment (which depends not only on the rate of growth of output but also labor productivity, which depends positively on h).

The model can also be used to examine the effects of a change in Λ which was taken to be exogenously given in our model. It can be seen that, depending on whether the increase in Λ has an overall effect of increasing or reducing the rate of capital accumulation, which is similar to what has been called wage-led or profit-led growth in the literature (see Bhaduri and Marglin, 1990), the long-run equilibrium growth rate will be positively or negatively affected. But if Figure 2.5 corresponds to the wage-led case and Figure 2.6 to the profit-led case, in the former case the long-run equilibrium level of h will be reduced, and the skill premium will rise, while in the latter the opposite will occur.

7. Summary and conclusions

Traditionally, growth theory has stressed the role of aggregate supply in determining the long-run growth of the economy. This was the case for much of classical growth theory of the type developed by Smith and Ricardo, although Malthus and Marx did offer important dissenting voices by incorporating the role of aggregate demand. It is even more the case for neoclassical growth theories, both of the "old" and "new" or endogenous variety, with their assumption of growth with fully-employed labor. In the older Solovian models, diminishing returns to capital imply that in the long-run steady state, the growth rate of output is determined by the exogenously fixed rates of growth of labor supply and labor productivity. In the newer endogenous growth models, increasing returns in one form or other leads to non-diminishing returns to capital, so that the growth rate is determined by savings and by the supply-side determinants of technological change. Although neoclassical macroeconomics does allow aggregate demand to have a role in the short run due to wage-price rigidity, in the long run aggregate demand plays no role because of market or government policy reactions.

Keynesian growth theory departs from this traditional focus on aggregate supply by making aggregate demand affect the rate of economic growth in the long run. The influence of Keynesian aggregate demand issues on growth theory was recognized in the early years of the development of modern growth theory, especially at the hands of Harrod and Robinson, but soon this was swept aside from mainstream growth theory by the neoclassical landslide. Perhaps the success of Keynesian policies nationally and globally under the Bretton Woods system – which maintained full employment growth in many advanced economies and with relatively few interruptions – had something to do with this. The inflationary periods of the 1970s and 1980s may also explain the lack of interest in aggregate demand issues as policymakers and economists became preoccupied with inflation control. Keynesian growth theory was alive only in some branches of heterodox economics. For most economists, aggregate demand issues may be relevant for the short run (though some, like the monetarists of different vintages, were unwilling to concede even this), but are considered to be irrelevant for the long run.

This neglect of aggregate demand issues for the long run has become almost second nature to mainstream economists, although the theoretical and empirical underpinnings of it are weak. Theoretically, aggregate demand issues are supposed to disappear in the long run because the unemployment resulting from deficient demand is supposed to be removed or reduced to some natural level due to long-run wage flexibility, which is supposed to increase the real supply of money and increase aggregate demand through real balance and interest rate effects. However, it is not clear whether wages in fact are flexible enough, or whether wage cuts are prevented by issues such as efficiency wages and insider–outsider effects and the existence of institutionalized wage bargaining in many countries. Moreover, even if wages became more flexible, it is unclear – as Keynes (1936) and post-Keynesian economists noted (see, for instance, Dutt and Amadeo, 1990) – whether problems such as debt deflation, reductions in real wages, and increases in uncertainty would in fact increase or reduce aggregate demand. Finally, governments have not had a great record, either because of unwillingness (by attaching too much weight to containing inflation, keeping small governments and perhaps driven by class interests favoring finance over labor), or inability to control financial markets. Empirically, the fact that the unemployment rate does not remain high for long periods of time has been used to argue for the long-run irrelevance of aggregate demand. However, the fact that the effective supply of labor as well as the demand for labor can adjust through immigration, changes in the participation rate, and, most importantly, technological change implies that aggregate demand adjusts to aggregate supply and we should not focus only on the latter in long-run analysis. Moreover, there have been significant shifts in the so-called natural rate of unemployment, shifts which appear to be related to changes in aggregate demand. Finally, long bouts with unemployment in countries such as Japan, and now apparently in many countries including the US, clearly due to aggregate demand issues, also undermine the empirical case for focusing on aggregate supply alone for the analysis of the long run.

This paper has argued that changes which have and are occurring in the world economy, including both short-term changes related to the global financial crisis, and long-term changes such as globalization and financialization related to the interactions between policy changes, technological changes, and the uneven spread of development around the world, are making Keynesian economics increasingly relevant in analyzing the economies of rich and poor countries and the global economy. In particular, Keynesian growth theory seems to have a promising future analyzing the dynamics of national and global economies. In addition to its increasing relevance, theoretical changes in both ortho-dox and heterodox growth economics – the increasing attention given to technological change and new developments in heterodox growth theory – are making it easier for Keynesian theories of economic growth to become more acceptable. In particular, as illustrated by the model of endogenous technological change and government investment dis-cussed in this paper, simple models of growth which combine aggregate supply issues and aggregate demand issues can be developed in which the unemployment rate is constant in the long run and yet aggregate demand has a long-run effect on the rate of economic growth.

This paper has also enumerated some important future directions for Keynesian growth theory. First, it can examine the long-run role of government fiscal policy, especially policy which increases government investment. The interesting feature of this model is that government investment – in infrastructure and research and development – can have an effect not only on the aggregate demand side, but also on the aggregate supply side, by affecting the responsiveness of the rate of technological change to aggregate depend pressures. Thus, Keynesian effective demand has consequences far beyond the short run. Second, it can examine the interaction between financial factors and expectational factors to show: how cyclical growth can occur; how changes in the financial system can make the cycles more dramatic; how, sometimes, the economy can become unstable; and how increasing financialization can affect the long-run growth of the economy. Third, it can examine the interaction between growth and distribution, not only increasing our understanding of the effects of distributional shifts between workers and capitalists, as in standard heterodox growth models, but also by dis-tinguishing between high-skilled and low-skilled workers and examin-ing the role of education. These are only meant to illustrate some useful future directions, and by no means exhaust the list of rich possibilities. Additional issues that require attention include environment-economy interactions, international trade and finance issues and global economic interdependence.

We have not stressed methodological aspects and policy implications of growth models in this paper, but we may conclude with three brief comments about them.

First, a distinction is sometimes made between the short and long runs in macroeconomics, and the distinction is used to relegate aggre-gate demand issues to the short run and to conduct the analysis of long-run growth by ignoring aggregate demand considerations right from the start. Our analysis suggests that the short-run/long-run distinction may be a useful one, and we indeed have used it in developing most of the models of this paper. However, the distinction simply allows us to distinguish between fast-moving and slow-moving variables, and our analysis suggests that there is nothing sacrosanct about specific definitions of these runs, such as those which can allow long-run theory to eschew aggregate demand considerations. Our model with endogenous technological change shows that this is not in general possible, and our other models have analyzed the growth process by emphasizing the role of aggregate demand in driving growth. Kalecki famously stated that the long run may be nothing but a collection of short runs, and this may well be true for real economies. However, the important message of Kalecki's statement is that factors that affect the short run may also drive long-run changes, and that has been a central message of our models.

Second, the ubiquitous optimizing agent of neoclassical theorizing has been conspicuously absent in our Keynesian growth models. Mainstream economic theory typically insists that all behavior must be explained in terms of optimization, and this is often justified with an appeal to the rationality of economic agents. Aside from the fact that in the real world, outside specific modeling environments, it is not clear what precisely is meant by rationality, behavioral economists have drawn attention to various kinds of predictable biases that are evident in individual behavior – even in simple environments. In the infinite horizon framework of much of neoclassical growth theory, intertemporal optimization seems to be nothing short of ludicrous, especially in a Keynesian world in which the future is uncertain. The claim that optimization is used only as a methodological tool and not as a description of reality robs optimization of much of its appeal. But even as a methodological device its desirability is limited because, given the bounded rationality of the analyst, introducing it in a dynamic setting requires omitting from the analysis many important aspects of reality, which are crowded out by the requirements of mathematical tractability. It is no wonder that growth theory featuring dynamic optimization has so little relevance for dealing with uncertainty, financial instability, and deficient aggregate demand in general.

Third, although we have not made many specific comments about policy issues, the Keynesian growth models certainly open up space for government policy, including fiscal policy, especially in relation to the expansion of government investment, financial regulation, policies for changing the distribution of income and education policy. This is not so say, of course, that government policies can always work as expected or as desired. Models can only give rough indicators about what can be done; especially in an uncertain environment in which the precise timing of expectational changes is unpredictable, and where much relevant empirical data is simply not known, policymaking is more art than science. Moreover, political factors – including the economic interests of powerful groups and classes, and the diverse motives of those in positions of power (including those of doing good and those which strengthen their power or fill their coffers) – will undoubtedly interact with the economic factors we have discussed to influence policy and their outcomes. Despite these complexities, however, our models strongly suggest that the fundamentalist dogma that free markets with minimum government intervention can promote equitable, stable and sustainable growth may be safely rejected.

Notes

1 Comments from participants of the SOAS Conference on Keynesian Economics in the 21st century, London, May 2009 and at a session on 21st century Keynesian economics at the 6th International Conference on Developments in Economic Theory and Policy, Bilbao, Spain, July 2009, and the editors are gratefully acknowledged.

2 There were a few early models, which can be called Keynesian, developed by such economists as Uzawa (1974) and Rose (1990). These models allowed unemployment to exist by introducing downward wage rigidity and in some cases using a version of the Philips curve, and explicitly incorporating asset markets into the analysis. But, for the most part, unemployment and aggregate demand issues are ignored in neoclassical growth models, both old and new. See Dutt (2003).

3 There may also be some models, which satisfy the first property but not the second. We will not call them Keynesian growth models.

4 For simplicity, we do not introduce any additional short-run variables, beyond u and g explicitly, but this framework allows such variables to be incorporated. Relevant variables could include an asset price or rate of return, or a relative price.

5 Models, which can be called Keynesian growth models in our sense, based on the Kalecki–Steindl model have been developed to analyze a broad range of issues, some of which will be discussed below. Taylor (2004) examines a number of such models.

6 Its only difference with that model lies with its investment function. Here we assume that investment depends positively on the rate of capacity utilization, whereas the standard neo-Keynesian model assumes that investment depends on the rate of profit.

7 Alternatively, we may retain the investment function and introduce a new variable, such as an interest rate, which has a negative effect on investment. The interest rate will vary to bring saving and investment to equality.

8 If the investment function is retained with the rate of interest rate as an argument, as in the function

$$g^I = \gamma_0 + \gamma_1 u - \gamma_2 i$$

where i is the rate of interest, a rise in γ_0 will produce and upward adjustment in i which will restore the equality given by $i = (\gamma_0 + \gamma_1 u_d - n)/\gamma_2$. There will be no other effect of the change in γ_0 for the model.

9 Neo-Marxian and classical-Marxian models are discussed in Foley and Michl (1999). See Dutt (2009) for a discussion of the neglect of aggregate demand issues in these models.

10 Auerbach and Skott (1988) and Committeri (1986) have criticized the model as being internally inconsistent because it implies that the long-run equilibrium u will not, in general, be equal to u_d.

11 Aschauer (1989) provides evidence for the US which suggests that taking into account both standard asset-market related crowding out effects, and the positive productivity effects of public capital on private profitability, the overall effect on private investment is positive. The model used here does not introduce public capital, but instead relies on a direct positive effect of public investment on private investment, following Taylor (1991), to simply the analysis by not introducing an additional stock variable into the model, that is, the stock of public capital as a ratio of private capital.

12 This formulation assumes that the level of "autonomous" investment depends on the level of the interest rate, which in turn, depends on the level of the unemployment rate. Thus changes in the unemployment rate result in changes in autonomous investment. An alternative specification can assume that the change in autonomous investment depends on the change in the interest rate, which depends on the level of the unemployment rate. In this case, if the rate of change in labor productivity growth also depends on the unemployment rate (rather than on changes in the unemployment rate, as assumed earlier), the qualitative properties of the model of the text will still hold. See Dutt (2006).

13 This model, or many of the other models discussed in this paper, address the issue about whether it is sensible to have models in which the actual rate of capacity is equal to some desired rate of capacity utilization. It should be noted, however, that the relevance of Keynesian models of growth does not rest on the endogeneity of the long run equilibrium rate of accumulation, since we have already discussed a Keynesian growth model – which can be used for a basis for others – in which actual and desired capacity utilization are in fact equal in long-run equilibrium. Moreover, many persuasive reasons have been given by several post-Keynesian growth theorists why the actual rate of capacity utilization may be endogenous in long-run equilibrium, including the endogeneity of the desired rate, and the existence of desired bands of capacity utilization. See, for instance, Lavoie (1995), Dutt (1997) and Dutt (2010). A contrary view may be found in Skott (2008).

14 In so doing we employ variables which have been used for similar purposes earlier in the heterodox Keynesian tradition. Taylor and O'Connell (1985), for instance, use a state of confidence variable in their analysis of a Minsky

crisis (see also Taylor, 2004). Skott (1994) uses a financial fragility variable in his model of financial innovation. Taylor and O'Connell, however, have a fast-moving interest rate variable in their model rather than a slow-moving financial fragility variable. Skott introduces a tranquillity variable as a fast-moving variable rather than a slow-moving confidence variable. The model of this section, in contrast to these contributions, takes both confidence or animal spirits and fragility as slow moving variables and examines their interaction in the long run. There are other differences between the model of this section and these other papers because of the way in which they model goods market adjustment (Skott makes output a slow-moving variable in his growth model) and the specificity of the treatment of assets (Taylor and O'Connell introduce a specific asset which yields an interest rate). The generality of the model has the virtue of being able to explore the effects of the accumulation of a range of assets and liabilities, but makes its relationships more difficult to interpret in a precise manner.

15 For open economies, a rise in the wage share can reduce competitiveness and reduce aggregate demand by reducing exports and increasing imports. See Blecker (1989).

16 See, for instance, Dutt (1992), Stockhammer (2004) and Hein (2008).

17 Thus the productivities of the two kinds of workers are assumed to be proportional to each other.

18 The model also emphasizes the fact that access to education has a major role in expanding education and skill formation, rather than stressing only individual choice, although an element of choice is incorporated into the model since an increase in the skill differential increases the rate of skill formation.

References

Akerlof, George and Shiller, Robert (2009), *Animal Spirits*, Princeton, NJ: Princeton University Press.

Aschauer, David Alan (1989), "Does public capital crowd out private capital?", *Journal of Monetary Economics*, 24, pp. 171–88.

Auerbach, Paul and Skott, Peter (1988), "Concentration, competition and distribution – a critique of theories of monopoly capital", *International Review of Applied Economics*, 2(1), pp. 44–61.

Bhaduri, Amit and Marglin, Stephen A. (1990), "Unemployment and the real wage: the economic basis of contesting political ideologies", *Cambridge Journal of Economics*, 14(4), pp. 375–93.

Blecker, Robert (1989), "International competition, income distribution, and economic growth", *Cambridge Journal of Economics*, 13(3), September, pp. 395–412.

Committeri, Marco (1986), "Some comments on recent contributions on capital accumulation, income distribution and capacity utilization", *Political Economy*, 2(2), pp. 161–86.

Dutt, Amitava Krishna (1984), "Stagnation, income distribution and monopoly power", *Cambridge Journal of Economics*, 8(1), pp. 25–40.

Dutt, Amitava Krishna (1990), *Growth, Distribution and Uneven Development*, Cambridge, UK: Cambridge University Press.

Dutt, Amitava Krishna (1992), "Rentiers in Post Keynesian models", in P. Arestis and V. Chick (eds), *Recent Developments in Post-Keynesian Economics*, Aldershot: Edward Elgar, pp. 95–122.

Dutt, Amitava Krishna (1997), "Equilibrium, path dependence and hysteresis in post-Keynesian models", in P. Arestis and M. Sawyer (eds), *Essays in Honour of G. C. Harcourt, Vol. 2: Markets, Unemployment and Economic Policy*, London: Routledge, pp. 238–53.

Dutt, Amitava Krishna (2003), "New growth theory, effective demand and Post Keynesian macrodynamics", in N. Salvadori (ed.), *Growth Theories: Old and New*, Aldershot: Edward Elgar, pp. 67–100.

Dutt, Amitava Krishna (2006), "Aggregate demand, aggregate supply and economic growth", *International Review of Applied Economics*, 20(3), pp. 319–36.

Dutt, Amitava Krishna (2008), "Education, growth and distribution: a heterodox macrodynamic perspective", paper presented at the 2nd Analytical Political Economic workshop, Queen Mary, London University, unpublished, Department of Economics and Policy Studies, University of Notre Dame.

Dutt, Amitava Krishna (2009), "The role of aggregate demand in classical-Marxian models of economic growth", paper presented at the 3rd Analytical Political Economy Workshop, Queen Mary, London University, unpublished, Department of Economics and Policy Studies, University of Notre Dame.

Dutt, Amitava Krishna (2010), "Equilibrium, stability and path dependence in post-Keynesian models of growth", in A. Birolo, et al., eds., *Production, distribution and trade: Alternative perspectives*, London: Routledge, forthcoming.

Dutt, Amitava Krishna and Amadeo, Edward J. (1990). *Keynes's Third Alternative? The Neo-Ricardian Keynesians and the Post Keynesians*, Aldershot, UK: Edward Elgar.

Foley, Duncan and Michl, Thomas (1999), *Growth and Distribution*, Cambridge, Mass.: Harvard University Press.

Godley, W. and M. Lavoie (2007), *Monetary Economics: An Integrated Approach to Credit, Money, Income, Production and Wealth*, London: Palgrave Macmillan.

Harrod, Roy F. (1939), "An essay in dynamic theory", *Economic Journal*, 49, pp. 14–33.

Hein, Eckhard (2008), *Money, Distribution Conflict and Capital Accumulation: Contributions to 'Monetary Analysis'*, Basingstoke: Palgrave Macmillan.

Kahn, Richard F. (1959), "Exercises in the analysis of growth", *Oxford Economic Papers*, 11, pp. 143–56.

Kalecki, Michal (1971), *Selected Essays on the Dynamics of the Capitalist Economy*, Cambridge, UK: Cambridge University Press.

Keynes, John Maynard (1936), *The General Theory of Employment, Interest and Money*, London: Macmillan.

Lavoie, Marc (1995), "The Kaleckian model of growth and distribution and its neo-Ricardian and neo-Marxian critiques", *Cambridge Journal of Economics*, 19(6), pp. 789–818.

Marglin, Stephen A. (1984), *Growth, Distribution and Prices*, Cambridge, Mass.: Harvard University Press.

Robinson, Joan (1962), *Essays in the Theory of Economic Growth*, London: Macmillan.

Rose, Hugh (1990), *Macroeconomic Dynamics: A Marshallian Synthesis*, Oxford: Blackwell.

Rowthorn, Robert (1982), "Demand, real wages and growth", *Studi Economici*, 18, pp. 3–54.

Skott, Peter (1994), "On the modelling of systemic financial fragility", in A.K. Dutt (ed.), *New Directions in Analytical Political Economy*, Aldershot, UK: Edward Elgar, pp. 49–76.

Skott, Peter (2008), "Growth, instability and cycle: Harrodian and Kaleckian models of accumulation and income distribution", unpublished, Amherst, Mass.: University of Massachusetts.

Solow, Robert M. (1956). "A contribution to the theory of economic growth", *Quarterly Journal of Economics*, 70, pp. 65–94.

Steindl, Josef (1952), *Maturity and Stagnation in American Capitalism*, Oxford: Blackwell.

Stockhammer, Engelbert (2004), "Financialisation and the slowdown of accumulation", *Cambridge Journal of Economics*, 28, 719–41.

Taylor, Lance (1991), *Income Distribution, Inflation and Growth*, Cambridge, Mass.: MIT Press.

Taylor, Lance (2004), *Reconstructing Macroeconomics*, Cambridge, Mass.: Harvard University Press.

Taylor, Lance and Stephen A. O'Connell (1985), "A Minsky crisis", *Quarterly Journal of Economics*, pp. 871–85.

Uzawa, Hirofumi (1974), "On the dynamic stability of economic growth: The neoclassical versus Keynesian approaches", in G. Horwich and P. Samuelson (eds), *Trade, Stability and Macroeconomics: Essays in Honor of Lloyd A. Metzler*, New York" Academic Press, pp. 523–53.

You, Jong-Il and Dutt, Amitava Krishna (1996), "Government debt, income distribution and growth", *Cambridge Journal of Economics*, 20(3), May, pp. 335–51.

3
21st Century Keynesian Economic Policies

Philip Arestis
University of Cambridge and University of the Basque Country
and
Malcolm Sawyer
University of Leeds

Abstract

This chapter starts from the idea that the ways in which macroeconomic policies are formulated are heavily conditioned by the underlying analysis of the macroeconomy. We develop a broad Keynesian approach to the macroeconomy analysis, which is relevant for the realities of the 21st century. The overall objectives of economic policy, which forms the basis of our approach, is squarely sustainable (environmental and otherwise) and equitable economic development and growth. And within it we identify the main objective of macroeconomic policy as the achievement of full employment of the available labour force (recognising that the available labour force depends on social conditions and is influenced by the path of economic activity). Achieving such an objective would require, inter alia, the maintenance of a high level of aggregate demand consistent with the full employment of labour, and the provision of sufficient productive capacity to enable that full employment, where sufficient is to be interpreted in terms of quantity, quality and geographical distribution.

JEL Classification: E12, E52, E62

Keywords: Keynesian economics, 21st century, macroeconomic policies, full employment

1. Introduction

The ways in which macroeconomic policies are formulated are heavily conditioned by the underlying analysis of the macroeconomy, which in its turn depends heavily on the perceptions of how the economy works. Our perception of how the economy works relies heavily on a broad

Keynesian approach to the macroeconomy aspect of it which is relevant for the realities of the 21st century. The objectives of macroeconomic policy are also heavily conditioned by the underlying analysis. An obvious example would be that full employment would not be an objective of macroeconomic policy if one's underlying analysis predicted strong market forces ensuring full employment. The macroeconomic analysis underpinning this paper is set out in the first main section.

The overall objectives of economic policy which forms the basis of our approach would be the sustainable (environmental and otherwise) and equitable economic development and growth. Within that general sweep, we identify the main objective of macroeconomic policy as the achievement of full employment of the available labour force (recognising that the available labour force depends on social conditions and is influenced by the path of economic activity). Achieving such an objective would require, *inter alia*, the maintenance of a high level of aggregate demand consistent with the full employment of labour, and the provision of sufficient productive capacity to enable that full employment, where sufficient, is to be interpreted in terms of quantity, quality and geographical distribution. The control of inflation is regarded as a side issue unless inflation is exhibiting tendencies to continue to rise and to exceed something of the order of 10 per cent (on the basis that inflation above 10 per cent begins to distort decision-making and that the evidence on the relationship between inflation and growth does not indicate detrimental effects of inflation on growth at rates less than (say) 10 per cent (see, for example, Ghosh and Phillips, 1998)).

The chapter is organised as follows. Section 2 focuses on the theoretical framework of our approach. The macroeconomic policy implications are dealt with in section 3. We visit open economy considerations in section 4 and counter-inflationary policies in section 5. The full-employment aspects and capacity are aspects of section 6. Finally, section 7 summarises and concludes.

2.   The theoretical framework

The general background to the theoretical framework is that the analysis is of a monetary production economy in which finance and credit plays a significant role. It relates to an economy which has degrees of instability in the sense of being subject to the ups and downs of the business cycle and prone to crisis. The theoretical framework which underpins the analysis of this contribution draws on five main elements, which we now outline.

2.1. Expenditure, income and employment

The first main element concerns the levels of expenditure, income and employment. The level of economic activity is set by the level of aggregate demand (in both the short run and the long run), which is the sum of intended consumer demand, investment demand and government expenditure plus the net trade balance. Since the propensity to consume depends on income source (wages vs profits) and investment is influenced by profitability for a variety of reasons, the distribution of income between wages and profits plays a significant role in the determination of aggregate demand. The level of economic activity is then seen to depend on a range of factors including the distribution of income.

Consumer expenditure is based on the proposition of differential savings propensities out of wages and profits. Hence consumer expenditure C is given by

$$C = C_0 + c_w WS + c_p \Pi = C_0 + c_w(1-m)Y + c_p mY$$
$$= C_0 + (c_w(1-m) + c_p m)Y \tag{1}$$

where WS is total wages, Π profits, m is the profit share in national income and hence $1 - m$ is the wage share. In the discussion on price formation below, the profit margin is treated as influenced, *inter alia*, by the level of output. Correspondingly there is a savings function of the form:

$$S = -S_0 + (s_w(1-m) + s_p m)Y \tag{2}$$

An extension to this approach would also consider the role of rentier income (see, for example, Hein and Stockhammer, 2007)

The approach to investment is rather eclectic, and seeks to reflect a range of ideas. The first relates to the role of profits and of capacity utilisation. The inclusion of profits comes from a range of considerations. Current profits provide a potential pool of funds for the internal financing of investment. They may also be used as a signal of future profitability. Capacity utilisation clearly relates to the idea that firms undertaking investment in order to add to the capital stock to be able to produce higher levels of output in the future. Underutilised capacity would dampen the need to undertake investment for that purpose. This can be viewed as a static expression of the accelerator mechanism which would help to generate cycles but which lies outside the scope of this paper.

The second is to reflect the notion that entrepreneurs' expectations on the future, and the bouts of 'optimism and pessimism' can have a strong influence on investment. This could be summed up under the heading of the role of 'animal spirits', and labelled A. This is included here to emphasise the role of perceptions of the future, and to negate the notion that economic agents adhere to 'rational expectations', that the future is well-known, and indeed that there is a predetermined evolution for the capital stock.

The third factor can be labelled technological opportunities, and labelled T. This is to represent the idea that new ideas (whether of products or processes) require investment for their generation and their implementation.

There is finally some allowance made for the availability and cost of finance. It has generally been assumed that banks would supply loans to creditworthy firms but ideas of credit rationing, application of the 'principle of increasing risk' (Kalecki, 1937) and the recent experience in the 'credit crunch' indicate that some allowance should be made for the availability of finance and the degree of credit rationing, and a parameter τ is included in the investment function for such a measure. The cost of finance is reflected in a real interest rate term, based on the interest rate on loans, i_L, as representative of the cost of borrowing. The rate of interest on loans is linked with the key interest rate set by the Central Bank.

This leads to a function for investment I of the form:

$$I = f(u, m, A, T, \tau, i_L - p) \tag{3}$$

where the rate of profit can be written as $= (m/1+m).(Y/Y_f)(Y^*/K)$ where m is the mark-up of price over costs, and hence $(m/1+m)$ is the profit share, $u = Y/Y_f$, with Y_f being capacity output, with an assumed constant capital–output ratio enables the rate of profit to be related with the mark-up m and capacity utilisation, and p is the rate of inflation.

Investment has a dual role. It is a relatively volatile component of aggregate demand and hence a factor in the generation of the business cycle. It is also a creator of future productive potential and helps to set out the path along which the economy develops. This establishes interdependence of demand and supply, which is closely related to path dependency (i.e. the path of the economy is not predetermined but rather it is built up step by step). In this macroeconomic analysis three mechanisms by which there is path dependency are postulated.[1] First, current demand, which in its turn adds to capital stock via its investment component. Second, the ways in which people are drawn into/out of the effective labour supply through demand. Thus, the evolution of the labour force cannot be understood without reference to demand. Third, the rate of productivity change is linked to the level of economic activity in the economy, which itself is determined by the level of demand.

Government expenditure is clearly an important component of aggregate demand, and tax structure and rates have a strong influence on aggregate demand. In this paper we say little about government expenditure and taxation and the factors influencing them. With regard to the balance between government expenditure and tax revenue, we discuss the role of fiscal policy in the short term and long term.

The nominal exchange rate e is defined as foreign currency per unit of domestic currency. The real exchange is then $E = eP/P_w$ where P_w is a measure of world prices and P of domestic prices (where, for simplicity, no distinction is made between the price of traded and the price of non-traded goods). We return to discuss the determination of the real exchange rate below. Exports X are taken as a function of world income Y_w and the real exchange rate, E, and in terms of domestic currency exports are $eP/P_w.X$. Imports M are taken to be a function of domestic income and the real exchange rate.

The level of aggregate demand is given by the sum of consumer expenditure, investment, government expenditure and the net trade balance, and in each case the current level of expenditure is determined by past values of the relevant economic variables (e.g. income, interest rate).

It is an important feature of our approach that there is no market-based mechanism whereby market forces would propel the level of aggregate demand to any specific level of output (including any supply-side determined equilibrium of output). As Hein and Stockhammer (2007) indicate how aggregate demand evolves over time depends on factors such as wage and price changes, the consequent changes in the distribution of income between wages and profits and the differential effects of wages and profits on the level of demand, and whether that is a movement towards or away from any supply-side equilibrium depends on the parameters involved.

2.2. Supply side of the economy

The supply side of the economy is viewed in terms of the interaction between production decisions of firms in the light of the (expected) level of aggregate demand and the consequent decisions on employment and the relationship between prices and wages, and the setting of wages.

2.2.1. Prices and production

The production side of the economy is characterised as oligopolistic and imperfectly competitive. Enterprises make interrelated decisions on price, output supply and employment offers in light of the demand conditions which they face and their own productive capacity. The way in which prices are decided upon and the influences on price no doubt vary between sectors of the economy, and there are numerous theories of price setting (Sawyer, 1983). For macroeconomic purposes the general approach to prices starts from the notion that a firm sets price as a mark-up over production costs. One representation of this is for price to be set as a mark-up over average direct costs (ADC), that is:

$$P = (1+m)ADC \qquad (4)$$

which can be written as

$$P = \left[\frac{W}{APL} + \frac{F}{APM} \right](1+m) \qquad (5)$$

or, dividing through by W:

$$\frac{P}{W} = (1+m)\left[\frac{1}{APL} + \frac{F}{W.APM} \right] \qquad (6)$$

where W is money wage, F is cost of materials, APL is the marginal product of labour, APM is the marginal product of materials, and m is the mark-up. Equation (6) can be used to generate a relationship between price:wage ratio and output drawn as the p-curve in Figure 3.1. This equation for the price:wage ratio clearly depends on the mark-up applied by enterprises, and any increase (decrease) in the market power of enterprises leading to a larger mark-up that would shift the p-curve upwards (downwards). An increase (decrease) in cost of materials would lead to an upward (downward) shift in the curve.

The target price P can then be seen to be a function of the money wages, the cost of materials and the level of output (which will influence

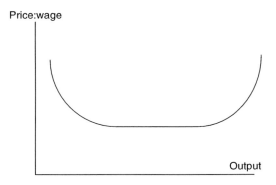

Figure 3.1   Relationship between price:wage ratio and output based on pricing considerations (p-curve)

the mark-up and the level of marginal costs). At the aggregate economy level, materials are those which are imported (as domestically produced material can be 'decomposed' into a labour input and a material input).

The move from the enterprise level to the economy level proceeds as follows. For a specified level of aggregate demand, there is a resulting amount of output which the enterprise seeks to produce, and adding those output decisions together gives the total level of output. There is also a price:wage ratio for each enterprise, and the average price:wage ratio is obtained by a suitably weighted average of the individual ratios. The relationship between the average price:wage ratio and the aggregate level of output is taken to be that of a 'flat-bottomed U-shape', similar to the shape drawn for the individual enterprise in Figure 3.1. At this aggregate level, the position of the p-curve will depend on the number of firms and capacity.

A move along the p-curve corresponds to variations in the (perceived) level of aggregate demand. It is not a matter of an enterprise choosing some combination of output and price:wage ratio, but rather that, for a particular level of aggregate demand, there is a combination of output and price:wage ratio that best serves the enterprises' interests. The expansion of output requires an expansion of aggregate demand, rather than a change in the price:wage ratio (though such a change in that ratio may come about as a consequence of the change in aggregate demand). But as the level of aggregate demand changes, so too will the price:wage ratio and the level of output, and those changes will map out the p-curve.

From the notion that price depends on wages, material costs and the level of output, the rate of price inflation (p) then depends upon the recent rate of change of money wages (w) and of imported materials (f), the rate of change of output q and a catch-up term which is a proportion of the difference between the desired price and the actual price. There may be a range of lags between costs and prices, but these lags are represented here in the simplest way. This can be expressed as:

$$p = bw_{-1} + (1-b)f_{-1} + cq + \vartheta \left[\left(\frac{P}{W} \right)^* - \left(\frac{P}{W} \right)_{-1} \right] \tag{7}$$

and subtracting w_{-1} from both sides of (10) can be readily re-written as:

$$p - w_{-1} = (1-b)(f_{-1} - w_{-1}) + cq + \vartheta \left[\left(\frac{P}{W} \right)^* - \left(\frac{P}{W} \right)_{-1} \right] \tag{8}$$

where c may be positive or negative.

The movement of price inflation relative to wage inflation then depends on three factors. The first is a measure of imported inflation $(f_{-1} - w_{-1})$, the second is the change in the level of output, q, and the third an adjustment factor related to the difference between desired price (relative to wages) and actual price (relative to wages).

The first term suggests that an upsurge in world inflation (which is not offset by appreciation of the domestic currency) would generate a form of cost-push inflation. The rate of change of output can influence price inflation in a positive or negative manner. For example, at relatively low levels of output, marginal costs fall as output expands, and from that perspective the prices fall (relative to money wages) as output expands, i.e. the c coefficient in the equation would be negative. The adjustment factor brings in the role of the level of output in that the output level influences the desired price:wage ratio.

In terms of the p-curve, for combinations of price:wage ratio and output below the curve, prices would tend to rise faster than wages, and for combinations above the curve prices tend to rise slower than wages, and this is signified in Figure 3.1. These tendencies would be modified by what was happening to foreign inflation and by the effects of recent changes in output.

The output produced and the employment offered in total by the enterprises depend on the amount of capacity possessed by the enterprises. Thus, the position of the aggregate p-curve depends on the amount of productive capacity. An increase in the capital stock increases the capital intensity of production and raises the average labour and material productivities, which, by reference to equation (6), can be seen to shift the aggregate p-curve downwards.

2.2.2.   *Wages and employment*

A relationship between price:wage ratio and output based on wage determination is now derived. The approach used here is based on the idea of efficiency wages.[2] At the enterprise level, money wages (W) are viewed as a set relative to alternative (expected) income (AY) of the workers. The mark-up μ of the wage over the alternative income (relative to the wage) can be viewed as depending on a variety of factors such as the bargaining strengths of the enterprise and trade unions, and/or on efficiency wage considerations. These alternative determinants lead to very similar formulations, and we work here with a general formulation. The alternative income is a weighted average of wages elsewhere and of the level of unemployment benefits (B) where the weights depend on the level of unemployment. The general form is then

$$\frac{W - AY}{W} = \mu \tag{9}$$

$$AY = (1 - \lambda\mu)W^e + \lambda UB \tag{10}$$

where W^e is the alternative wage outside of the enterprise and U the level of unemployment and λ a factor reflecting the rate of labour turnover and the rate of discount (and hence the cost of job search). The formulation of the alternative income reflects the idea that a worker leaving the enterprise may expect to spend sometime unemployed during which unemployment benefits B would be received and other time in employment paying the alternative wage W^e.

The equilibrium is characterised by all enterprises paying the same wage, and hence the condition that $W = W^e$, and solving the equations yields $W/B = \lambda U/(\lambda U - \mu)$. This provides a negative relationship between the ratio of wages to unemployment benefits and the level of unemployment. In terms of logs of relevant variables, this can be written as $\log W - \log B = h(U)$, which can be expanded and expressed in terms of employment as $(\log W - \log P) - (\log B - \log P) = H(L)$ with the first derivative of H assumed to be positive. For a given productive capacity, output and employment are related, and we derive a w-curve as $(\log P - \log W) - (\log P - \log B) = J(Y)$. The precise mapping between employment and output will change as productive capacity changes, and this is further discussed below.

In Figure 3.2, the top half of the diagram illustrates the relationship between real wage and employment which is viewed as a positive one. The bottom half translates this into a relationship between price:wage ratio and output, and this price:wage–output relationship is labelled the w-curve in Figure 3.2.

The wage dynamics would be expected to be that enterprises would raise money wages faster than prices (so that real wage rises) when wages are low relative to the alternative income, that is when either wages are low or unemployment low (and hence employment and output high). In terms of the second half of Figure 3.2, for points above the w-curve, where price:wage ratio is relatively high (and hence real wage relatively low) and output (and hence also employment) relatively high, wages would tend to rise relative to prices and wage increases exceed price increases. For points below the w-curve, price:wage ratio and output relatively low, and wages would tend to fall relative to prices, and wage increases less than price increases.

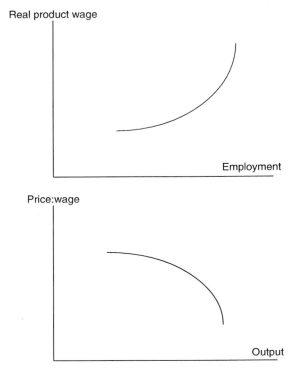

Figure 3.2   Relationship between real product wage and employment, and between price:wage ratio and output (w-curve)

2.2.3.   *Constant inflation level of output (CILO)*

The price and the wage determination processes can now be brought together in Figure 3.3 to provide a supply-side equilibrium. Along the p-curve, prices would rise in line with wages from price determination considerations, whereas along the w-curve wages would rise in line with prices from wage determination considerations. The intersection of the two curves at point A in Figure 3.3 would provide the constant inflation level of output (CILO) where prices and wages rise at the same rate. This level of output is now labelled Y+.

This figure is drawn in price:wage, output space rather than wage: price, employment space to seek to avoid suggestions that the labour market plays the key role in the determination of the supply-side equilibrium. This could be seen as akin to a non-accelerating inflation rate of unemployment (NAIRU), but the CILO differs from the NAIRU in

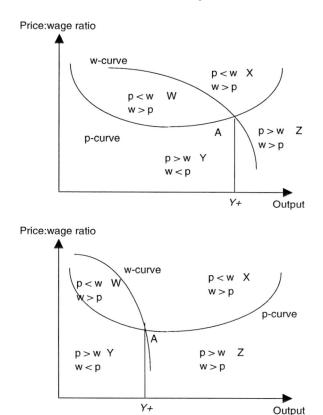

Figure 3.3 The constant inflation level of output (CILO) and inflationary pressures

(at least) two major respects. First, the interaction of prices and wages do not take place in what may be described as 'the labour market', and hence the supply-side equilibrium is not set by the features of the labour market. Instead the emphasis is placed on the role of productive capacity. Second, there is no presumption that the CILO acts as a strong (or even weak) attractor for the actual level of economic activity. As wages and prices change, the distribution of income would be changing, and in general it is not possible to say whether those changes would lead aggregate demand towards or away from the CILO. It should also be emphasised that there is no presumption here that the supply-side equilibrium is 'natural' or remains unchanged over time.

Figure 3.3 appears in two parts. In the upper part the intersection of the two curves occurs where the p-curve is downward-sloping which would be where unit costs are declining; this is in the lower part where the p-curve is upward-sloping. It can also be readily envisaged that there could be multiple equilibria points.[3]

The CILO clearly depends on the position of the p-curve and the w-curve. In particular, this means that increases in productive capacity, which shift the p-curve outwards, lead to a higher level of CILO. There would be a level of employment corresponding to the CILO level of output Y+. But there would be no strong reason why that level of employment would correspond to full employment (or indeed to any particular level of employment).

The level of the CILO would be influenced by a range of factors which we briefly list here. The p-curve would shift upwards leading to a lower CILO with an increase in the degree of market power (raising the mark-up of price over cost) and with an increase in foreign prices. The w-curve would shift inwards (to the south west) also leading to a lower CILO with an increase in the mark-up m.[4] An increase in the number of enterprises in an economy would cause some shift in the p-curve towards the right, leading to an increase in the CILO. An increase in capital intensity of production which raises labour productivity would be associated with a downward shift in the p-curve.

The CILO has been drawn as though it is a precise point. However, the p-curve may well be horizontal over a considerable range which would correspond to constant unit costs with a constant mark-up. The w-curve may also be relatively flat. In those circumstances, there may be a CILO range; or at least, output above Y+ would involve only rather small increases in inflation. In effect, zone Z in Figure 3.3 could be relatively small, and the pace with which inflation accelerates in that zone relatively low.

2.3.   The inflationary process

Inflation is viewed as multi-causal and the sources of inflationary pressure vary over time and economy. The range of factors which impact on the rate of inflation includes a struggle over income shares, the level of and rate of changes of the level of aggregate demand and cost-push factors coming notably from the foreign sector (change in import prices and the exchange rate). This is all summarized in equation (10) above.

In Figure 3.3, there are four distinct zones. In each zone, there are two inequalities, transferred from Figures 3.1 and 3.2. The top inequality indicates the relative changes in prices and wages resulting from price determination and the bottom inequality from wage determination. Zone Z is one of rising inflation (associated with relatively high levels of output), whereas zone W is one of falling inflation (associated with relatively low levels of output). These zones correspond to the positive association between price inflation and level of economic activity. In zone X (Y) the price:wage ratio tends to fall (rise); price inflation would tend to fall (rise) but wage inflation tend to rise (fall).

Changes in the rate of inflation appear to depend on the level of output. For an output other than the CILO, there is a difference between the actual price:wage ratio and at least one of the equilibrium ratios given by the p-curve and the w-curve. It is the difference between the price:wage ratio and the equilibrium ratio which generates a change in inflation. The pace of inflation, however, has a range of other influences besides the level of output. One of these would be the influence of changes in output, whereby on the downward-sloping part of the p-curve, increases in price would tend to reduce prices. Hence the effects of an increase in output there would reduce the rate of inflation (as can be seen from the inflation equation given above). For the upward-sloping portion of the p-curve, an increase in output would tend to increase the rate of inflation.

Equation (10) also indicates another influence on inflation, namely imported inflation. It comes as no surprise that domestic prices will tend to rise faster when imported material costs are rising. This introduces an element into the inflationary process which is not directly effected by the level of demand.

2.4. Money, credit and finance

The fourth component relates to the interplay between money, credit and finance. Money is endogenously created within the private sector with loans created by banks generating bank deposits. Their willingness or otherwise to provide loans and the terms upon which they are provided impact on the level and structure of demand. Consequently, since money comes into existence via the credit process, the ways in which credit is created impacts on investment, and thereby the productive potential of the economy. Money is thereby created through the credit system, where the manner in which loans are provided by the banking system becomes central to the analysis: banks provide credit 'off their own bat'. The expansion of the stock of money is driven by the demand for loans, which leads to the expansion of bank deposits in so far as the demand for loans is met by the banking sector. However, the stock of money has to be held by people, and the stock of money is largely determined by the 'demand for money', as money is destroyed by the repayment of loans. The Central Bank sets the key policy interest rate, which governs the terms upon which the Central Bank provides the 'base' money to the banking system. The way in which the Central Bank sets its policy interest rate impacts on the manner in which the economy performs. In an inflation targeting setting, the Central Bank can be viewed as seeking to vary the policy interest rate according to its perceptions of the inflationary environment. The pursuit of inflation targeting may contribute to the short-term interest rate changes, but does not indicate how the average or underlying rate of interest is set. Different central banks approach this in different ways. It should, though, be remembered that central banks do pursue other objectives (or may just muddle through). However, it is significant that the policy interest rate is set, which raises the question of the relationship between the policy rate and the rates of interest which matter for economic decision making, e.g. rate of interest on bank loans, long-term interest rate of bonds. Further, the policy interest rate and the general level and structure of interest rates can have a range of effects, both predictable and unpredictable. There are effects on interest-sensitive components of demand (including investment), the size of which may be relatively small. Other important effects can be on the exchange rate and on asset prices. Wide gyrations in interest rates required in a regime where the Central Bank sets them for inflation purposes, create circumstances for potential bubbles. Consequently, the dangers with this type of conduct of monetary policy are clear: frequent changes in interest rates can have serious effects; low interest rates may contribute to asset price bubbles; high interest rates work through applying economic pressures on vulnerable social groups; there are, thus, severe distributional effects. Regulatory and prudential controls become, then, necessary. The credit creation process can itself be a source of instability with credit booms and credit crunches, and the generation of asset price bubbles.

2.5. Foreign sector

The fifth component is concerned with the foreign sector and an open economy. One significant aspect of that has been included above where imports and exports were included in the aggregate demand equation, and reflected the effects on demand (and hence employment) of variations in the exchange rate. The current account position may be thought of in terms of p_d X $(Y_w, p_d.ner/p_f) - (p_f/ner)$. M(Y, $p_d.ner/p_f$) where X is exports, M is imports, ner is nominal exchange rate, p_d is domestic prices and p_f is foreign prices, Y is domestic income and Y_w is world income.

It is a requirement that CA + FA + DR = 0 where CA is current account position, FA is financial (capital) account position and DR the change in official reserves. In a floating exchange rate regime DR is taken to be zero. A current account deficit implies a financial account inflow, and hence accumulating debts and future interest and other payments. Whilst the recent experience is that countries may run substantial current account deficits over a number of years, there may be limits to how long that can continue. But in any event it is unlikely that a current account (more accurately trade) deficit can grow continuously which places a constraint that the growth of imports and of exports are in line. The 'balance of payments' constrained' growth rate is then given by

$$y_B = (1/\zeta)\Big[(1-\eta-\psi)\big(p_d - p_f + e\big) + \varepsilon y_w\Big] \tag{11}$$

where η is price elasticity of demand for exports, ε is income elasticity, ψ is price elasticity of demand for imports and ζ income elasticity and $1-\eta-\psi < 0$ is the Marshall-Lerner condition. If it is further assumed that the real exchange rate is constant, then $y_B = \varepsilon y_w / \zeta$.

The effects of exchange rate variations will depend on the extent of pass-through. There are several approaches to modelling the exchange rate, but notoriously movements in the exchange rate are difficult (impossible) to predict. It can be readily observed that there is considerable volatility in exchange rates with consequent effects on the current account position. What we can argue, though, is that there are serious difficulties with a floating market-determined exchange rate system. A high real exchange rate contributes to 'imbalances' in the economy through its impact on the domestic composition of output: declines in manufacturing and exports, and increases in services and current account deficit, occur, and the corresponding capital account inflow. The pass-through effect of a change in the exchange rate first on import prices and subsequently on the generality of prices, both goods and services, has weakened since the late 1980s. Consequently, the stronger real exchange rate has had less offsetting effect on domestic prices than in earlier periods. The argument normally used to justify appreciation in the exchange rate that such a move slows inflation is no longer valid under such circumstances. The impact of interest rate changes may have become more ambiguous. Evidence seems to show that capital movements are based more on equities than on other assets. A change in interest rates then may have the opposite effect on capital movements than otherwise. A secondary instrument in the form of direct intervention is necessary. Central Baks should engage in intervention on their own as a monetary mechanism. In this sense we may treat the exchange rate as an exogenous variable.

2.6.   Cycles and fluctuations in economic activity

In terms of our approach there will be fluctuations in economic activity (cycles, 'boom and bust') and full employment will be at best a rather infrequent occurrence at the top of the cycle. There has been a range of mechanisms for the generation of cycles which are by no means contradictory and indeed all of these mechanisms are likely to be at work and interacting. Investment expenditure plays a significant role in at least two ways. First, the relationship between investment decisions and variables, which are related to the level of and the rate of change of economic activity (e.g. the accelerator approach to investment), reinforce movements in economic activity whether in the upward or the downward direction. The simple multiplier–accelerator approach provides one of the simpler views on the generation of the business cycle. Second, investment decisions are subject to the vagaries of 'animal spirits' and the effects of bouts of optimism and pessimism which will also lead to fluctuations in investment expenditure.

In the approach sketched above, the level of and change in economic activity have an impact on the rate of change of prices and of wages, and there would then be consequent changes in the distribution of income between wages and profits. Changes in the distribution of income will have effects on the level of aggregate demand, with the nature of the effects depending on whether there is a wage-led or a profit-led regime. These interactions can also help to generate cycles. In the hands of Goodwin (1967) the interactions between price determination (and the implications for profit share) and investment in a predator–prey model were capable of generating limit cycles.

The approach of Minsky (1986) and others indicates the 'boom and bust' nature of the financial system. It does not lead to regular uniform cycles but does indicate the ways in which a period of apparent stability leading to optimism, encouragement of risk taking, development of asset bubbles etc., leads into a fragile financial system.

3.   Macroeconomic policy implications

The objectives of economic policy should be: full employment of the available labour supply; constant rate of inflation rather than target inflation, in view of the evidence that inflation and output move together up to around 10–15 percent inflation rate; and financial stability. The instruments of economic policy may be briefly summarised: (i) fiscal policy is paramount. We consider the operation of fiscal policy in terms of movements in the fiscal stance in the short run and also in respect of the long-run setting. In the short term, variations in the fiscal stance can be used in conjunction with automatic stabilisers to offset fluctuations in economic activity arising from, inter alia, variations in private sector aggregate demand. In the longer term, the general fiscal stance should be set to underpin the desired level of output and employment; (ii) interest rate policy should be set so that the real rate of interest is as low as possible in line with the trend rate of growth. In this sense, a real rate of interest in line with the perceived trend rate of growth could be targeted so that the nominal rate is set by the Central Bank equal to the target rate plus the expected rate of inflation. Further, the operations of the Central Bank should ultimately be directed towards financial stability and this objective of financial stability should be placed as the most significant one for the Central Bank, requiring the development of alternative policy instruments alongside the downgrading of interest rate policy and of any notion of inflation targeting; and (iii) exchange rate policy is also important. Changes in the exchange rate affect the domestic economy: primarily in terms of the level of demand and hence economic activity and, rather weakly, in terms of inflation. Intervention by the Central Bank in the foreign exchange market with the specific aim to stabilise the exchange rate may be important in this respect as argued above, where we suggested control and direct manipulation of the exchange rate by the Central Bank. We elaborate in what follows on these economic policies.

3.1. The role of fiscal policy

Since the forces ensuring that the level of aggregate demand is in line with the productive potential (or full employment) are, at best, weak, there is a requirement for aggregate demand policies. Fiscal policy is a much more potent instrument than interest rate policy for setting the level of demand (Arestis and Sawyer, 2003). The operation of fiscal policy is considered in both a long-term setting and in terms of movements in the fiscal stance in the short term. In the short term, variations in the fiscal stance can be used to offset fluctuations in economic activity arising from, *inter alia*, variations in private sector aggregate demand. At the extreme this leads to the fine tuning of fiscal policy. In the longer term, the general fiscal stance can be set to support the level of aggregate demand consistent with high level of economic activity.

3.1.1. Coarse tuning

For the long term we adopt the approach of Lerner (1943) and Kalecki (1944) and aim to achieve a budget position to achieve a high target level of economic activity (labelled here Y_f). This is represented as a budget deficit in equation (12):

$$G - T = S(Y_f) - I(Y_f) + M(Y_f) - X(Y_w) \qquad (12)$$

where G is government expenditure, I investment, X exports, T tax revenue, S savings and Q imports, Y_f is the target level of income, and Y_w is world income.

The budget deficit is to be used to mop up 'excess' private savings (over investment), and the counterpart budget surplus used when investment expenditure exceeds savings (at the desired level of economic activity). A budget deficit would not be required when there is a high level of private aggregate demand such that investment equals savings at a high level of economic activity (and a surplus would be required when investment exceeds savings at the desired level of economic activity). The budget deficit required to achieve Y_f can be seen clearly to depend on the propensities to save, invest, import and the ability to export, and these over country and across time. The underlying budget position should then be set in accordance with the perceived underlying values of the propensities to save, invest, import and export (see Sawyer, 2007b). This approach to fiscal policy can be said to incorporate a clear rule: set the underlying budget deficit compatible with the desired level of output. But it is clear that the estimation of the relevant budget stance would involve substantial difficulties and disputes. Although whether the latter difficulties are any greater than the estimation of key variables in the current orthodoxy such as the 'equilibrium rate of interest' and the 'non-accelerating inflation rate of unemployment' is an interesting question.

This approach raises the issue of the sustainability of the deficit (see Arestis and Sawyer, 2006, 2009), which we view as not a significant issue for two basic reasons. First, in this approach governments borrow because the private sector wishes to lend; if there were no potential excess of savings over investment, then there would be no need for a budget deficit. Savings (over and above investment) can only be realised if there is a budget deficit or overseas lending, which absorbs those savings. Second, a total budget deficit of d' (relative to GDP) is always sustainable in the sense that the corresponding debt to GDP ratio stabilises at $b = d'/g$ with g as the growth rate. The budget deficit, which is relevant for the level of demand, is the overall budget position rather than the primary deficit (or surplus). To the extent that a budget deficit is required to offset an excess of private savings over investment, then it is the overall budget deficit which is relevant. Bond interest payments are a transfer payment and add to the income of the recipient, and similar in that respect to other transfer payments (though the propensity to consume out of interest payments is likely to be less than that out of many other transfer payments). In terms of sustainability, then, of a fiscal deficit the condition under 'functional finance' is generally readily satisfied being the requirement of a positive nominal growth rate.

3.1.2. Fine tuning

The ultimate in fine tuning would arise when the budget stance was changed continuously in response to variations in economic activity. This would be comparable to the fine tuning that is currently attempted through interest rate changes, with decisions on interest rates being made on a frequent (e.g. monthly) basis, even if the decision is one of no change. The problems of fine tuning are well-known in terms of the various lags involved, including those of recognition, decision making, implementation and effect. However, the automatic stabilisers of fiscal policy already perform part of that task in the sense that a downturn is met by reduced tax and increased expenditure, which modify but do not eliminate the degree of fluctuations in economic activity.[5] The tax and expenditure regime could be designed in a manner to increase the extent of stabilisation and a more progressive tax system would enhance the stabilisation properties. But that should be argued for on grounds of equity and income distribution, albeit that there would be the additional benefits for stabilisation.

The question to be addressed is whether discretionary fiscal policy can and should also be used to help stabilise the economy. A Fiscal Policy Committee (FPC) analogous with a Monetary Policy Committee (MPC) has been suggested in a number of forms (see, for example, Arestis, 2009; Wren-Lewis, 2000). If interest rates can be varied to seek to fine tune the economy, then cannot fiscal policy be used in a similar way? There can be seen to be a basic similarity between interest rate policy and fiscal policy in this respect. For example, it has been argued that "the literature stemming from Barro and Gordon that is often cited by economists as justifying ICBs [Independent Central Banks], does not specify what instrument is used to control output and inflation, and so it applies equally to fiscal countercyclical policy" (Leith and Wren Lewis, 2005, p. 595).

It is often objected that the politically sensitive nature of tax and expenditure decisions and the need for those to be taken by Parliament prevents this. Further whilst lowering taxes and raising transfers may be an acceptable way of responding to a downturn, it is unlikely to be an acceptable way of dealing with an upturn. The statement 'your benefit has been cut this week as the economy is growing too fast' would not be well received; though, of course, a similar argument is put in the case of interest rates: 'your mortgage payments will rise because the economy is growing too fast'. But there are taxes, such as value added tax, social security contributions, which could be varied in this manner. The role of FPC would be to judge on say a six-monthly basis whether a change in tax rates would be warranted. It would require institutional arrangements, which would enable these decisions to be taken in a timely manner under operating procedures agreed through the democratic process. The key role of a FPC would be to use their discretion to adapt the fiscal stance in the face of significant short-run movements in the economy.

There are, of course, other ways by which government policy may be able to influence the level of demand. Interest rate policy is one of those, but we would argue that such a policy is not an effective one as compared with fiscal policy (Arestis and Sawyer, 2003). From a Kaleckian perspective two others have to be considered, namely shifts in the distribution of income and the stimulation of investment (Kalecki, 1944). The effects of a shift in the distribution of income as between wages and profits would depend on whether the economy was in a wage-led or a profit-led regime. The stimulation of investment may tend to raise the capital–output ratio, leading to a decline in the rate of profit. In both cases, we would suggest that a demand policy has to take into account the prevailing distribution of income and propensity to invest, and in terms of the coarse tuning approach outlined above the required budget deficit depends on the distribution of income (via its effects on savings and investment behaviour) and on the propensity to invest. However, we would argue that income distribution policies and encouragement or otherwise of investment should not be undertaken for reasons of their effects on aggregate demand but rather assessed in their own terms. For example, there are strong reasons to advocate a less egalitarian distribution of income in social and ethical terms, rather than because such a policy would stimulate demand.

3.2. The role of monetary policy

Until recently, many would claim that inflation targeting had been able to provide a nominal anchor for the economy. After a number of other policies designed to provide nominal stability – notably control of the money supply, fixed exchange rates – had largely failed, inflation targeting appeared to have delivered. The experience of 2008, with inflation rising well above the target levels, should raise considerable question marks against inflation targeting as it proved impotent in the face of cost-push inflation. For the present, inflation targeting (here seen to involve an independent Central Bank with the objective of achieving a stated target rate, or band, of inflation using the policy interest rate as the instrument) remains nominally in place, though whether decisions made by Central Banks over the past 12 months could be said to be independent of central government or directed towards inflation is rather doubtful.

In previous writings we have cast doubt on inflation targeting along four lines (see, for example, Arestis and Sawyer, 2008). First, the difference in inflation performance between inflation targeting and non-inflation targeting countries appears small in a general environment where inflation had been declining, and that inflation targeting was often introduced after inflation had been reduced (see also Angeriz and Arestis, 2007). Roger Ferguson, then Vice Chairman of the Board of Governors of the Federal Reserve System, argues that 'Unfortunately, the empirical evidence for industrial countries available to date generally appears insufficient to assess the success of the inflation-targeting approach with confidence. For example, it is unclear whether the announcement of quantitative inflation targets lessens the short-run trade-off between employment and inflation and whether it helps anchor inflation expectations. In addition, some research, controlling for other factors, fails to isolate the benefits of an inflation target with respect to the level of inflation or its volatility over time, and output does not seem to fluctuate more stably around its potential for countries that have adopted numerical targets' (Ferguson, 2005, p. 297).

Second, variations in the rate of interest appear to have little effect on the rate of inflation (though rather more on the level of output). The evidence on this is typically obtained from econometric estimation results undertaken within Central Banks or by those closely associated with them. A 1 per cent hike in policy interest rate leads to a significant drop in output but a reduction in inflation of the order of 0.1 to 0.2 per cent (Arestis and Sawyer, 2004). Goodhart (2005b), drawing on his experience on the Monetary Policy Committee and the work done within the Bank of England, commented that 'unless the shocks hitting the system were really quite small, the extent of policy-induced demand management, even if perfectly calibrated, could not be responsible for the achievement of the stability and successful growth that we have enjoyed' (p. 169). A number of words of caution: the interest rate change is applied for a year, but this may be because the nature of the model is such that a departure from the equilibrium interest rate within the model would eventually cause the model to explode. And second, inflation in these models is tied down by expectations, and with assumption of some form of forward-looking 'rational expectations' and that the inflation target is met. This does though point to the notion that the success or otherwise of monetary policy with respect to inflation comes not from variations in the policy rate of interest but through generation of low inflationary expectations, and specifically that expectations are 'locked down' even in the face of changes in actual inflation.

Third, there is the attempt at ultra fine tuning in the sense that monthly decisions (and hence potential change) on interest rates are made seeking to target inflation up to two years ahead. Fourth, the lack of strong theoretical link running from interest rate to economic activity to inflation. Sawyer (2009) examines a number of the proposed links. The essence of the argument is that the interest rate and the level of economic activity are in levels whereas inflation is a rate of change (of prices). It is more usual in economics to relate levels with levels, and specifically the rate of interest with the level of prices (as initially postulated by Wicksell, 1898), and the level of demand (or level of economic activity) with the level of prices. For example, theories of price behaviour by firms focus on the determination of the price-cost margin, and that margin and costs themselves may vary with the level of demand (but not with the rate of change of demand).

A higher level of demand may then lead to higher prices, but that does not mean higher inflation, that is a persistent rise in prices. There are two situations where this could lead to inflation. First, in the period of higher prices there is inflation and, if expectations of inflation jump in line with the experience of inflation, then the initially higher price could set out inflation (in the sense of persistent rise in prices). Second, wages (or similar) also come into the picture and if higher output and employment means higher prices and higher wages, the intended increase in at least one of price/wage or wage/price cannot occur. In effect a wage–price spiral is set off.

It can therefore be disputed whether monetary policy is an effective means to control inflation. There may be an exception to this argument in that having a 'credible' central bank with an inflation mandate influences people's expectations somehow, which produces an inflation rate that hits eventually the target set by it. But even this argument is not backed by persuasive empirical backing.

3.2.1.   *Setting the policy interest rate*

The attempt has been made to fine tune the economy (or at least the rate of inflation) through the frequent change of the policy rate of interest (with monthly or thereabouts decisions on the policy interest rate). We have cast doubt above on the effectiveness of that policy with regard to inflation. The changes in the policy interest rate have implementation costs. But the most significant argument here is that the policy rate has effects on a range of variables, notably the exchange rate and asset prices. Indeed those variables are part of the channels through which changes in the policy rate of interest is supposed to influence the level of demand and thereby the rate of inflation. There are questions of the strength and reliability of those channels, but the point here is that there can be effects, and some of them may be adverse. For example, Goodhart (2005a) argues that a focus on domestic variables only in interest rate determination may provide 'a combination of internal price stability and exchange rate instability' (p. 301). In recent times, an important aspect of this can be the influence of low interest rates on asset prices, and whether the stimulus to asset price rises coming from low interest rates can be the spark setting off a price bubble. The argument of Wicksell (1898), and others, could be seen as one that suggests interest rate policy has an effect on asset price inflation – or at least some subset of asset prices; asset prices develop a speculative element (meaning here purchase of asset to benefit from expected rise in price, rather than for income stream from asset); it is obvious to say that asset price bubbles have developed – dot.com, house prices, etc. Current arrangements are powerless to deal with those bubbles.

One of the curiosities of the present approach to monetary policy is that all attention is paid to 25 basis point variations in the interest rate on a monthly basis, and little attention is paid to what in the monetary central bank policy rule is the key, namely the average/equilibrium/natural rate. There is virtually no discussion – there may be attempts to estimate 'natural rate' but those are little more than the average of what has been actually observed. Yet a number of arguments point to the average rate being around the rate of growth – in Taylor's original formulation, the 'golden rule' of accumulation, the distributional argument (real rate = growth rate preserves the relative position of savings) and that (cf. Pasinetti, 1997) $b = d/g$ where b is debt/bonds, g is the GDP growth rate, and d is total deficit = primary deficit (d') + interest payments ($b.i$); and hence, $b.g = d = d' + i.b$, and hence $d' = 0$ and deficit = interest payments.

The rule of 'rate of interest equal to the rate of growth' can be linked with other considerations. The 'golden rule of capital accumulation' in the framework of a neoclassical model with the marginal productivity of capital equal to the rate of interest generates such an outcome. Another is the 'fair rate of interest' (Pasinetti, 1981), which 'in real terms should be equal to the rate of increase in the productivity of the total amount of labor that is required, directly or indirectly, to produce consumption goods and to increase productive capacity' (Lavoie and Seccareccia, 1999, p. 544).

The setting of the interest rate has some clear and obvious implications ·for the operation of fiscal policy. The sustainability of a budget deficit depends on the level of interest rates (and specifically the post-tax rate of interest on government bonds, labelled r). If $r < g$, then any primary budget deficit of d (relative to GDP) would lead to an eventual debt ratio (to GDP) of $b = d/(g - r)$ (either both of g and r in real terms or both in nominal terms). If $r > g$ then a primary budget deficit would lead to growing debt ratio. In a similar vein, a continuing total budget deficit of d (including interest payments) leads to a debt to GDP ratio stabilising at d'/g where here g is in nominal terms. This implies that $b + rd = gd$, i.e. $b = (g - r)d$ and hence if g is less than r the primary budget deficit is negative (i.e. primary budget is in surplus). The case where $g = r$ is of particular interest. Pasinetti (1997, p. 163) remarks that this case 'represents the 'golden rule' of capital accumulation. ... In this case, the public budget can be permanently in deficit and the public debt can thereby increase indefinitely, but national income increases at the same rate (g) so that the D/Y ratio remains constant. Another way of looking at this case is to say that the government budget has a deficit, which is wholly due to interest payments' (p. 163).

The simplest way to implement such a policy would be to set the nominal policy interest rate at the beginning of the year, taking into account the expected rate of inflation for the coming year (with perhaps some adjustment based on the difference between actual and expected inflation in the preceding year). Outside of crisis (and perhaps even then) the nominal policy interest rate would be maintained for the year, with avoidance of costs of further decision-making and implementation of interest rate changes. In some respects this could be seen as the equivalent to the monetarist constant growth of money supply rule to avoid problems of fine tuning, but applied to the rate of interest!

There are some issues with such a policy approach to be resolved. The arguments for a constant real rate equal to the rate of growth relate to some market rate of interest, which is not equal to the policy rate, and which may bear a varying relationship with the policy rate. There can be international complications in so far as domestic interest rate relative to interest rates elsewhere can have implications for the exchange rate. This is neither to suggest some simple uncovered interest rate parity idea nor to suggest that the effects of interest rate differentials on exchange rate are firm and predictable.

In effect, we wish to put forward two lines of argument here. First, to argue that the view against fine tuning applies to the setting of interest rates, and that such fine tuning should be foregone and rather the nominal rate of interest should be set to achieve a constant target real rate of interest. Second, there are a number of arguments to support the view that the target real rate of interest be the underlying rate of growth of the economy.

3.2.2. Independence of the Central Bank

There has, of course, been a world-wide move over the past two decades towards the adoption of an 'independent' Central Bank generally with the objective of achieving (or maintaining) low inflation. Ever since Kydland and Prescott (1977) and Barro and Gordon (1983), where the notion of time-inconsistent behaviour and the inflation bias syndrome are introduced, there has been a sustained trend towards Central Bank Independence (CBI) in the world economy. The arguments for a Central Bank with operational independence (specifically from politicians) were based on two interconnected propositions. First, that the single instrument (interest rate) affecting the single objective (inflation) was a viable one. This in turn rested on the long-run vertical Phillips curve type approach in that interest rate could influence the rate of inflation and that there is an equilibrium rate of interest, which is simultaneously compatible with constant inflation and with supply-side equilibrium (expressed in the form of either the 'natural' rate of unemployment or a zero output gap). The achievement of a constant rate of inflation would secure the achievement of supply-side equilibrium (which was assumed to be uninfluenced by the path of aggregate demand and to have some desirable properties). The ability of the equilibrium rate of interest, along with market flexibility, especially flexibility in the labour market, to secure the supply-side equilibrium was in effect sufficient to rule out any requirement for active fiscal policy.

Second, the short-run Phillips curve suggests that lower unemployment (higher output) comes with a higher rate of inflation, and that elected politicians at times will be tempted to boost demand with its benefits of lower unemployment and higher output at the cost of higher inflation. Central Bankers are then viewed as uniquely able to influence the level of demand without falling to the temptation to raise demand at inappropriate times, to be more committed to low inflation and to avoid the problems of time inconsistency. The notion that the Central Bank has, or can acquire, credibility in terms of its commitment to the control of inflation, and that it is the Central Bank alone (the 'conservative' central bankers' argument) that has this creditability with respect to the control of inflation are central themes in the Central Bank theoretical framework.

Taylor (2008) claims to have been able to provide empirical evidence 'that government actions and interventions caused, prolonged, and worsened the financial crisis. They caused it by deviating from historical precedents and principles for setting interest rates, which had worked well for 20 years' (p. 18). This could suggest that the bankers were not 'conservative', at least as judged against Taylor's rule. In this context such a judgement may be warranted in that an operational rule akin to Taylor's rule would be needed to ensure the stability of the economy in terms of the macroeconomic model that is compatible with it.

The operational 'independence' of a Central Bank in any serious sense would preclude co-operation between the Central Bank and other public authorities. In a one instrument–one objective framework (bearing in mind the first point above, namely that constant inflation and the supply-side equilibrium are in effect two sides of the same coin) this could be acceptable. But once it is recognised that the interest rate tool is not adequate to achieve the objective so that more tools are required, and that there is more to life than low inflation, and that (at least intermediate) objectives such as the exchange rate and the level of and growth of output are on the agenda, then doubt must be cast on this isolation of the Central Bank. It can be argued that (as to some degree illustrated by the present crisis) there are 'get out' clauses, which enable co-ordination in times of crisis. But the argument would be that the institutional arrangements for co-ordination need to be in place, and further that the co-ordination is required at all times, not just in times of crisis.

3.2.3.   *The objectives of monetary policy and financial stability*

The argument made here is that financial stability should become the central objective of the Central Bank. Buiter (2008) indicates that 'financial stability means (1) the absence of asset price bubbles; (2) the absence of illiquidity of financial institutions and financial markets that may threaten systemic stability; (3) the absence of insolvency of financial institutions that may threaten systemic stability' (p. 10). It can be noted that the recent Banking Act 2009 in the UK establishes that 'an objective of the Bank [of England] shall be to contribute to protecting and enhancing the stability of the financial systems of the United Kingdom (the "Financial Stability Objective")', with the Bank working with other bodies such as the Treasury and the Financial

Services Authority (FSA) and the establishing of a Financial Stability Committee. At present this is placed alongside the monetary stability objective under the heading of inflation targeting. This could be seen a significant step away from the operational independence of the Bank of England and from the single inflationary objective. Our argument here is that the financial stability objective should be the prime objective and the operational independence of the Bank of England ended.

Current events and the general record on financial crises (see Laeven and Valencia, 2008, for details of crises over the past three decades and their costs) indicate the substantial costs associated with financial crisis and financial instability (which would far outweigh any costs associated with inflation). In terms of the general multiple instruments–multiple objectives framework it may not be possible to uniquely assign each instrument to a specific objective. Nevertheless, it may be possible to link an instrument mainly with a specific objective, recognising that co-ordination in the use of instruments can be advantageous. In this context, the argument is that the main link should be monetary policy – monetary and financial stability. However, we have argued above for the policy of seeking to target a specified real rate of interest and to seek to maintain a constant rate of interest. Such a policy may have some beneficial effects on financial stability in that lowering interest rates can be seen to inflate asset prices with the possibility of setting off an asset price bubble which will burst at some point. Further, as recent experience suggests, asset price inflation may be inimical to financial stability given the interrelationships between asset price inflation and credit expansion.

One approach to financial stability was expressed by Greenspan (2002) when considering how to respond to asset price bubbles. He argued that 'the degree of monetary tightening that would be required to contain or offset a bubble of any substantial dimension appears to be so great as to risk an unacceptable amount of collateral damage to the wider economy' (p. 4). But further his general attitude was that policy should be directed towards cleaning up after a crisis rather than seeking to prevent a crisis. 'Faced with this uncertainty, the Federal Reserve has focused on policies that would, as I testified before the Congress in 1999,[6] "... mitigate the fallout [of an asset bubble] when it occurs and, hopefully, ease the transition to the next expansion"'. The costs (in terms of lost output, unemployment and fiscal costs) as well as the sheer difficulties of propping up the financial system following the financial collapse indicate that this approach should not be one to be applied in the future.

The argument here is made more relevant by Goodhart (2007), who in fact suggests that

> [i]n so far, therefore, as the central bank has a prime concern for systemic financial stability, it should want to promote a program of counter-cyclical prudential regulations, where these latter become restrictive during asset price bubbles and relax during asset price downturns. Unfortunately the system of financial regulation is developing in a manner which will have exactly the reverse proclivity. Under the Basel II accord for financial regulation, this will become more pro-cyclical. (p. 68)

Goodhart goes on to point out problems with the national adoption of standards different from Basel II.

There are already in place a variety of regulatory policies, which are intended to develop financial stability, but it could be said that these are often focused on the stability and viability (or otherwise) of individual banking institutions rather than on systemic factors. As D'Arista (2009) argues in the context of the use of capital requirement,

> As a strategy for ensuring that market forces rather than regulations and quantity controls would determine the volume of bank lending, capital requirements became the rationale for – and poster child of – deregulation. But they have subsequently been seen as its Achilles heel because of their focus on the individual institution rather than the system as a whole. William R. White describes this "fallacy of composition" as one that can exacerbate a system-wide problem when recommendations for a sale of assets by one institution in a stressful situation could reduce prices and the value of remaining assets, leaving other institutions weaker (White 2007, p. 83). (p. 10)

The argument here is:

  (i) monetary and financial stability should be adopted as an objective of macroeconomic policy. This is argued in part on the basis of the relative frequency of financial instability and the significant costs associated with financial crisis.
  (ii) the objective relates to the whole of the financial system, and not – as has generally been the case – to the banking system. It is now generally recognised that the financial system has evolved and changed

such that the banking system has become a (relatively) smaller part of the overall financial system. The key point here is to bring to the forefront a form of monetary and financial policy, which is focused on financial stability. The key elements of such a policy would be tools to influence and control the activities of financial firms as they bear on the issue of financial stability. This firstly suggests that such a policy, financial regulation, has to be comprehensive in its coverage, and this applies to the range of financial institutions, which are covered and also to its international coverage. It may further suggest that the policy would need to act in a counter-cyclical manner and to be potentially differentiated. This points away from the capital adequacy ratios of the Basle II system in light of its pro-cyclical nature of operation and the way in which the required capital depends on risk assessment. In contrast an asset based reserve requirement (see, for example, D'Arista, 2009, Palley, 2004 for proposals) system has counter-cyclical features and can apply differential reserve requirements against different classes of assets.

There is an element here of the end of monetary policy, and its replacement by (or incorporation into) financial stability policy. Monetary policy is about money and involves banks since they are the financial institutions whose liabilities are regarded as part of the stock of money. Monetary policy in the simple IS-LM type framework is viewed in terms of the (policy) rate of interest and the stock of money and the notion that the Central Bank could set one of the variables and then had to accept the consequential value of the other variable. In the endogenous money framework the Central Bank sets the policy interest rate as the terms on which it will supply reserves (monetary base). One of the key roles of the Central Bank has been viewed as the lender of last resort, which would involve supplying liquidity to the banking system as and when required.

With an objective of financial stability, the Central Bank would become more like a Central Financial Agency (CFA). It would be responsible for policies, which seek to influence the credit and lending policies of the full range of financial institutions by, for example, assets-based reserve requirements.

4. Exchange rate and open economy considerations

The level, rate of change and the volatility of the exchange rate have significant effects on the domestic economy in terms of both the level of demand (and hence economic activity) and of inflation. The exchange rate has significant implications for the real standard of living and to some degree the distribution of income, and can be seen as an intermediate rather than final target for economic policy. With regard to the exchange rate, policy concerns would involve the volatility of the exchange rate (in both nominal and real terms) and general level of the real exchange rate. In terms of policy objectives we would argue for the benefits of a stable (real) exchange rate set at a level which is most conducive for the level of demand. But in an era of market-determined exchange rates and high capital mobility what are the possibilities of achieving a stable exchange rate? Or is it a matter of letting the exchange rate roam where the market determines, and seeking to deal with the consequences?

The ability of policy to influence the (nominal) exchange rate may be doubted. Interest rate policy can be viewed as one way in which the exchange rate could be influenced. The uncovered interest rate parity notion suggests that the rate of change of the nominal exchange rate is equal to the interest rate differential between the rest of the world and country concerned. Casual observation suggests that large movements in an exchange rate (say of the order of 10 per cent per annum or more changes) go alongside relatively small interest rate differentials (say of the order of 1 or 2 percentage points). As the Bank of England (2006) states on its website,

> changes in interest rates can also affect the exchange rate. An unexpected rise in the rate of interest in the UK relative to overseas would give investors a higher return on UK assets relative to their foreign-currency equivalents, tending to make sterling assets more attractive. That should raise the value of sterling, reduce the price of imports, and reduce demand for UK goods and services abroad. However, the impact of interest rates on the exchange rate is, unfortunately, seldom that predictable.

The argument sketched above points in the direction of setting a real interest rate broadly in line with the rate of growth. If that is accepted, then the interest rate could not also be varied for exchange rate purposes. It would, however, need to be recognised that the general global level of interest rates may constrain the domestic rates. Despite the lack of evidence supporting uncovered interest rate parity, the degree to which a country's real interest rate could persistently diverge from real interest rates around the world can be doubted.

It seems rather unlikely that any single country can secure a stable exchange rate without tightly controlling it. The use of the domestic interest rate does not appear to be an effective instrument, and in any event depends on some co-operation from others since it is the relative interest rate which would be relevant. This suggests that securing a stable exchange rate requires international co-operation and agreement, and this is particularly relevant for stability between the major currencies (dollar, euro, yen and perhaps sterling and yuan).

5. Counter-inflationary policies

The approach to inflation which underpins this paper is a multifaceted approach and can be briefly summarized. The equations underlying our approach to inflation are for price setting and for wage setting. The latter indicate the influence of foreign prices, of the level of economic activity (reflected in the level of output and the rate of change of unemployment). Thus inflation has a conflict element to it (the target real wage), and involving cost push elements and changes in the level of economic activity.

A significant aspect can be viewed by reference to Figure 3.1. With the level of economic activity above Y+ in Figure 3.1, whether inflation tends to rise or not depends on the real wage (reflecting the distribution of income). The pace of wage and price changes depend on the experience and expectation of price and wage changes. A general belief that inflation will be low provides a substantial boost to the actual achievement of low inflation.

The inflationary problem occurs particularly in zone Z in that with output above the CILO, there is something of a wage–price spiral. The severity of the inflation problem depends not only on the level of output and the distribution of income but also on rate of change of output and employment and imported inflation. The inflationary pressures in zone Z can be interpreted in terms of demand-pull inflation in that the level of demand leads to output which is above the CILO. But the other interpretation is that there is a conflict over the distribution of income which at output Y+ is indicated by the gap between price:wage ratio at C and at D.

The ways in which demand influences inflation are not straightforward. It can first be seen by reference to Figure 3.1 that how a specific level of demand (as reflected in the level of output) influences price and wage changes depends on the prevailing price:wage ratio, and that there is not a unique relationship between level of output and price (or wage) changes. Further, the change of output (and hence of demand) may also have an impact, and that the sign of that impact may be positive or negative. This reflects the ambiguity of the effects of higher output on unit costs: when firms are operating with excess capacity, higher output may well be associated with lower unit costs (see also Arestis and Sawyer, 2005). The interaction of the p-curve and the w-curve as above also serves to illustrate the role of income distribution and the struggle over income shares. An attempt by one group to increase their share in income (e.g. firms seeking higher profits, which would push up the p-curve) could spark some increase in inflation, and as other groups seek to restore their income shares inflation persists and may rise further. Cost-push pressures can clearly arise and can emanate from the foreign sector through changes in the price:wage ratio, which would be consistent with constant inflation in this model provided that output was at the CILO. This distribution of income becomes inconsistent with import prices and in the exchange rate.

Distribution of income represented by the price:wage ratio would be consistent with constant inflation in this model provided that output was at the CILO. This distribution of income becomes inconsistent with constant inflation at output above the CILO through the decentralised nature of wage and price determination and the opening up of differences between the claims on national income. A policy (for example, incomes policy) which maintained the distribution of income at a price: wage ratio consistent with Y+ (as in Figure 3.1) through agreement that wages and prices rise together (or in the growth setting wages rise in line with productivity plus prices), would clearly be consistent with levels of output higher than CILO.

The generally low inflation of the past decade in many industrialised countries is often ascribed to the use of monetary policy and inflation targeting. However, monetary policy cannot address cost inflation and its impact on demand inflation, as argued above, is rather small. Monetary policy may have the effect of locking in low inflationary expectations. An alternative explanation of generally low inflation comes from a combination of the spillover effects of lowering inflation from one country to another and the 'China effect' with declining prices for many manufactured products. The decline in and then low inflation would for any individual country have elements of a cost disinflation. Any reversal of this downward pressure on costs (in the form of import prices) would leave monetary policy helpless.

This brings us to the heart of this section, that is, the design of an anti-inflationary policy. The analysis above suggests that low inflation can be maintained provided that there is not a rapid expansion of demand, that demand does not go way beyond the CILO level and that there are no substantial external cost pressures. Demand management policies can help to address the first two sources of inflation, though the limitations of the estimated CILO levels have to be borne in mind to avoid setting demand too low through a fear of inflation. It is also necessary to stress the role of policies to ensure productive capacity in line with full employment, as discussed in the next section, and also to recognise the positive effects which high levels of demand have on capacity creation.

The clear requirement is for the development of a policy instrument which help address cost inflation without resorting to deflation and which can help to anchor inflationary expectations. The present policy arrangements do not address the first. They may foster the belief in low inflation though the experience of low inflation and the 'China effect' are alternative routes through which a belief in low inflation is maintained. The development of some form of incomes policy is then required to replace the present policy arrangements.

6. Full employment and capacity

It has been emphasised above that what may be termed as an inflation barrier (or, more generally, a supply-side equilibrium at which the claims for wages and for profits appear to be mutually compatible) does not act as a strong, or even a weak, attractor for the level of economic activity. Nevertheless, it does form a barrier in the sense that economic activity significantly higher than Y+ could be expected to generate some inflationary pressures, though the extent of those pressures may be relatively small and would depend on many other factors including the conflict over income shares and the speed of expansion. At the same time, the inflationary barrier at any moment in time depends on the size of the capital stock. The inflationary barrier will shift in a favourable direction as and when there are additions to the capital stock, that is investment. But investment itself responds to the level of economic activity, and a low level of economic activity which may tend to reduce inflation has an adverse effect on investment, capital formation and the future position of the inflation barrier. Deflationary policies designed to reduce inflation in the short run can make the longer-term problems worse. There are path dependency effects with regard to the capacity of the economy through the simple device of investment impacting on the capital stock. This also indicates that substantial downturns in economic activity, for whatever reason they occur, will lower investment and the development of the capital stock, leading to a lower (than otherwise) capital stock over the long haul.

There is no strong reason to think that the inflation barrier (as represented by point A in Figure 3.1) corresponds to any notion of the full employment of labour. We would further add that buried behind the single p-curve in Figure 3.1 there are regional and industrial p-curves; this becomes clear once it is appreciated that the p-curve is an aggregation of micro behaviours. The inflation barrier could well represent a situation in which there was sufficient capacity to ensure full employment of labour in some regions but a lack of capacity in others (this should be interpreted as effective capacity: a shift in the composition of demand may leave a lack of demand for some goods even though there is capacity and labour available to produce them). A lack of capacity may arise following a recession, which has led to plant closures. The reopening of plants does not just require the 'turning of a switch' to bring the plant to life but also the re-establishment of the firm and its infrastructure (as an organisation).

The creation of the required capacity can be approached through many routes, and the routes to be followed would depend on specific circumstances as well as the capabilities of government. For example, the replacement of capacity lost as a result of recession may be generated by the re-establishment of high levels of demand. The loss of capacity through regional concentrated closures in 'sunset industries' may require specific regional measures focused on the regions affected. The structure of public expenditure may also help in so far as it can focus demand onto areas where there is underutilised capacity and by the creation of capacity, notably in the area of infrastructure but more generally.

The situation in many EU countries prior to the onset of the financial crisis is an illustration where unemployment rates of the order of 7 to 8 per cent coexisted with estimates of the output gap close to zero. The latter could be interpreted as indicating that the actual level of output was around that consistent with the absence of inflationary pressures, yet near 8 per cent of the workforce was without work. The aligning of productive capacity with the size and distribution of the workforce is, of course, a major task, and one which is rarely accomplished. Nothing here should be taken to suggest that accomplishing the task is easy. The purpose of the present argument is to indicate that there are generally supply-side (as well as demand-side) constraints on the achievement of the full employment of labour. But the nature of those constraints comes from the lack of productive capacity rather than any notion of them arising from inflexible or rigid labour markets. The particular significance of this line of argument is that policies designed to improve the production side of the economy and to create the supply-side conditions, which are compatible with full employment are industrial and regional policies, and not labour market policies along the lines of de-regulation and increased 'flexibility'.

The disparities in capital stock (in terms of quantity, quality and relevance for the current composition of demand) between geographical locations is a significant constraint on the achievement of the full employment of labour. When some locations have reached full employment, others will not, and the further expansions of demand would not readily lead to increases in employment and output.

7. Summary and conclusions

This contribution has put forward a way of analysing the macroeconomy, which we would regard as Keynesian/Kaleckian in spirit. Our approach is based on the proposition that the way macroeconomics and the policy implications that emanate from it are heavily dependent on the objectives of the underlying vision ('model') of the economy and of the economic policies that follow from it. The level of economic activity and the associated level of (un)employment are at the centre of the economic policy concerns. In the longer term sustainable economic growth would be the centre of attention, though we consider that high levels of economic activity in the short term are conducive to high rates of economic growth. The theoretical framework that underpins our approach is based firmly on the proposition that the level of economic activity is set by the level of aggregate demand. Indeed aggregate demand determines the level of output in the short run and in the long run. The level of economic activity depends on a range of factors including, most importantly, the distribution of income. There is no mechanism whereby market forces would push the level of aggregate demand to a supply-side determined equilibrium. Aggregate demand in this model has a dual role. It is a relatively volatile component; and it is also a creator of productive potential. This establishes interdependence of demand and supply, which is closely related to path dependency.

We draw five sets of economic policy conclusions from this analysis. First, the long-run fiscal stance should be set to underpin the desired level of output and employment. We have argued that a budget deficit (including interest payments) which bears a constant relationship with GDP is always sustainable (and leads to a debt ratio equal to the deficit ratio divided by the nominal growth). This approach replaces monetary policy as the mechanism which seeks to ensure the desired level of economic activity.

Second, discretionary variations in the fiscal stance should be used in conjunction with automatic stabilisers to modify the business cycle. The hyper fine tuning currently associated with monetary policy where the policy instrument (policy rate of interest) is set on a monthly basis is not sought here. Automatic stabilisers should be re-enforced (through the adoption of more progressive taxation) and arrangements (such as a Fiscal Policy Committee as noted above; see, however, Sawyer, 2007a for further discussion) should be put in place, which enable adjustments to be made to the fiscal stance on a relatively frequent basis (say six monthly) in light of macroeconomic developments.

Third, industrial and regional policies are required to ensure that any inflation barrier is compatible with the full employment of labour. Public expenditure, particularly investment, can also be structured to ease supply constraints. It is argued here and elsewhere (e.g. Arestis and Sawyer, 2005) that there is often a mismatch between available productive capacity and the labour force and its geographical distribution. Specifically, the zero output gap (where output equals trend output) and the full employment of labour cannot be used interchangeably. Higher levels of employment require more productive capacity.

Fourth, interest rate policy should be to set the real interest rate in line with the trend rate of growth, but this may be constrained by world levels of interest rates. Another constraint in this regard is the requirement of a fixed exchange rate. However, the main operations of the Central Bank should be directed towards financial stability. Insofar as the control of inflation is pursued through demand deflation, then monetary policy is a rather ineffectual policy instrument, and fiscal policy would be more effective. At most, a belief in the 'high priests' of the Central Bank locks in inflationary expectations, and an alternative set of 'high priests' may be required. Enabling the government to borrow at a post-tax rate of interest, which is at or below the rate of economic growth, gives more leeway to fiscal policy.

Fifth, there is the need to develop an inflation policy which is not dependent on demand deflation. Under the present arrangements the only policy aimed at the control of inflation is monetary policy, and we have argued that is an ineffective policy instrument in terms of the influence of interest rates on the pace of inflation. Monetary policy may have some success in terms of generating low inflation expectations, and the search should be on for a policy which can have a similar effect without the threat of deflation.

The prevailing orthodoxy in macroeconomic policy can be summarised as: use interest rates to address demand issues with fiscal policy left in neutral; use the 'credibility' of the Central Bank to hold down inflationary expectations and to 'reform' labour markets to lower the non-accelerating inflation rate of unemployment. The alternative perspective advanced here can be summarised as: use fiscal policy in the short term and in the long term to address demand issues; use regional and industrial policies to create the required capacity and to develop incomes policy to maintain low inflation.

Notes

1 For more general discussion on path dependency see papers in Arestis and Sawyer (2009).
2 This is not the only approach to adopt. See Arestis and Sawyer (2005) and Sawyer (2001) for comprehensive summaries of the prevailing approaches.
3 The p-curve at the aggregate level is drawn as a smooth U-shape. But the aggregation from the enterprise level to the economy level could easily lead to a p-curve, which was far from smooth. This would increase the possibility of multiple equilibria.
4 In the case of the target real wage approach, an increase in the target real wage would lead the curve to shift inwards.
5 It should be noted, though, that automatic stabilisers can change. Creel and Saraceno (2008), for example, argue that the automatic stabilisers in EU countries have diminished over the past years.
6 *Committee on Banking and Financial Services*, US House of Representatives, July 22, 1999.

References

Angeriz, A. and Arestis, P. (2007), "Monetary Policy in the UK", *Cambridge Journal of Economics*, 31(6), pp. 863–84.
Arestis, P. (2009), "Fiscal Policy Within the NCM Framework", in J. Creel and M. Sawyer (eds), *Current Thinking on Fiscal Policy*, Basingstoke: Palgrave Macmillan.
Arestis, P. and Sawyer, M. (2003), "On the Effectiveness of Monetary and Fiscal Policy", *Review of Social Economics*, 62(4), pp. 441–63.
Arestis, P. and Sawyer, M. (2004), "Can Monetary Policy Affect the Real Economy?", *European Review of Economics and Finance*, 3(3), pp. 9–32.
Arestis, P. and Sawyer, M. (2005), "Aggregate Demand, Conflict and Capacity in the Inflationary Process", *Cambridge Journal of Economics*, 29(6), pp. 959–74.
Arestis, P. and Sawyer, M. (2006), "Fiscal Policy Matters", *Public Finance*, 54(1), pp. 133–53.
Arestis, P. and Sawyer, M. (2009), "The Intertemporal Budget Constraint and the Sustainability of Budget Deficits", in J. Creel and M. Sawyer (eds), *Current Thinking on Fiscal Policy*, Basingstoke: Palgrave Macmillan.
Arestis, P. and Sawyer, M. (2008), "New Consensus Macroeconomics and Inflation Targeting: Keynesian Critique", *Economia & Sociedade*, vol. 17 (Special Issue), pp. 631–56.

Arestis, P. and Sawyer, M. (eds) (2009) *Path Dependency and Macroeconomics*, Basingstoke: Palgrave Macmillan.

Bank of England (2006), "From interest rates to inflation", http://www.bankofengland.co.uk/monetarypolicy/how.htm.

Barro, R.J. and Gordon, D.B. (1983), "A Positive Theory of Monetary Policy in a Natural Rate Model", *Journal of Political Economy*, 91(3), 589–619.

Buiter, W.H. (2008), "Central Banks and Financial Crises", paper presented at the Federal Reserve Bank of Kansas City's Symposium on "Maintaining Stability in a Changing Financial System", Jackson Hole, Wyoming, August.

Creel, J. and Saraceno, F. (2008), "Automatic Stabilisation, Discretionary Policy and the Stability Pact", in J. Creel and M. Sawyer (eds), *Current Thinking on Fiscal Policy*, Basingstoke: Palgrave Macmillan.

D'Arista, Jane (2009), "Setting an Agenda for Monetary Reform", Political Economy Research Institute, University of Massachusetts, Amherst, Working Paper series, Number 190.

Ferguson, R. (2005), "Monetary Credibility, Inflation, and Economic Growth", speech at the Cato Institute 23rd Annual Monetary Conference on Monetary Institutions and Economic Development, Washington, DC, 3 November.

Ghosh, A. and Phillips, S. (1998), "Warning: Inflation May be Harmful to Your Growth", *IMF Staff Papers*, 45(4), pp. 672–710.

Goodhart, C.A.E. (2005a), "Safeguarding good policy practice' in "Reflections on Monetary Policy 25 Years after October 1979", *Federal Reserve Bank of St Louis Review*, March/April 2005, 87(2, Part 2), pp. 298–302.

Goodhart, C.A.E. (2005b), "The experience of inflation targeting since 1993", in P. Arestis, M. Baddeley and J. McCombie (eds), *The New Monetary Policy*, Cheltenham: Edward Elgar.

Goodhart, C.A.E. (2007), "The Future of Central Banking", in P. Arestis (ed.), *Is There a New Consensus in Macroeconomics?*, Basingstoke: Palgrave Macmillan, pp. 61–81.

Goodwin, R.M. (1967), "A growth cycle", in C.H. Feinstein (ed.), *Socialism, Capitalism and Growth*, Cambridge: Cambridge University Press.

Greenspan, A. (2002), "Opening remarks", in *Rethinking Stabilization Policy*, Kansas: Federal Reserve Bank of Kansas City, pp. 1–10.

Hein, E and Stockhammer, E (2007), "Macroeconomic policy mix, employment and inflation in a Post-Keynesian alternative to the New Consensus Model", mimeo.

Kalecki, M. (1937), "The Principle of Increasing Risk', *Economica*, 4(4), pp. 440–7.

Kalecki, M. (1944), "Three Ways to Full Employment", in *The Economics of Full Employment*, Oxford: Blackwell for Oxford University Institute of Statistics.

Kydland, F. and Prescott, E.C. (1977), "Rules Rather than Discretion: The Inconsistency of Optimal Plans", *Journal of Political Economy*, 85(3), 473–92.

Laeven, L. and Valencia, F. (2008), "Systemic Banking Crises: A New Database", IMF Working Paper WP/2008/0224.

Lavoie, M. and Seccareccia, M. (1999), "Interest rate – Fair", in P.A. O'Hara (ed.), *Encyclopedia of Political Economy*, London: Routledge, pp. 543–5.

Layard, R., Nickell, S. and Jackman, R. (1991), *Unemployment: Macroeconomic Performance and the Labour Market*, Oxford: Oxford University Press.

Leith, S. and Wren-Lewis, S. (2005), "Fiscal Stabilization Policy and Fiscal Institutions", *Oxford Review of Economic Policy*, 21(4), pp. 584–97.

Lerner, A. (1943), "Functional Finance and the Federal Debt", *Social Research*, 10, pp. 38–51. Reprinted in M.G. Mueller (ed.), *Readings in Macroeconomics*, New York: Holt, Rinehart and Winston, 1966, pp. 353–60.

Minsky, H.P. (1986), *Stabilizing an Unstable Economy*, New Haven: Yale University Press.

Palley, T.I. (2004), "Asset-based reserve requirements: reasserting domestic monetary control in an era of financial innovation and instability", *Review of Political Economy*, 16(1), pp. 43–58, January.

Pasinetti, L. (1981), *Structural Change and Economic Growth*, Cambridge: Cambridge University Press.

Pasinetti, L. (1997), "The Social 'Burden' of High Interest Rates", in P. Arestis, G. Palma and M. Sawyer (eds), *Capital Controversy, Post-Keynesian Economics and the History of Economics: Essays in Honour of Geoff Harcourt*, London: Routledge.

Sawyer, M. (1982), "Collective Bargaining, Oligopoly and Macro-economics", *Oxford Economic Papers*, 34(4), pp. 428–48.

Sawyer, M. (1983), *Business Pricing and Inflation*, London: Macmillan.

Sawyer, M. (2001), "The NAIRU, Aggregate Demand and Investment", *Metroeconomica*, 53(1), pp. 66–94.

Sawyer, M. (2007a), "Towards a New Framework for Fiscal and Interest Rate Policy", mimeo.

Sawyer, M. (2007b), "Fiscal Policy Under New Labour", *Cambridge Journal of Economics*, 31(6), pp. 885–900.

Sawyer, M. (2009), "Interest rates and inflation: what are the links?", *Intervention*, forthcoming.

Taylor, J.B. (2008), "The Financial Crisis and the Policy Responses: An Empirical Analysis of What Went Wrong", mimeo, November.

White, W.R. (2007), "The Need for a Longer Policy Horizon: A Less Orthodox Approach", in J.J. Teunissen and A. Akkerman (eds), *Global Imbalances and Developing Countries: Remedies for a Failing International Financial System*. The Hague: Forum on Debt and Development (FONDAD).

Wicksell, K. (1898), *Geldzins und Güterpreise*, Frankfurt: Verlag Gustav Fischer. English translation in R.F. Kahn (1965), *Interest and Prices*, New York: Kelley.

Wren-Lewis, S. (2000), "The Limits to Discretionary Fiscal Stabilisation Policy", *Oxford Review of Economic Policy*, 16, pp. 92–105.

4
A Keynesian Perspective on 'Financialisation'*

Eckhard Hein
Berlin School of Economics and Law

Abstract

Keynesian and Kaleckian demand driven distribution and growth models, based on the notion of distribution conflict between different groups, have been critical regarding the macroeconomic effects of 'financialisation'. In the present paper, firstly, we attempt to identify theoretically and empirically the main channels of influence of 'financialisation' on investment, saving and distribution in order to obtain a precise macroeconomic meaning of 'financialisation' in a distribution and growth context. Secondly, we analyse the effects of 'financialisation' in a simple stock-flow consistent distribution and growth model and we show that with 'normal' parameter constellations 'financialisation' generates systemic instability.

JEL Classification Codes: E12, E21, E22, E25, E44

Keywords: 'Financialisation', distribution, growth, instability, Keynesian and Kaleckian models

*This study summarises some results of a research project at the Macroeconomic Policy Institute (IMK), Hans Boeckler Foundation, on 'Financial systems and economic growth'. For helpful discussions and comments, and for assistance in the collection of literature and data, I would like to thank Katharina Dröge, Petra Dünhaupt, Till van Treeck, and Klara Zwickl. I am also grateful for the comments and suggestions by the participants in the conferences at the School of Oriental and African Studies (SOAS), London, and at the University of the Basque Country, Bilbao, and in particular by Philip Arestis and Malcolm Sawyer. Remaining errors are, of course, my own.

1. Introduction

The recent decades have seen major changes in the financial sectors of developed and developing countries.[1] Generally, we have observed a rapid development of new financial instruments, triggered by national and international legal liberalisation and by the development of new communication technologies. The overall importance of financial factors for distribution, consumption, investment and growth seems to have increased considerably. And the instability potential arising from the financial sector has increased dramatically, as suggested most recently by the experience of the financial crisis, which started in the US subprime mortgage market in 2007 and has spread all over the world since then.

The changes in the financial sector and in the relationship between the financial and the real sectors of the economy have been broadly summarised as 'financialisation' by some authors (Epstein, 2005; Krippner, 2005; Lavoie, 2008; Palley, 2008; Skott/Ryoo, 2008a, 2008b; Stockhammer, 2004; van Treeck, 2009a, 2009b).[2] Epstein (2005, p. 3), for example, argues that '[...] financialization means the increasing role of financial motives, financial markets, financial actors and financial institutions in the operation of the domestic and international economies'. This is a rather broad definition of 'financialisation' which lacks analytical precision. In this paper we therefore attempt to give 'financialisation' a more precise meaning from a macroeconomic and distribution and growth perspective.

Generally, today there seems to be a broad consensus among macroeconomists of different schools of thought with regard to the macroeconomic real effects of the financial system. It is now broadly accepted that the development of the financial sector of an economy is crucial for real economic growth. However, there remains equally wide disagreement as to which kind of financial structure and institutions are conducive to growth, and which are not. Therefore, it comes as no surprise that the effects of the recent trends in the development of the financial sector on distribution and growth are also viewed differently.

Modern mainstream models, based on a synthesis of new 'endogenous' growth theory and new information economics, generally hold – albeit with different emphasis with respect to the relative importance of banks and financial markets – that the degree of financial intermediation should be positively associated with long-run growth.[3] However, these models are rather limited when it comes to taking into account the recent 'financialisation' processes as sketched above because they allow for at best only a very limited role for effective demand in the long run or for distribution conflict between different social groups or classes. Keynesian and Kaleckian demand-driven distribution and growth models, based on the notion of distribution conflict between different groups, have been more critical with respect to the real effects of 'financialisation'.[4] In the present paper we attempt to identify – theoretically and empirically – the main channels of influence of 'financialisation' on distribution and growth from a demand-led growth perspective in order to obtain a more precise macroeconomic meaning of 'financialisation'. These channels of influence will then be integrated into a simple analytical stock-flow consistent distribution and growth model and the macroeconomic effects of 'financialisation' will be derived. The remainder of the paper is therefore organised as follows. In section 2 we deal with the channels of influence of 'financialisation' on the macroeconomy focussing on the effects on firms' investment, on households' consumption and on income distribution, and we briefly review the integration of these transmission channels into demand-led growth models. Section 3 then develops a simple stock-flow consistent closed-economy distribution and growth model, as an extension of the model proposed by Bhaduri/Marglin (1990), and discusses the short- and medium-run effects of 'financialisation'. Section 4 summarises the main results and concludes.

2.   'Financialisation': transmission channels and potential growth regimes

In order to discuss potential growth regimes in a period of 'financialisation' within a demand-led distribution and growth model, we first have to analyse the effects of 'financialisation' on the main building blocks of such a model. This concerns, firstly, the effects on firms' investment in capital stock, secondly, the effects on households' consumption, and, thirdly, the effects on income distribution.

2.1.   'Financialisation' and firms' investment

Regarding the effects of 'financialisation' on investment decisions of the corporate sector, some authors, such as Crotty (1990), Dallery (2008), or Stockhammer (2005–6), have highlighted the importance of the 'owner–manager conflict' inherent to large corporations.[5] This conflict arises from the postulation of a 'growth–profit trade-off' at the firm level, implying that shareholder value orientation is likely to be associated with a high preference for short-term profitability and with a low propensity to invest in real capital stock by firms. Due to diversified portfolios, 'stockholders typically have only a fleeting relation with any particular enterprise', as Crotty (1990, p. 534) has argued, and care much more about the current profitability than the long-term expansion and survival of a particular firm. In fact, with 'financialisation', various mechanisms have been designed, on the one hand, to impose restrictions on management's ability to seek expansion, and, on the other hand, to change management's preferences themselves and align them to share-holders' profit maximisation objective. Management's desire for growth is contained through, in particular, higher dividend payouts demanded by shareholders, a weaker ability of firms to obtain new equity finance through stock issues (which tend to decrease share prices), a larger dependence on leverage, and an increased threat of hostile takeovers in a liberalised market for corporate control. Simultaneously, financial market-oriented remuneration schemes have been developed to align management's preferences to shareholders' objectives. As an overall result, it has been argued that the traditional managerial policy of 'retain and invest' is replaced by the shareholder-oriented strategy of 'downsize and distribute' (Lazonick/O'Sullivan, 2000).

Graphically, these new developments can be analysed on the basis of Figure 4.1. The lines given by FF_i reflect different finance constraints faced by the managers of the firm in their investment decision. These finance frontiers indicate the maximum rate of accumulation (g) that

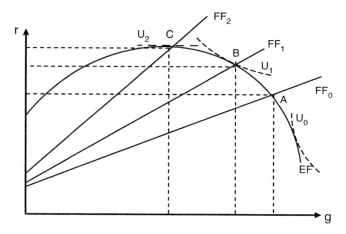

Figure 4.1 Shareholder value orientation and investment decisions at the firm level
Source: Hein/van Treeck (2010a).

firms can finance with a given profit rate (r). Seen from a different angle, they determine the profit rate that is necessary for firms to be able to finance the desired accumulation rate under the conditions of incompletely competitive financial markets, as has been suggested by Kalecki's (1937) 'principle of increasing risk'.

The second constraint faced by managers is the expansion frontier (*EF*). It indicates the profit rate that can be realised with a particular growth strategy. The expansion frontier is assumed to be upward sloping for low accumulation rates and downward sloping for higher rates (Lavoie, 1992, pp. 114–16). The upwards-sloping part is caused by dynamic economies of scale and scope allowing for a higher rate of profit when accumulation is rising: Investment in capital stock allows for the introduction of new and more productive means of production; profitability and survival of the firms in an uncertain environment will depend on sheer size; and rapid expansion in novel markets will allow for temporary monopoly profits. The negatively sloped segment of the expansion function is due to managerial inefficiencies reducing the rate of profit: At a certain speed of expansion, management will have difficulties in handling the expansion process (Penrose effect); internal expansion in a certain market may be costly because of rising advertising, product innovation and research and development costs; and external expansion and diversification into further markets, in particular foreign markets, may be limited by management's lack of knowledge about new markets and products.

In the traditional Post-Keynesian analysis of the firm, the accumulation decision is determined by the point of intersection of the finance frontier and the expansion frontier (Lavoie 1992, p. 117). In this view, firms are interested in the profit rate only insofar as a higher profit rate eases the finance constraint and hence allows for faster expansion. In contrast, with 'financialisation' it seems more appropriate to consider the possibility that the desired accumulation rate, given by preferences, is below the maximum rate, given by the finance constraint. Therefore, Figure 4.1 is completed by a set of indifference curves, U_i, reflecting different preferences of managers faced with the growth–profitability trade-off in the downward-sloping segment of the expansion frontier (see also Dallery, 2008; Stockhammer, 2005–6).[6]

With higher shareholder value orientation, one may expect two things to happen:

1. Shareholders impose higher distribution of profits on firms, i.e. a higher dividend payout ratio and hence a lower retention ratio

and/or a lower contribution of new equity issues to the financing of investment, or even share buybacks.

2. Managers' (firms') preference for growth is weakened as a result of remuneration schemes based on short-term profitability and financial market results.

The first effect will imply a counter-clockwise rotation of the finance frontier in Figure 4.1. The second effect can be represented as a flattening of the indifference curve. Starting from a situation (point A) in which shareholders' influence on the firm's preferences is very weak (U_0) and the firm's accumulation decision is restricted only by a relatively loose finance constraint (FF_0), the effects of increasing shareholder value orientation can be interpreted as follows. The new accumulation decision will be determined either by the new preferences alone (U_2 with FF_0 or FF_1 (point C) or U_1 with FF_0 (point B)), or by the new finance constraint alone (U_0 with FF_1 (point B) or U_0 or U_1 with FF_2 (point C)), or by preferences fully compatible with constraints (U_1 with FF_1 (point B) or U_2 with FF_2 (point C)).

Econometric evidence in favour of the hypothesis that 'financialisation' has caused a slowdown in capital accumulation has been presented by Stockhammer (2004), van Treeck (2008) and Orhangazi (2008). Stockhammer (2004) takes the share of interest and dividends in profits of non-financial business as an indicator for the dominance of short-term profits in firms' or in management's preferences. Short-term financial investment is hence preferred over long-term real investment in capital stock and the share of dividends and interest in profits should therefore be negatively associated with real investment. Using annual data for the business sector and applying time series estimations for France (1978–97), Germany (1963–90), the UK (1970–96), and the US (1963–97), Stockhammer finds evidence in favour of his hypothesis for France, the US and perhaps also the UK, but not for Germany. Van Treeck (2008) introduces interest and dividend payments, each in relation to the capital stock, into the estimation of the determinants of the rate of capital accumulation in the non-financial corporate sector of the US (1965–2004) using annual data for his time series estimations. He finds that dividend and interest payments each have a statistically significant negative effect on capital accumulation, indicating the finance constraint given by internal means of finance. The value of the negative coefficient on dividend payments also exceeds the one on interest payments which is interpreted as evidence for 'shareholder value orientation' of management: Dividend payments thus do not only negatively affect investment via internal means of finance but also via firms' (or management's) preferences. Different from Stockhammer and van Treeck, Orhangazi (2008) has used firm-level data on non-financial firms in the US (1972–2003) with a focus on the manufacturing sector in a dynamic panel-estimation approach. He finds that financial profits have a negative impact on real investment for large firms, indicating short-termism in favour of short-term financial profits and at the expense of long-term profits from investment in capital stock. For small firms, however, the effect of financial profits (the sum of interest and equity income in net earnings) on real investment is positive, because financial profits seem to ease the financing constraint for these firms. The effect of financial payments (interest expense, cash dividends, purchase of firms' own stock) on investment is negative for the whole panel.

2.2. 'Financialisation' and households' consumption

A second aspect of 'financialisation' stressed in various models is the link between wealth, household indebtedness and consumption. Such a mechanism has already been included by Palley (1994; 1996, pp. 201–15) into a business cycle model: Rising debt is initially stimulating aggregate demand transferring purchasing power from high income households with a low marginal propensity to consume to low income households with a high propensity to consume. But interest payments on debt then become a burden on aggregate demand, because purchasing power is redistributed into the opposite direction.

Dutt (2005, 2006) has analysed the effects of easier access to consumer credit associated with deregulation of the financial sector within a Steindlian model of growth and income distribution making use of a similar mechanism as Palley did. Credit-based consumption is facilitated by the deregulation of the financial system allowing home equity lending, adjustable consumer loans and securitization, thus stimulating effective demand and growth. However, since in the model the burden of servicing debt falls exclusively upon workers, the potentially contractive long-run effect of consumer borrowing is corroborated because income is redistributed to the rich, who receive the interest income and have a lower propensity to consume.

Bhaduri/Laski/Riese (2006) focus explicitly on the wealth effects on consumption, implying that increases in financial wealth stimulate households' willingness to consume. However, stock market wealth is purely 'virtual wealth' and increasing consumption is hence associated with increasing indebtedness of private households. Therefore, financial deregulation may improve the perspectives of maintaining a wealth-based credit boom over a considerable period of time. However, finally the expansive effects of consumer borrowing may be overwhelmed in the long run by rising interest obligations, which reduce households' creditworthiness and may eventually require higher saving by households.

Econometric studies have shown that (financial) wealth is a statistically significant determinant of consumption, in particular in those countries with a capital-market based financial system, but also in bank-based financial systems. For the US, Boone/Giorno/Richardson (1998), Ludvigson/Steindel (1999), Davis/Palumbo (2001), and Mehra (2001) have estimated marginal propensities to consume out of wealth between 3 and 7 percent, applying time series econometrics to different periods.[7] Edison/Slok (2001) find that the marginal propensity to consume out of wealth in North American countries and the UK (1990–2000) has been between 4 and 5.2 percent, whereas in Continental European countries the range of this value has been between 1 and 3.8 percent. The study by Boone/Girouard (2002) does not confirm this difference. The authors find marginal propensities to consume out of wealth between 2 and 4 percent for the US, the UK, France, Italy and Japan (1980–1999), with a higher value only for Canada. Applying dynamic panel regression for 14 OECD countries (1979–1999), Dreger/Slacalek (2007) obtain that the marginal propensity to consume out of financial and housing wealth in capital-market based countries has been 3.7 percent, whereas in bank-based countries it has only been 0.7 percent. Ludwig/Slok (2001; 2004) get a qualitatively similar result for 16 OECD countries (1960–2000) making use of cointegrated panel estimations. The elasticity of consumption with respect to an increase in stock and house market prices in capital-market based countries is considerably higher than the one in bank-based countries, according to their estimations. They also find that the elasticities have increased over time for both country groups.

2.3. 'Financialisation' and distribution

A third channel of influence of 'financialisation' is on different forms of income redistribution. Regarding functional distribution of income between gross profits, including retained profits, dividends and interest, on the one hand, and wages, on the other hand, it may be expected that shareholders' demand for higher distributed profits will be passed through to workers with the effect of a declining share of wages in national income (Boyer, 2000). Hein (2008b, 2010) and Hein/van Treeck (2010b) have argued that at least in the medium run, when rising dividend payments to rentiers have become a permanent feature, the mark-up in firms' price setting is likely to become dividend-elastic. Decreasing price competition in the goods market associated with mergers and acquisitions and hostile takeovers in the corporate sector, and in particular the weakened bargaining power of labourers and increasing (threat of) unemployment caused by a policy of 'downsize and distribute' (Lazonick/O'Sullivan, 2000) will improve the conditions for a rising mark-up in the face of a rising dividend rate. Therefore, in the medium to long run increasing shareholder power favours redistribution at the expense of the labour income share.

There is some empirical support for this assumption regarding the effects of 'financialisation' on functional income distribution. In a study focussing on the distribution effects of changes in the interest rate, Argitis/Pitelis (2001) find that a falling wage share in the non-financial business sector was accompanied by a rising share of interest payments in profits in this sector until the early 1990s in the UK, but not in the US. Applying time series econometrics, however, they obtain the general result that the nominal interest rate has a negative effect on the share of industrial profits in both countries. Further determinants are nominal wages and the bargaining power of labour unions, measured by unemployment and strike intensity. Therefore, according to these results, a rise in interest payments to rentiers does not seem to harm the wage share directly but rather seems to compress industrial profits. However, if rising interest payments are accompanied by weakened bargaining power of labour unions and lower wage demands, the redistribution will take place at the expense of labour income.

Studying the development of the profit rate of non-financial corporations in France and the US (1960–2001), Duménil/Lévy (2001, 2005) have shown that the rise in this profit rate since the early 1980s has been mainly due to the rise in net real interest payments. Excluding net real interest payments from profits, the profit rate of the non-financial corporate sector has remained constant in France and has increased only slightly in the US.[8] Therefore, rising interest payments have had to be paid for by a reduction in the labour income share and it has thus been mainly the rentiers' class which has benefited from redistribution at the expense of labour.

In a more general study on 29 OECD countries (1960–2000) focussing on the development of the share of rentiers' income in GDP, Epstein/Power (2003) confirm the results by Duménil/Lévy. Epstein/Power show that the share of rentiers' income in GDP increased at the expense of the wage share in most countries during the 1980s until the early 1990s. In their study, rentiers' income is more broadly defined as the sum of profits of the financial sector plus interest income of the non-financial sector and households. Since nominal interest payments also compensate for capital losses due to inflation, Epstein/Jayadev (2005) have extended the analysis for 15 OECD countries (1960–2000), correcting the share of rentiers' income in GDP for inflation. Applying this method, they mainly confirm the earlier results by Epstein/Power (2003).

A further implication of 'financialisation' and increasing shareholder value orientation for income distribution appears to be an increasing gap between manager salaries and blue-collar wages. Palley (2006) and Lavoie (2009) have introduced this phenomenon of 'cadrisme' (Lavoie, 2009) into Post-Keynesian models of growth and distribution and have derived different potential regimes for the effect of increasing manager salaries vis-à-vis blue collar wages. Empirically, Piketty/Saez (2003, 2006), in a long-run study for the US (1913–2002) based on income tax data, have shown that the increase in the income share of the 0.01 percent richest households from the early 1980s until 2000 was due mainly to the increase in top-management salaries. Increasing income inequality since the early 1980s has hence been associated with the phenomenon of the 'working rich'.[9]

2.4. 'Financialisation' and the macroeconomic regime

Based on the contradictory effects of 'financialisation' on investment and consumption and on its impact on distribution, different potential macroeconomic growth regimes have been derived in the literature. We sketch these regimes in turn.

1. Some authors have considered the possibility of a 'finance-led growth' regime (Boyer, 2000), in which shareholder value orientation has an overall positive impact on growth. The condition for this is a very high propensity to consume out of rentiers' income and/or a very strong wealth effect on consumption, implying a strong effect of credit-financed consumption. This compensates for the loss of consumption caused by the redistribution at the expense of labour. In turn, it also stimulates investment via the accelerator mechanism and over-compensates the direct negative effect of shareholder value orientation on real investment.[10]
2. Other authors, starting with Cordonnier (2006), have argued that a regime of 'profits without investment' might emerge. In this regime, rising interest or dividend payments of firms to rentiers are associated with a rising profit rate and with a rising rate of capacity utilisation, but with a falling rate of capital accumulation. Due to a high propensity to consume out of rentiers' income and/or out of wealth,

again implying rising importance of credit-financed consumption, redistribution in favour of rentiers is able to compensate for the loss of consumption demand caused by a falling labour income share. But it is insufficient to stimulate capital accumulation in the face of increasing shareholder value orientation of management and the decrease of firms' internal means of finance associated with high dividend payments or share buybacks.[11]

3. Finally, some authors have shown that a 'contractive' regime may arise, in which rising interest and dividend payments to rentiers have a restrictive effect on the rates of capacity utilisation, profit and capital accumulation (Hein, 2008b; Hein/van Treeck, 2010b; van Treeck, 2008). Due to a low rentiers' propensity to consume, and implicitly low wealth effects and hence little importance of credit-based consumption, rising rentiers' income is unable to compensate for the reduction in consumption demand caused by redistribution at the expense of labour in this regime. And management's shareholder value orientation together with the loss of internal means of finance also causes a slowdown in capital accumulation.

Empirically, the 'profits without investment' regime of weak investment in the face of prospering profits seems to have dominated the development of the US since the early 1980s, interrupted only by the 'new economy' boom in the second half of the 1990s when investment soared as well, as for example the estimations by van Treeck (2008) and the case studies by van Treeck/Hein/Dünhaupt (2007) and van Treeck (2009b) suggest.

Given a specific parameter constellation a regime of 'profits without investment' seems to be a viable accumulation regime for a considerable period of time. However, major drawbacks of the analysis of the papers mentioned so far have to be noticed. In particular, in these papers the effects of changes in interest and dividend payments on firms' debt– and equity–capital ratios and hence on the financial structure are not considered explicitly. That is why recently some authors have started to study the impacts of 'financialisation' in stock-flow-consistent models, pioneered by Lavoie/Godley (2001–2). These models take into account stock-flow interactions of financial and real variables, either analytically or by means of model simulations (Godley/Lavoie, 2007, pp. 378–444; Hein, 2010; Lavoie, 2008; Skott/Ryoo, 2008a, 2008b; Taylor, 2004, pp. 272–8; van Treeck, 2009a).[12]

As has been reviewed in more detail in Hein/van Treeck (2010a), these stock-flow consistent models are also able to generate the three potential accumulation regimes mentioned above. In order to obtain a 'finance-led growth' regime, these models usually rely on strong effects of Tobin's q (or Kaldor's valuation ratio) in the investment function and on a strong wealth effect in the consumption function.[13] Under these conditions, the increase in stock market prices, associated with a higher target rate of profit imposed on the firm by shareholders, share buybacks, increasing dividend payments to rentiers and redistribution at the expense of labour, feeds back positively both on investment and consumption spending and may dominate the overall result (Skott/Ryoo, 2008a, 2008b; van Treeck, 2009a). However, if the models do away with a strong coefficient on Tobin's q in the investment function, 'profits without investment' (van Treeck, 2009a) or even 'contractive' accumulation regimes are generated (Godley/Lavoie, 2007, pp. 378–444; Lavoie, 2008).

We doubt that in an era of 'financialisation' an increase in Tobin's q triggered by increasing shareholder power, share buybacks, increasing dividend payments and enforced changes in management's preferences should be considered to cause rising real investment. Medlen (2003) provides empirical support for our doubts. According to his observations, there was a positive correlation in the US (1968–2001) between Tobin's q, on the one hand, and the relationship between mergers to new real investment, on the other hand. This is the exact opposite of what Tobin's q would suggest, because a rise in Tobin's q should be correlated with higher real net investment relative to mergers and acquisitions.[14]

The stock-flow consistent models referred to above do not pay much attention to changes in distribution between capital and labour caused by changes in the financial regime and the related macroeconomic effects via consumption and investment. And, finally, also instability problems regarding the financial structure of the corporate sector have been hardly addressed in these models. Therefore, in the following section we present a simple model which tackles some of these issues.

3. 'Financialisation' in a simple comparative static, stock-flow consistent distribution and growth model

In this section we develop a simple analytical stock-flow consistent distribution and growth model. In this model, the transmission channels of financialisation discussed above are integrated in the following way. 1. 'Financialisation' is assumed to affect distribution between firms and rentiers in the short run, and distribution between capital and labour through a dividend-elastic mark-up in firms' price setting in the medium run. 2. Firms' investment is affected through the channels discussed above, the 'preference channel' and the 'internal means of finance channel'. 3. Consumption is influenced via distribution of dividends in the short run and via a reduction in the labour income share in the medium run of the model. 4. The development of firms' outside finance–capital ratio is endogenised in order to check the medium-run stability and viability of the potential accumulation regimes.

Our model has a medium-run horizon, because we allow debt and equity held by rentiers to vary relative to the capital stock. But we do not consider any effect of changes in the dividend payments (relative to interest payments) on households' portfolio choice between credit/bonds and shares. In our view, portfolio choice seems to be dominated by long-run institutional and habitual factors, such as the pension system (pay as you go vs capital-based), the stock market culture, and sentiments towards risk.[15] Therefore, what we consider in the medium-run analysis of our model is the development of the ratio of debt plus equity held by rentiers relative to the capital stock and its feedback effects on capital accumulation, without any deeper investigation into the composition of rentiers' financial wealth. For the reasons given in the previous section, our model also does neither include any positive effect of Tobin's q on firms' investment in capital stock. Nor do we consider wealth effects on consumption and credit-financed consumption expenditures, in order to keep the model as simple as possible.

The model we employ in this section is an extension of the basic Kaleckian model suggested by Bhaduri/Marglin (1990), into which financial variables are integrated in a way similar to the integration of monetary variables into this model by Hein (2007). We have chosen the Bhaduri/Marglin model as a starting point, because the basic structure of this model allows for 'wage-led' or 'profit-led' demand and growth regimes. The model results are hence not restricted to the usual Kaleckian wage-led demand and growth regimes.[16]

3.1. The basic model

We assume a closed economy without economic activity of the state. Under given conditions of production, there is just one type of commodity produced which can be used for consumption and investment purposes. There is a constant relation between the employed volume of labour (L) and real output (Y), i.e. there is no overhead-labour and no technical change, so that we get a constant labour–output ratio (a). The capital–potential output ratio (v), the relation between the real capital stock (K) and potential real output (Y^v), is also constant. The capital stock is assumed not to depreciate. The rate of capacity utilisation (u) is given by the relation between actual real output and potential real output. The basic model can be described by the following equations.

Pricing and distribution

$$p = \left[1 + m(e)\right]wa, \quad m > 0, \frac{\partial m}{\partial e} \geq 0, \tag{1}$$

$$h = \frac{\Pi}{pY} = 1 - \frac{1}{1 + m(e)}, \quad \frac{\partial h}{\partial e} \geq 0, \tag{2}$$

$$r = \frac{\Pi}{pK} = \frac{\Pi}{pY} \frac{Y}{Y^v} \frac{Y^v}{K} = hu\frac{1}{v}, \tag{3}$$

Financing of capital stock and rentiers' income

$$pK = B + E^R + E^F, \tag{4}$$

$$\gamma = \frac{B + E^R}{pK}, \tag{5}$$

$$\phi = \frac{E^F}{pK}, \tag{6}$$

$$\Pi = \Pi^F + R, \tag{7}$$

$$R = e\left(E^R + B\right), \tag{8}$$

Saving, investment and goods market equilibrium

$$\sigma = \frac{S}{pK} = \frac{\Pi - R + s_R R}{pK} = r - (1 - s_R)e\gamma, \quad 0 < s_R \leq 1, \tag{9}$$

$$g = \frac{I}{pK} = \alpha + \beta u + \tau h - \theta e \gamma, \quad \alpha, \beta, \tau, \theta \geq 0, \tag{10}$$

$$g = \sigma \tag{11}$$

$$\frac{\partial \sigma}{\partial u} - \frac{\partial g}{\partial u} > 0 \quad \Rightarrow \quad \frac{h}{v} - \beta > 0. \tag{12}$$

Variables

p: price; m: mark-up; e: rentiers' rate of return on equity and bonds; w: nominal wage rate; a: labour–output ratio; h: profit share; Π: gross profits; Y: real income; r: rate of profit; K: real capital stock; Y^V: full capacity output determined by the capital stock; u: rate of capacity utilisation; v: capital–full capacity output ratio; B: bonds held by rentiers; E^R: equity held by rentiers; E^F: equity held by firms/owner-managers; γ: outside finance–capital ratio; ϕ: inside finance–capital ratio; Π^F: retained profits by firms; R: rentiers' income; σ: saving-capital rate; S: saving; s_R: propensity to save out of rentiers' income; g: rate of capital accumulation; I: investment; α, β, τ, θ: coefficients in the investment function.

Writing w for the nominal wage rate, we assume that firms set prices (p) according to a mark-up (m) on constant unit labour costs up to full capacity output. Following Kalecki (1954, pp. 17–18), the mark-up is determined by the degree of price competition in the goods market and by the relative powers of capital and labour in the labour market (equation 1). The profit share (h), i.e. the proportion of profits (Π) in nominal output (pY), is therefore determined by the mark-up (equation 2). The mark-up and the profit share may become elastic with respect to the rentiers' rate of return on equity and bonds (e) in the medium run, as will be discussed in more detail below. The profit rate (r) relates the annual flow of profits to the nominal capital stock and can be decomposed into the rate of capacity utilisation, the profit share, and the inverse of the capital–full capacity output ratio (equation 3).

The pace of accumulation in our model is determined by firms' decisions to invest, independently of saving, because firms have access to short-term (or initial) finance for production purposes supplied by a developed banking sector.[17] We assume that long-term finance of the capital stock consists of firms' accumulated retained earnings (E^F), long-term credit granted by rentiers' households (B), and equity issued by the firms and held by rentiers' households (E^R) (equation 4). Part of firms' liabilities ($B+E^R$) is therefore held by 'outsiders' to the firm, i.e. rentiers' households, whereas another part (E^F) is controlled by 'insiders', either by the management or by owner-managers. Since in our model we assume prices in goods and financial markets to be constant – capital gains are hence omitted from the analysis – rentiers are interested in short-run maximum dividend and interest payments, whereas management favours long-term growth of the firm, following the arguments presented in section 2.1. The rentiers' share in capital stock, the outside finance–capital ratio, is given by γ (equation 5), whereas ϕ denotes the accumulated retained earnings-capital ratio or the inside finance–capital ratio (equation 6). We assume these ratios to be constant in the short run, but to be variable and hence to be endogenously determined in the medium run.

Total profits (Π) split into firms' retained profits (Π^F), on the one hand, and dividends plus interest paid to rentiers' households (R), on the other hand (equation 7). Interest payments to rentiers' households are given by the rate of interest and the stock of debt, with the rate of interest as a distribution parameter being an exogenous variable for income generation and capital accumulation, mainly determined by monetary policies and risk and liquidity assessments of banks and rentiers, following the Post-Keynesian 'horizontalist' view of endogenous money and credit.[18] Dividend payments, given by the dividend rate and the stock of equity held by rentiers' households, are also determined by the power struggle between rentiers (shareholders) and firms (management), with rentiers being interested in high dividends for income purposes and management being in favour of retained earnings for firms' real investment and growth purposes. Since we omit the effects of rentiers' portfolio choice from our considerations – and in order to simplify further analysis – in what follows we synthesise dividend and interest payments to rentiers and consider just one rentiers' rate of return on bonds and equity (e), which together with the stock of equity and bonds held by rentiers determines rentiers' income (equation 8). The rentiers' rate of return is determined by the power struggle between managers and rentiers and is hence the crucial variable when it comes to the discussion of the effects of increasing shareholder power vis-à-vis management and labourers.

Changes in the rentiers' rate of return may cause a change in the mark-up in firms' pricing in incompletely competitive goods markets (equation 1), if the determinants of the mark-up are affected as well by the rise of shareholder power, in particular the degree of price competition in the goods market and the relative power of workers and labour unions in the labour market.[19] If these changes occur, distribution between gross profits, as the sum of retained firms' profits, and interest and dividends received by rentiers' households, on the one hand, and wages, on the other hand, will be affected (equation 2). Discussing the effects of a rising rentiers' rate of return caused by rising shareholder power, we distinguish two cases: 1. the dividend-inelastic mark-up in which a rising rentiers' rate of return leaves the gross profit share in national income untouched and only affects firms' retained profits adversely, and 2. the dividend-elastic mark-up in which an increasing rentiers' rate of return affects distribution between gross profits and wages.

In the face of increasing shareholder power, we consider the mark-up to be dividend-inelastic in the short run. Therefore, in the short run only the distribution of income between firms and rentiers is affected by rising shareholder power. But in the medium run, the mark-up is likely to become dividend-elastic because of decreasing price competition in the goods market associated with mergers and acquisitions and hostile takeovers in the corporate sector, and in particular because of weakened bargaining power of labourers caused by a policy of 'downsize and distribute' and increasing (threat of) unemployment (Lazonick/O'Sullivan, 2000). The profit share, and therefore distribution between capital and labour, will hence become elastic with respect to the rentiers' rate of return in our model.

In order to simplify the analysis, we assume a classical saving hypothesis, i.e. labourers do not save. The part of profits retained is completely saved by definition. The part of profits distributed to rentiers' households, the interest and dividend payments, is used by those households according to their propensity to save (s_R). Therefore, we get the saving-capital rate (σ) in equation (9) which relates total saving to the nominal capital stock. Note that an increase in the rentiers' rate of return, *ceteris paribus*, decreases the saving-capital rate because income is transferred from firms with a saving propensity of unity to rentiers' households with a saving propensity of presumably less than unity. In our model, we consider only rentiers' consumption out of current income flows. As argued in section 2.2, increasing stock prices and rising (stock market) wealth will further lower the overall saving rate, in particular when households can borrow extensively against collateral. However, this will be associated with increasing household debt which might feed back negatively on consumption. These aspects are not modelled here.

The accumulation rate (g), relating net investment (I) to the capital stock (equation 10) is based on the investment function proposed by Bhaduri/Marglin (1990). Investment decisions are assumed to be positively affected by expected sales and by unit profits (or the profit share), because both increase the (expected) profit rate. Distributed profits, the dividends and interest payments to rentiers, have a negative impact on investment, because they reduce retained earnings and firms' own means of finance. Expected sales are determined by the rate of capacity utilisation. Unit profits are given by the profit share and are thus determined by the mark-up in firms' pricing in the goods market. Distributed profits are given by the rentiers' rate of return and the stocks of debt and equity held by rentiers, each variable being normalised by the capital stock. An increase in the rentiers' rate of return has a negative impact on investment because firms' internal funds for investment finance are adversely affected. This also limits the access to external funds in imperfect capital markets, according to Kalecki's (1937) 'principle of increasing risk'. As argued in section 2.1, given shareholders' desire for profits – compared to management's desire for growth of the firm – increasing shareholder power vis-à-vis management will increase the rentiers' rate of return and reduce available funds for real investment and growth of the firm. But increasing shareholder power will affect not only internal funds and thus firms' finance constraints but will also affect management's preferences: Management's 'animal spirits', reflected in the constant α in the investment function, will decline and might even become negative when managers are aligned with shareholders through stock option programmes and the threat of hostile takeovers in an active market of corporate control. Therefore, as argued in section 2.1, even if the availability of internal funds were irrelevant for firms' investment decisions, increasing shareholder power would affect investment nonetheless in the negative through this 'preference channel'. Our investment function hence captures the two channels of transmission of increasing shareholder power on real investment: the 'internal finance channel' and the 'preference channel'.

As mentioned above, we refrain from integrating a positive effect of Tobin's q or Kaldor's valuation ratio (or of the relationship between the dividend rate and the rate of interest) into our investment function, because an increase in the dividend rate (relative to the interest rate) indicates rising shareholder power vis-à-vis management and can hence not be seen as a stimulus for real investment, we rather assume the opposite. In our model, the shares of internal and external investment finance matter for firms' real investment, but the source of external finance (issue of shares or debt) is of minor relevance for investment decisions.

The goods market equilibrium is determined by the equality of saving and investment decisions (equation 11). The goods market stability condition requires that the saving-capital rate responds more elastically to changes in capacity utilisation than the capital accumulation rate does (condition 12).

Our model generates the following goods market equilibrium values:

$$u^* = \frac{\alpha + \tau h + e\gamma\left(1 - s_R - \theta\right)}{\dfrac{h}{v} - \beta}, \tag{13}$$

$$r^* = \frac{\dfrac{h}{v}\left[\alpha + \tau h + e\gamma\left(1 - s_R - \theta\right)\right]}{\dfrac{h}{v} - \beta}, \tag{14}$$

$$g^* = \frac{\dfrac{h}{v}(\alpha + \tau h) + e\gamma\left[\beta(1 - s_R) - \theta\dfrac{h}{v}\right]}{\dfrac{h}{v} - \beta}. \tag{15}$$

In what follows, the effects of increasing shareholder power on stable goods market equilibria only in an era of 'financialisation' will be discussed. Increasing shareholder power will, firstly, affect management's preferences regarding growth and hence 'animal spirits' in the negative, and, secondly it will be associated with an increasing rentiers' rate of return.

3.2.   Short-run effects of 'financialisation' and increasing shareholder power

For the discussion of the short-run effects of 'financialisation' and increasing shareholder power we assume γ and ϕ to be given and constant. For the medium run these ratios will be endogenised, the stability will be checked, and the effects of changes in management's 'animal spirits' and the rentiers' rate of return on these ratios will be examined. For the short run, we will also assume that firms are unable to shift increasing dividend payments to prices, because the determinants of the mark-up will change rather slowly. The mark-up and the profit share will therefore remain constant in the short run, too. This restriction will also be lifted for the medium-run considerations, and the effects of redistribution between capital and labour on investment and saving will be taken into account.

An increase in shareholder value orientation of management, and hence a decrease in 'animal spirits', as indicated by α in the investment function, has uniquely negative effects on the endogenous variables. This is so, because 'animal spirits' display unambiguously positive relationships with the equilibrium rates of capacity utilisation, profit and capital accumulation, as can easily be seen from equations (13)–(15):
$\dfrac{\partial u}{\partial \alpha} > 0$, $\dfrac{\partial r}{\partial \alpha} > 0$ and $\dfrac{\partial g}{\partial \alpha} > 0$.

An increase in the rentiers' rate of return, however, has ambiguous effects. It affects firms' investment through the availability of internal funds and the access to external financing, but it also has an influence on the income of rentiers' households and hence on consumption. With the outside finance–capital ratio, as well as the mark-up and the profit share, being constant in the short run, we obtain the following effects of a change in the rentiers' rate of return on the equilibrium rates of capacity utilisation, profit and capital accumulation:

$$\frac{\partial u^*}{\partial e} = \frac{(1 - s_R - \theta)\gamma}{\frac{h}{v} - \beta}, \tag{13a}$$

$$\frac{\partial r^*}{\partial e} = \frac{\frac{h}{v}(1 - s_R - \theta)\gamma}{\frac{h}{v} - \beta}, \tag{14a}$$

$$\frac{\partial g^*}{\partial e} = \frac{\gamma\left[\beta(1 - s_R) - \theta\frac{h}{v}\right]}{\frac{h}{v} - \beta}. \tag{15a}$$

The effects of a change in the rentiers' rate of return may be positive or negative, depending on the parameter values in the saving and investment functions of the model. We obtain the following conditions for positive effects on the short-run equilibrium values of the system:

$$\frac{\partial u^*}{\partial e} > 0, \quad \text{if:} \quad 1 - s_R > \theta, \tag{13a'}$$

$$\frac{\partial r^*}{\partial e} > 0, \quad \text{if:} \quad 1 - s_R > \theta, \tag{14a'}$$

$$\frac{\partial g^*}{\partial e} > 0, \quad \text{if:} \quad 1 - s_R > \theta\frac{h}{v\beta}. \tag{15a'}$$

Assuming the stability condition (12) for the goods market equilibrium to hold implies for equation (15a'): $\frac{h}{v\beta} > 1$. Therefore, we get the following cases for the short-run equilibrium in Table 4.1.

The 'normal' case of a negative impact of an increase in the rentiers' rate of return throughout on the equilibrium values of capacity utilisation, the profit rate and the rate of capital accumulation will be given if: $1 - s_R < \theta$. Therefore, this case is the more likely the higher the rentiers' propensity to save and the higher the responsiveness of firms' real investment with respect to distributed profits and hence to internal funds. With this parameter constellation, the increase in consumption demand associated with redistribution of income from fitrms to rentiers' households is insufficient to compensate for the negative effects on firms' investment. In the 'normal' case, the effect of an increasing

Table 4.1   Short-run cases for a change in the rentiers' rate of return

	'Normal' case	'Intermediate' case	'Puzzling' case
	$1 - s_R < \theta$	$\theta < 1 - s_R < \dfrac{\theta h}{v\beta}$	$\dfrac{\theta h}{v\beta} < 1 - s_R$
$\dfrac{\partial u}{\partial e}$	–	+	+
$\dfrac{\partial r}{\partial e}$	–	+	+
$\dfrac{\partial g}{\partial e}$	–	–	+

Table 4.2   Short-run accumulation regimes under the conditions of 'financialisation' and rising shareholder power

	'Contractive' regime	'Profits without investment' regime	'Finance-led growth' regime
Effect via management's animal spirits	weak/strong	weak	weak
Effect via rentiers' rate of return	'normal' case	'intermediate' case	'puzzling' case

rentiers' rate of return on the equilibrium rates of capacity utilisation, profit and capital accumulation amplifies the negative effects of rising shareholder power via management's 'animal spirits' on these variables and we obtain the overall 'contractive' regime (Table 4.2).

In the 'puzzling' case, we have an opposite parameter constellation: $1 - s_R > \theta \dfrac{h}{v\beta}$. A low propensity to save out of rentiers' income, a low responsiveness of investment with respect to distributed profits and internal funds, and a high elasticity with respect to capacity utilisation allow for a positive effect of an increasing rentiers' rate of return on the equilibrium rates of capacity utilisation, profit and capital accumulation. In the 'puzzling' case, the effect of an increasing rentiers' rate of return on the equilibrium rates of capacity utilisation, profit and capital accumulation may over-compensate the negative effects of rising shareholder power via management's 'animal spirits'. If this condition holds, we will obtain a 'finance-led' accumulation regime, and hence an overall positive effect of increasing shareholder power on the rates of capacity utilisation, profit and capital accumulation (Table 4.2).

Finally, an 'intermediate' case may arise if: $\theta < 1 - s_R < \theta \dfrac{h}{v\beta}$. In this case, an increase in the rentiers' rate of return is accompanied by rising rates of capacity utilisation and profit, but by a falling equilibrium rate of capital accumulation. What is required for the 'intermediate' case, on the one hand, is a low rentiers' propensity to save, which boosts consumption demand in the face of redistribution in favour of rentiers, and a low responsiveness of firms' investment with respect to distributed profits and hence internal funds, which limits the negative effects of redistribution on firms' investment. On the other hand, however, in the 'intermediate' case we also have a low responsiveness of investment with respect to capacity utilisation which, in sum, is not able to over-compensate the negative effects of a rise in the rentiers' rate of return through internal funds. Under the conditions of the 'intermediate' case, the negative effects of increasing shareholder power via management's preferences ('animal spirits') may be over-compensated by the effects of a rising rentiers' rate of return with respect to capacity utilisation and the profit rate, but the negative effect on capital accumulation is not. For the former, it is again required that increasing shareholder power is associated with a strong effect of the increase in the rentiers' rate of return but with a low effect via management's 'animal spirits'. If these conditions hold, we will obtain a 'profits without investment' regime (Table 4.2).

3.3. Medium-run equilibrium and stability

In the medium run of our model we have to take into account that firms may be able to shift a higher rate of return demanded by rentiers to prices and that the mark-up, and hence the gross profit share (including dividend and interest payments), may increase. Therefore, with a dividend-elastic mark-up we have $\dfrac{\partial h}{\partial e} \geq 0$, and the labour income share will decrease in the face of a rising rentiers' rate of return. The income share of retained profits by firms will then not have to carry the whole burden or may even remain constant. A dividend-elastic mark-up is made possible by decreasing price competition in the goods market and weakened labour unions in the labour market. In particular, the latter seems to be closely related to increasing shareholder value orientation and decreasing 'animal spirits' of management associated with the policy of 'downsize and redistribute' which has negative effects on real investment, the expansion of the firm and hence on employment at the firm level. However, at the macroeconomic level, there may be countervailing forces at work if a rising rentiers' rate of return has expansive effects on capacity utilisation and capital accumulation, as in the 'puzzling' and partly in the 'intermediate' case. These may thus limit the elasticity of the mark-up and the profit share with respect to the rentiers' rate of return.

In the medium-run analysis, the effects of a change in the rentiers' rate of return on the stocks of debt and equity held by rentiers, and hence on the inside and outside finance–capital ratios, have to be considered as well. Since $\gamma + \phi = 1$, it is sufficient to analyse the dynamics of γ. As mentioned above, we do not consider households' portfolio choice between bonds and equity in the face of relative changes in dividend and interest rates. On the one hand, this is to simplify the analysis, on the other hand, we hold that households' portfolio choice seems to be dominated by institutional and historical factors which only change slowly in the course of time despite short- and medium-run variations in the dividend rate (relative to the interest rate). Further on, changes in households' portfolio decisions would only affect firms' investment decisions in our model if firms' internal means of finance were affected. But there is no effect via Tobin's q or Kaldor's valuation ratio in our investment function, different from other stock-flow consistent approaches referred to above. For these reasons it seems to be sufficient to treat the effects of changes in the rentiers' rate of return on the outside finance–capital ratio, and then to analyse the related effects on capital accumulation.

The accumulation of bonds and equity held by rentiers is given by rentiers' income and the propensity to save out of this income:

$$\Delta\left(E^{R} + B\right) = s_{R}e\left(E^{R} + B\right). \tag{16}$$

For the growth rate of debt plus equity held by rentiers we get:

$$\frac{\Delta\left(E^{R} + B\right)}{\left(E^{R} + B\right)} = s_{R}e. \tag{17}$$

If we assume that prices remain constant, which means that mark-ups and distribution may change but not the price level, the growth rates of the outside finance–capital ratio depends on the growth rate of outside finance and on the growth rate of the real capital stock. From equation (6) we get:

$$\hat{\gamma} = \frac{\Delta\left(E^{R} + B\right)}{\left(E^{R} + B\right)} - \hat{K} = s_{R}e - g. \tag{18}$$

In medium-run equilibrium the endogenously determined value of γ has to be constant, hence $\hat{\gamma} = 0$ has to hold. Introducing this condition into equation (18) and making use of equation (15) yields the following medium-run equilibrium value for the outside finance–capital ratio:

$$\gamma^* = \frac{s_R e\left(\dfrac{h}{v} - \beta\right) - \dfrac{h}{v}(\alpha + \tau h)}{e\left[\beta(1 - s_R) - \theta\dfrac{h}{v}\right]}. \tag{19}$$

This medium-run equilibrium will be stable if: $\dfrac{\partial\hat{\gamma}}{\partial\gamma} < 0$. Starting from equations (18) and making use of equation (15) yields:

$$\frac{\partial\hat{\gamma}}{\partial\gamma} = \frac{-e\left[\beta(1 - s_R) - \theta\dfrac{h}{v}\right]}{\dfrac{h}{v} - \beta}. \tag{20}$$

Taking into account that we assume the goods market equilibrium to be stable, it follows for the medium-run stability condition of the outside finance–capital ratio:

$$\frac{\partial\hat{\gamma}}{\partial\gamma} < 0 \quad \text{if:} \quad \beta(1 - s_R) - \theta\frac{h}{v} > 0$$
$$\Leftrightarrow 1 - s_R > \theta\frac{h}{v\beta}. \tag{20'}$$

Stability of γ requires a low rentiers' propensity to save, a low responsiveness of firms' investment with respect to distributed profits and internal funds, and a high elasticity with respect to capacity utilisation. This is tantamount to a positive relationship of the rate of capital accumulation with the outside finance–capital ratio. From equation (15) we obtain:

$$\frac{\partial g^*}{\partial\gamma} = \frac{e\left[\beta(1 - s_R) - \theta\dfrac{h}{v}\right]}{\dfrac{h}{v} - \beta}, \tag{15b}$$

$$\frac{\partial g^*}{\partial\gamma} > 0 \quad \text{if:} \quad \beta(1 - s_R) - \theta\frac{h}{v} > 0$$
$$\Leftrightarrow 1 - s_R > \theta\frac{h}{v\beta}. \tag{15b'}$$

Most importantly, it has to be noted that medium-run stability of the outside finance–capital ratio requires a 'puzzling' case effect of a change in the rentiers' rate of return on the short-run equilibrium rate of capital accumulation, as can be seen in condition (15a').

3.4. Medium-run effects of 'financialisation' and rising shareholder power

We are now in a position to discuss the medium-run effects of a rising rentiers' rate of return and decreasing management's 'animal spirits'. We start with the effects of a rising rentiers' rate of return on the outside finance–capital ratio and on the rate of capital accumulation in medium-run equilibrium, and then we discuss the effects of decreasing management's 'animal spirits' on the medium-run equilibrium.

From equation (19) we obtain the following effects of a change in the rentiers' rate of return on the equilibrium outside finance–capital ratio:

$$\frac{\partial \gamma^*}{\partial e} = \frac{s_R\left(\dfrac{h}{v} - \beta\right) - \gamma\left[\beta(1-s_R) - \theta\dfrac{h}{v}\right] + \dfrac{\partial h}{\partial e}\dfrac{1}{v}\left[e(\theta\gamma + s_R) - \alpha - 2\tau h\right]}{e\left[\beta(1-s_R) - \theta\dfrac{h}{v}\right]} . (19a)$$

For the evaluation of the effects of an increasing rentiers' rate of return we have to distinguish the 'medium-run stable' from the 'medium-run unstable' case.

For the stable case, in which $\beta(1-s_R) - \theta\dfrac{h}{v} > 0$ has to hold, we obtain:

$$\frac{\partial \gamma^*}{\partial e} > 0$$

$$\text{if:} \quad \beta(1-s_R) - \theta\frac{h}{v} > 0, \tag{19a'}$$

and:
$$\frac{s_R\left(\dfrac{h}{v} - \beta\right) + \dfrac{\partial h}{\partial e}\dfrac{1}{v}(s_R e - \alpha - 2\tau h)}{\left[\beta(1-s_R) - \theta\dfrac{h}{v}\right] - \dfrac{\partial h}{\partial e}\dfrac{1}{v}e} > \gamma.$$

In the medium-run stable case, the effect of a change in the rentiers' rate of return on the outside finance–capital ratio depends on the initial value of the rentiers' share in the capital stock. If γ is below the value defined in condition (19a'), an increase in the rentiers' rate of return, hence rising dividend payments, will raise γ; if γ is above this value it will fall; and if γ is exactly equal to this value there will be no effect of a change in the rentiers' rate of return.

In the medium-run unstable case, we have $\beta(1-s_R)-\theta\dfrac{h}{v}<0$ and the inspection of equation (19a) yields:

$$\frac{\partial\gamma^*}{\partial e}<0$$

$$\text{if:}\quad \beta(1-s_R)-\rho s_R\frac{h}{v}<0, \tag{19a''}$$

$$\text{and:}\quad \frac{s_R\left(\dfrac{h}{v}-\beta\right)-\gamma\left[\beta(1-s_R)-\theta\dfrac{h}{v}\right]+\dfrac{\partial h}{\partial e}\dfrac{1}{v}e(\theta\gamma+s_R)}{\dfrac{\partial h}{\partial e}\dfrac{1}{v}}>\alpha.+2\tau h.$$

A change in the rentiers' rate of return will have an adverse effect on the equilibrium outside finance–capital ratio, provided that 'animal spirits' (α) are not too strong and the effect of the profit share on firms' investment is weak. Otherwise, the effect of a change in the rentiers' rate of return on the equilibrium outside finance–capital ratio may be zero or positive as well.

Evaluating the effects of an increasing rentiers' rate of return on the medium-run equilibrium rate of capital accumulation, we obtain from equation (18), in which the condition $\hat{\gamma}=0$ has to hold:

$$g^{**}=s_R e. \tag{21}$$

The effect of a rising rentiers' rate of return on the medium-run equilibrium rate of capital accumulation, given the propensity to save out of rentiers' income, is thus by necessity positive in all cases:

$$\frac{\partial g^{**}}{\partial e}=s_R>0. \tag{21a}$$

This finding follows straightforwardly from the condition for medium-run equilibrium, which requires the constancy of γ and hence that capital stock has to grow at the same rate as the sum of debt plus equity held by rentiers' households. An increase in dividend (and also in interest) payments to rentiers in relation to the capital stock therefore requires increasing capital stock growth in order to obtain a medium-run equilibrium.[20] We call this medium-run equilibrium rate of capital accumulation the 'warranted rate' (g**), because it is the rate of accumulation which is required for the constancy and thus stability of the outside finance-capital ratio. However, it is by no way guaranteed that the goods market equilibrium rate of capital accumulation will adjust to that rate. Our 'warranted rate' of accumulation is thus reminiscent of Harrod's (1939) 'warranted rate of growth'. However, in our case it is neither related to goods market equilibrium, nor to desired capacity utilisation, but to a constant financial structure of the firm sector.

As shown above, under the conditions of the short-run 'puzzling' case regarding the effects of a rising rentiers' rate of return (15a'), the stability condition for the medium-run equilibrium outside finance–capital ratio (20') is met. The goods market equilibrium rate of capital accumulation will thus adjust to the 'warranted rate' when the rentiers' rate of return increases, and the new medium-run equilibrium will be reached. This adjustment process may be disturbed but not prevented by the two additional effects of rising shareholder power in our model.

First, in the short and the medium run, the negative effects of falling animal spirits associated with rising shareholder power reduce the positive impact of a rising rentiers' rate of return on capital accumulation. Second, in the medium run, the mark-up and hence the profit share is assumed to be elastic with respect to the rentiers' rate of return. This has an additional effect on the goods market equilibrium rate of capital accumulation (for a given γ), as can be derived from equation (15):

$$\frac{\partial g^\star}{\partial e} = \frac{\gamma\left[\beta(1-s_R)-\theta\dfrac{h}{v}\right]+\dfrac{\partial h}{\partial e}\dfrac{1}{v}(\tau h-\beta u)}{\dfrac{h}{v}-\beta}. \tag{15c}$$

As can be seen from the second term in the numerator, the effect of an increasing profit share on capital accumulation may be positive or negative, depending on the relative importance of unit profits and demand in firms' investment decisions. If capital accumulation is profit-led, medium-run redistribution in favour of gross profits will give an extra push to the goods market equilibrium rate of capital accumulation. If accumulation is wage-led, however, redistribution in favour of gross profits will reduce the short-run positive effect of a rising rentiers' rate of return.

If for one of these reasons the increase in capital accumulation following an increase in the rentiers' rate of return is not sufficient to meet the increased 'warranted rate' in equation (21), the outside finance–capital ratio will grow according to equation (18), and this will push up the goods market equilibrium rate of capital accumulation according to equation (15) and thus stabilise the system. Therefore, the conditions for the short-run 'puzzling' case are sufficient for medium-run stability of the 'finance-led growth' regime. The effects of shareholder value orientation on management's animal spirits and the distribution effects of a rising rentiers' rate of return regarding the labour income share may prolong the adjustment process but will not prevent it – as long as the condition for medium-run stability is not violated. Note, however, that an increase in the profit share may turn a long-run stable outside finance-capital ratio unstable, according to condition (20').

Under the conditions of the short-run 'normal' and 'intermediate' cases, capital accumulation will fall when the rentiers' rate of return increases and the new equilibrium will not be reached; the stability condition for medium-run equilibrium (20') is not met. With the short-run 'normal' and 'intermediate' cases prevailing, which implies instability of the medium-run outside finance–capital ratio, the 'warranted rate' of capital accumulation in equation (21), therefore, contains a kind of Harrodian 'knife-edge' instability property (Harrod, 1939). However, this instability is not related to the actual and the goods market equilibrium rate of capital accumulation, as in Harrod, but to the goods market equilibrium rate of capital accumulation and the rate of accumulation required for a constant outside finance–capital ratio. If the goods market equilibrium rate of capital accumulation in equation (15) by accident is equal to the 'warranted rate' in equation (21), capital stock will keep on growing at that rate. But any deviation from the 'warranted rate' will cause exploding deviation from this rate. If the goods market equilibrium rate of capital accumulation falls short of the 'warranted rate', the outside finance–capital ratio will rise, according to equation (18), and this will feed back negatively on capital accumulation, according to equation (15), making capital accumulation fall further below the 'warranted rate' and the outside finance–capital ratio rises further above the equilibrium rate. If the goods market equilibrium rate of capital accumulation exceeds the 'warranted rate', the outside finance–capital ratio will fall (equation 18), and this will feed back positively on capital accumulation (equation 15), making it diverge even further from the 'warranted rate' and so on. The medium-run cumulative disequilibrium process will hence be characterised either by rising outside finance–capital ratios and by falling rates of capital accumulation, or it will show decreasing outside finance–capital ratios and increasing rates of capital accumulation. We therefore attain a 'paradox of outside finance' reminiscent of Steindl's (1976, pp. 113–22) 'paradox of debt'.[21]

Falling (rising) rates of capital accumulation induce firms to attempt to reduce (raise) the outside finance–capital ratio, but the macroeconomic effects of such a behaviour is that this ratio will increase (fall).

In the 'contractive' and the 'profits without investment' regimes, an increase in the rentiers' rate of return shifting the 'warranted rate' upwards will thus trigger a cumulatively downward process of the goods market equilibrium rate of capital accumulation and a cumulatively upwards process of the outside finance–capital ratio. A decrease in managements' animal spirits associated with rising shareholder power will exacerbate this process. Redistribution at the expense of labour in the medium run via the dividend-elastic mark-up will also reinforce this process if accumulation is wage-led, and it will dampen it without being able to prevent it, if accumulation is profit-led.

Finally, we have to examine the effects of falling management's 'animal spirits'. From equation (19) we obtain for the effect of 'animal spirits' on the medium-run equilibrium outside finance–capital ratio:

$$\frac{\partial \gamma^*}{\partial \alpha} = \frac{-\dfrac{h}{v}}{e\left[\beta(1-s_R)-\theta\dfrac{h}{v}\right]}. \qquad (19b)$$

In the medium-run stable case, in which $\beta(1-s_R)-\theta\dfrac{h}{v} > 0$, we get $\dfrac{\partial \gamma^*}{\partial \alpha} < 0$. Falling 'animal spirits' associated with rising shareholder value orientation will hence increase the equilibrium outside finance–capital ratio. Medium instability implies $\beta(1-s_R)-\theta\dfrac{h}{v} < 0$ and hence $\dfrac{\partial \gamma^*}{\partial \alpha} > 0$. Decreasing 'animal spirits' will thus shift the (unstable) equilibrium outside finance-capital ratio downwards.

For the effects of 'animal spirits' on the medium-run 'warranted rate' of capital accumulation we obtain from equation (21):

$$\frac{\partial g^{**}}{\partial \alpha} = 0. \qquad (21b)$$

Since the 'warranted rate' of capital accumulation required for a constant outside finance–capital ratio is determined exclusively by rentiers' saving out of dividend and interest payments relative to the capital stock, changes in management's 'animal spirits' have no effect on this rate. A change in animal spirits will only affect the goods market equilibrium rate of capital accumulation. As discussed above, this will exacerbate cumulatively diverging processes of the goods market equilibrium rate of capital accumulation from the 'warranted rate' in the medium-run unstable case, and it will modify, but not prevent the adjustment process in the medium-run stable case.

3.5. Summary of the main model results

We can now summarise the effects of 'financialisation' in our distribution and growth model. For our purposes, 'financialisation' has been understood as meaning increasing shareholder power vis-à-vis management and labourers, causing lower management's 'animal spirits' regarding real investment and a higher rentiers' rate of return in the short run, and a falling labour income share in the medium run. Summarising the main findings in Table 4.3, we distinguish between short- und medium-run effects, between a stable medium-run equilibrium and an unstable one, and between 'contractive', 'profits without investment' and 'finance-led growth' regimes. The short-run equilibrium condition is assumed to be fulfilled in each case.

Table 4.3 Effects of increasing 'financialisation' and rising shareholder power in the short and the medium run

		'Contractive' regime	'Profits without investment' regime	'Finance-led growth' regime
		$$\beta\left(1-s_R\right)-\theta\frac{h}{v}$$		
		−	−	+
Short run				
Rentiers' rate of return, profit share and outside finance-capital ratio	$\dfrac{\partial h}{\partial e},\dfrac{\partial \gamma}{\partial e}$	0	0	0
Animal spirits and goods market equilibrium	$\dfrac{\partial u^*}{\partial \alpha},\dfrac{\partial r^*}{\partial \alpha},\dfrac{\partial g^*}{\partial \alpha}$ (13, 14, 15)	+	+	+
Rentiers' rate of return and equilibrium rates of capacity utilisation and profit	$\dfrac{\partial u^*}{\partial e},\dfrac{\partial r^*}{\partial e}$ (13a, 14a)	−	+	+

(Continued)

Table 4.3   Continued

		'Contractive' regime	'Profits without investment' regime	'Finance-led growth' regime
		$\beta\left(1-s_R\right)-\theta\dfrac{h}{v}$		
		–	–	+
Rentiers' rate of return and equilibrium rate of capital accumulation	$\dfrac{\partial g^*}{\partial e}$ (15a)	–	–	+
Medium run				
Rentiers' rate of return and profit share	$\dfrac{\partial h}{\partial e}$	+	+	+
Stability of equilibrium outside finance-capital ratio	$\dfrac{\partial\hat{\gamma}}{\partial\gamma}$ (20)	+ (unstable)	+ (unstable)	– (stable)
Rentiers' rate of return and equilibrium outside finance-capital ratio	$\dfrac{\partial\gamma^*}{\partial e}$ (19a)	+/0/–	+/0/–	+/0/–
Rentiers' rate of return and equilibrium rate of capital accumulation ('warranted rate')	$\dfrac{\partial g^{**}}{\partial e}$ (21a)	+	+	+
Animal spirits and equilibrium outside finance-capital ratio	$\dfrac{\partial\gamma^*}{\partial\alpha}$ (19b)	+	+	–
Animal spirits and equilibrium rate of capital accumulation ('warranted rate')	$\dfrac{\partial g^{**}}{\partial\alpha}$ (21b)	0	0	0

In the parameter constellation generating the medium-run stable case and a 'finance-led growth' regime, we obtain that decreasing management's 'animal spirits' have a negative effect on the equilibrium rates of capacity utilisation, profit and capital accumulation in the short run. These negative effects, however, are over-compensated by the positive effects of an increasing rentiers' rate of return, provided that increasing shareholder power is associated with a relatively weak decline in management's 'animal spirits'. In the medium run, the mark-up and the profit share will increase, and the equilibrium outside finance–capital ratio will rise, fall or even remain constant, depending on the initial value of this ratio. This implies that, in the face of a continuously rising rentiers' rate of return, the equilibrium outside finance–capital ratio will converge towards a definite value and then remain inelastic with respect to further changes in the rentiers' rate of return. The effect of a rising rentiers' rate of return on the medium-run equilibrium rate of capital accumulation, on the 'warranted rate', is positive. And since we are dealing here with a stable equilibrium outside finance–capital ratio, the 'warranted rate' of capital accumulation is stable, too, because it has been derived from the constancy condition for the outside finance–capital ratio. Changing 'animal spirits' have no effect on the medium-run equilibrium rate of capital accumulation (the 'warranted rate') but only affect the equilibrium outside finance–capital ratio in an adverse way, i.e. the medium-run equilibrium value of this ratio will rise in the face of falling management's 'animal spirits'.

From this it follows that a 'finance-led growth' regime, which is characterised by high or rising rates of capacity utilisation, profit and capital accumulation in the face of low 'animal spirits' and a high and rising rentiers' rate of return, may be a viable regime, not only in the short but also in the medium run, under special conditions. In a 'finance-led growth' regime, medium-run viability, in the sense of a medium-run stable outside finance–capital ratio, requires a low rentiers' propensity to save, a low elasticity of investment with respect to distributed profits and hence to internal funds, and a high responsiveness with respect to capacity utilisation, on the one hand. On the other hand, redistribution at the expense of labour has to be limited, because a strong increase in the profit share might turn a medium-run stable equilibrium unstable.

In the parameter constellation yielding the medium-run unstable case and the 'profits without investment' or the 'contractive' regimes, the short-run negative effects of rising shareholder power on the real equilibrium via management's preferences are reinforced by the effects of an increasing rentiers' rate of return with respect to capital accumulation. The effects of the increasing rentiers' rate of return on the rates of capacity and profit may be negative, which will then give the short-run 'normal' case and the 'contractive' regime. Or they may be positive, which yields the short-run 'intermediate' case, and over-compensate the negative effect of increasing shareholder power on management's 'animal spirits', which then gives the 'profits without investment' regime. In the medium run with a rising mark-up and an endogenously determined outside finance–capital ratio, a rising rentiers' rate of return reduces the equilibrium outside finance–capital ratio, provided managements 'animal spirits' are weak and the effect of unit profits on investment is not too strong. A rising rentiers' rate of return increases the medium-run equilibrium rate of capital accumulation, the 'warranted rate'. The depressing effect of rising shareholder power on management's 'animal spirits' reinforces the diminishing effect of the rising rentiers' rate of return on the equilibrium outside finance–capital ratio.

Since we are dealing with a medium-run unstable equilibrium, the equilibrium values of the outside finance–capital ratio and of the rate of capital accumulation in the 'profits without investment' and the 'contractive' regimes will only be attained by a fluke. If by accident the economy is in such an equilibrium, the effects of rising shareholder power – via falling 'animal spirits' and a rising rentiers' rate of return – will most probably reduce the equilibrium outside finance–capital ratio and increase the 'warranted' rate of capital accumulation. The actual value of the outside finance–capital ratio will then exceed its new equilibrium value, whereas the actual rate of capital accumulation will fall short of the respective new 'warranted rate'. We will hence see a disequilibrium process with rising outside finance–capital ratios and falling rates of capital accumulation which reinforce each other. The medium-run equilibrium, therefore, displays 'knife-edge'-instability properties and the disequilibrium process contains a 'paradox of outside finance'. Redistribution at the expense of labour will reinforce this disequilibrium process if capital accumulation is wage-led, and it will dampen it without being able to preventing it if capital accumulation is profit-led.

4.   Summary and conclusions

From a Keynesian/Kaleckian macroeconomic perspective we have identified theoretically and empirically the main channels of influence of 'financialisation' on investment, saving and distribution in order to obtain a precise macroeconomic meaning of 'financialisation' in a distribution and growth context. Regarding investment, 'financialisation' has been associated with increasing shareholder power vis-à-vis management and labourers, an increasing rate of return on equity and bonds held by rentiers, and decreasing managements' animal spirits with respect to real investment in capital stock, which each have partially negative effects on firms real investment. Regarding consumption, 'financialisation' has been considered to imply increasing potential for wealth-based and debt-financed consumption. And regarding distribution, 'financialisation' has been viewed to be conducive to a falling labour income share and to increasing inequality of wages and salaries.

As in the preceding literature, introducing (some of) these channels into a demand-led growth model may yield different potential accumulation regimes for the era of 'financialisation'. Depending on the values of the model parameters 'finance-led growth', 'profits without investment' and 'contractive' regimes may emerge. Analysing the medium-run stability and viability of these regimes in a simple stock-flow consistent distribution and growth model has given the following results: Only the 'finance-led growth' regime yields medium-run stability of the financial structure of the firm sector and of capital accumulation. But this regimes requires a very special parameter constellation: only weakly negative effects of increasing shareholder power on management's 'animal spirits', a low rentiers' propensity to save, a low elasticity of investment with respect to distributed profits and internal funds, a high responsiveness with regard to capacity utilisation, and only weak redistribution at the expense of labour. Even if such a parameter constellation persisted for a certain period of time, it remains questionable whether a 'finance-led' growth regime would remain stable in the medium to long run if a low overall propensity to save, as a crucial precondition for such a regime, were associated with increasing (workers') households' debt. The analysis by Bhaduri/Laski/Riese (2006), Dutt (2005, 2006) and Palley (1994) briefly reviewed in section 2.2 raises major doubts. The explicit introduction of household debt into the model presented in this paper, however, remains as a task for future research.

More realistic parameter constellations giving rise to 'profits without investment' or 'contractive' regimes have turned out to yield cumulatively unstable medium-run results regarding the financial structure of the firm sector and the rate of capital accumulation. In the face of rising shareholder power, a rising rentiers' rates of return and falling management's 'animal spirits', these regimes are liable to systemic instability characterised by rising outside finance–capital ratios, i.e. rising debt plus rentiers' equity–capital ratios, and falling goods market equilibrium rates of capital accumulation and hence to a macroeconomic 'paradox of outside finance'.

Of course, this is not to argue that economies with a 'profits without investment' or a 'contractive' regime are cumulatively unstable, because there may be other forces in the economy at work (in particular, monetary and fiscal policies) which contain this instability. However, based on the results of our simple model, we would argue that under the conditions of the 'contractive' and the 'profits without investment' regimes there exists a considerable systemic medium-run instability potential regarding the financial structure of the economy and capital accumulation. Therefore, a regime of 'profits without investment' in the face of rising shareholder power, as observed in the US from the early 1980s until the recent crisis, may emerge under specific conditions. In the medium to long run, however, the financial structure of this regime and the rate of capital accumulation will turn out to be fragile and unstable. It can be expected that introducing household debt for consumption purposes into our model, along the lines of Bhaduri/Laski/ Riese (2006), Dutt (2005, 2006), and Palley (1994), might even increase this instability potential inherent to the 'profits without investment' regime (and also in the 'contractive' regime).

Finally, it should also be noted that the instability properties emerging from the financial structure in the 'profits without investment' regime are supplemented by further problems, not explicitly addressed in the present paper: This regime will be characterised by weak real investment, weak capital stock growth and slow productivity growth, as far as the latter is embodied in capital stock. Generating a high level of activity and a high profit rate in the short run, the 'profits without investment' regime will therefore face medium- to long-run growth, employment, and inflation problems caused by its weak capital stock and productivity growth.[22]

Notes

1. See for example the overview in Eatwell/Taylor (2000) for an early analysis, Krippner (2005), Orhangazi (2008), Duménil/Lévy (2004a), Palley (2008), and the contributions in Epstein (2005) for a detailed treatment of the development in the US and other countries, van Treeck (2009b) and van Treeck/Hein/Dünhaupt (2007) for a comparison of the macroeconomics of 'financialisation' in the US and Germany, and Stockhammer (2008) for the development in Europe.
2. Other authors have used different terms, with sometimes different meanings: 'finance-led growth regime' (Boyer, 2000), 'financial wealth-induced growth regime' (Aglietta, 2000), 'finance-led economies' (van Treeck, 2008),

'finance-dominated regime' (Stockhammer, 2008), 'neo-liberalism' (Duménil/ Lévy, 2001, 2005), 'shareholder value orientation' (Hein, 2010; Stockhammer, 2005–6), 'maximizing shareholder value' (Lazonick/O'Sullivan, 2000), or 'rising shareholder power' (Hein, 2008b).
3. See the surveys by Arestis/Sawyer (2005a), Demetriadis/Adrianova (2004), Hein (2005), and Levine (2003; 2005).
4. Whereas the earlier Post-Keynesian and Kaleckian models of distribution and growth were missing an explicit introduction of monetary and financial variables at all, with the exception of Pasinetti's (1974, pp. 139–41) natural rate of growth models, these variables have been introduced into those models since the late 1980s/early 1990s by different authors. However, the focus in these models has mainly been on the introduction of the rate of interest, as an exogenous distribution parameter determined by central bank policies and liquidity and risk assessments of commercial banks and rentiers, and bank credit, created endogenously by a developed banking sector on demand by creditworthy borrowers. See the overview and the analysis in Hein (2008a).
5. The following arguments on 'financialisation' and the Post-Keynesian theory of the firm draw on Hein/van Treeck (2010a).
6. One may also interpret the indifference curves as reflecting the preferences of the firm as a whole, determined by a compromise between shareholders and managers.
7. See also the discussion in Poterba (2000).
8. The profit-rate of the financial sector in the US, however, has increased significantly since the early 1980s exceeding the profit rate of the non-financial sector by a considerable amount since then (Duménil/Lévy, 2004a).
9. See Duménil/Lévy (2004b) for more extended interpretation of the results by Piketty/Saez (2003) against the background of 'financialisation'.
10. See also Aglietta (2000), Hein (2008b), Hein/van Treeck (2010b), Stockhammer (2005–6) and van Treeck (2008) for the discussion of the conditions for such a regime within different model frameworks.
11. See Hein (2008b), Hein/van Treeck (2010b) and van Treeck (2008) for such a regime within different model setups.
12. See also the earlier approach by Skott (1988; 1989, pp. 114–40).
13. On Tobin's q see Brainard/Tobin (1968) and Tobin (1969). For a discussion see Crotty (1990) and Tobin/Brainard (1990). On Kaldor's valuation ratio see Kaldor (1966) and the discussion in Lavoie (1998).
14. Generally, empirical studies have difficulties in finding a statistically significant and empirically relevant effect of Tobin's q on investment. See, for example, Bhaskar/Glyn (1995), Chirinko (1993) and Ndikumana (1999).
15. See van Treeck/Hein/Dünhaupt (2007) for a comparison of the development in Germany and the US. In Germany, direct and indirect holding of stock and shares by private households is still very low compared to the US and has developed rather slowly, although stock market prices have increased more than tenfold since the early 1980s.
16. For a similar approach integrating 'financialisation' issues into the 'stagnationist' version of the Kaleckian distribution and growth model, which is more in line with the original ideas of Kalecki, see Hein (2010).
17. The distinction between short-term (or initial) finance for production purposes and long-term (or final) finance for investment purposes, not dealt

with in the present paper, can be found in the monetary circuit approach. See Graziani (1989; 1994), Hein (2008a, pp. 70–9), Lavoie (1992, pp. 151–69), and Seccareccia (1996; 2003).
18. The Post-Keynesian 'horizontalist' view of endogenous money was pioneered by Kaldor (1970; 1982; 1985), Lavoie (1984; 1992, pp. 149–216; 1996), and Moore (1988; 1989). For a survey of the Post-Keynesian endogenous money approach and its implementation into Post-Keynesian models of distribution and growth see Hein (2008a).
19. See Hannsgen (2004; 2006a; 2006b) and Lima/Setterfield (2008) for empirical work on the cost-push channel of changes in the interest rate ('Gibson's paradox' or 'Wright Patman effect'), and Hein (2008a) for an overview of the development and implementation of this idea in Neo-Ricardian, Marxian and Post-Keynesian economics. The effects of changes in the dividend rate and hence also in the overall rentiers' rate of return can be seen from a similar angle: From the perspective of the firm these payments are costs which have to be covered by the prices set by the firm. In the face of a rising rentiers' rate of return, either the firm manages to raise the mark-up on unit labour costs and labour bears the brunt, or retained profits will have to give way, or conflict inflation will accelerate. See Hein (2008a), Hein/Stockhammer (2010), and Lima/Setterfield (2008) for theoretical models including the cost-push effects of monetary policies.
20. Since an increasing rentiers' rate of return also affects the value of the equilibrium outside finance-capital ratio, as shown above, the required increase in capital stock may initially not need to be proportionate to the increase in outside finance.
21. On the 'paradox of debt' see also Dutt (1995) and Lavoie (1995).
22. For the effects of capital stock growth on GDP growth, employment and inflation see for instance. Arestis, Baddeley and Sawyer (2006, 2007), Arestis and Biefang-Frisancho Mariscal (2000), Arestis and Sawyer (2005b), Rowthorn (1995, 1999) and Sawyer (2002). And for the effects of 'financialisation' on productivity growth and long-run 'potential growth' see Hein (2009).

References

Aglietta, M. (2000), 'Shareholder value and corporate governance: some tricky questions', *Economy and Society*, 29, pp. 146–59.
Arestis, P., Baddeley, M. and Sawyer, M. (2006), 'Is capital stock a determinant of unemployment?', in E. Hein, A. Heise and A. Truger (eds), *Wages, Employment, Distribution and Growth. International Perspectives*, Basingstoke: Palgrave Macmillan.
Arestis, P., Baddeley, M. and Sawyer, M. (2007), 'The relationship between capital stock, unemployment and wages in nine EMU countries', *Bulletin of Economic Research*, 59, pp. 125–39.
Arestis, P. and Biefang-Frisancho Mariscal, I. (2000), 'Capital stock, unemployment and wages in the UK and Germany', *Scottish Journal of Political Economy*, 47, pp. 487–503.
Arestis, P. and Sawyer, M. (2005a), 'Financial liberalization and the finance-growth nexus: what have we learned?', in P. Arestis and M. Sawyer (eds), *Financial Liberalization. Beyond Orthodox Concerns*, Basingstoke: Palgrave Macmillan.

Arestis, P. and Sawyer, M. (2005b), 'Aggregate demand, conflict and capacity in the inflationary process', *Cambridge Journal of Economics*, 29, pp. 959–74.

Argitis, G. and Pitelis, C. (2001), 'Monetary policy and the distribution of income: evidence for the United States and the United Kingdom', *Journal of Post Keynesian Economics*, 23, pp. 617–38.

Bhaduri, A., Laski, K. and Riese, M. (2006), 'A model of interaction between the virtual and the real economy', *Metroeconomica*, 57, pp. 412–27.

Bhaduri, A. and Marglin, S. (1990), 'Unemployment and the real wage: the economic basis for contesting political ideologies', *Cambridge Journal of Economics*, 14, pp. 375–93.

Bhaskar, V. and Glyn, A. (1995), 'Investment and profitability: the evidence from the advanced capitalist countries', in G.A. Epstein and H.M. Gintis (eds), *Macroeconomic Policy after the Conservative Era*, Cambridge/UK: Cambridge University Press.

Boone, L., Giorno, C. and Richardson, P. (1998), 'Stock market fluctuations and consumption behaviour – some recent evidence', OECD Economics Department Working Papers No. 208, Paris.

Boone, L. and Girouard, N. (2002), 'The stock market, the housing market and consumer behaviour', *OECD Economic Studies*, no. 35, pp. 175–200.

Boyer, R. (2000), 'Is a finance-led growth regime a viable alternative to Fordism? A preliminary analysis', *Economy and Society*, 29, pp. 111–45.

Brainard, W. and Tobin, J. (1968), 'Pitfalls in financial model building', *American Economic Review. Papers and Proceedings*, 58, pp. 99–122.

Chirinko, R.S. (1993), 'Business fixed investment spending: modelling strategies, empirical results and policy implications', *The Journal of Economic Literature*, 31, pp. 1875–911.

Cordonnier, L. (2006), 'Le profit sans l'accumulation: la recette du capitalisme dominé par la finance', *Innovations. Cahiers d'Economie de l'Innovation*, 23, pp. 51–72.

Crotty, J. (1990), 'Owner–management conflict and financial theories of investment instability: a critical assessment of Keynes, Tobin, and Minsky', *Journal of Post Keynesian Economics*, 12, pp. 519–42.

Dallery, T. (2008), 'Post-Keynesian theories of the firm under financialization', paper presented at the Workshop 'Financialization: Post-Keynesian Approaches', University of Lille 1 (April).

Davis, M.A. and Palumbo, M. (2001), 'A primer on the economics and time series econometrics of wealth effects', Finance and Economics Discussion Series, 2001–09, Federal Reserve Board, Washington, DC.

Demetriades, P. and Adrianova, S. (2004), 'Finance and growth: what we know and what we need to know', in C. Goodhart (ed.), *Financial Development and Economic Growth. Explaining the Links*, Basingstoke: Palgrave Macmillan.

Dreger, C. and Slacalek, J. (2007), 'Finanzmarktentwicklung, Immobilienpreise und Konsum', *DIW Wochenbericht*, 74, pp. 533–6.

Duménil, G. and Lévy, D. (2001), 'Costs and benefits of neoliberalism: a class analysis', *Review of International Political Economy*, 8, pp. 578–607.

Duménil, G. and Lévy, D. (2004a), 'The real and financial components of profitability (USA 1948–2000)', *Review of Radical Political Economics*, 36, pp. 82–110.

Duménil, G. and Lévy, D. (2004b), 'Neoliberal income trends. Wealth, class and ownership in the USA', *New Left Review*, 30, pp. 105–33.

Duménil, G. and Lévy, D. (2005), 'Costs and benefits of neoliberalism: a class analysis', in G.A. Epstein (ed.), *Financialization and the World Economy*, Cheltenham: Edward Elgar.

Dutt, A.K. (1995): 'Internal finance and monopoly power in capitalist econo mies: a reformulation of Steindl's growth model', *Metroeconomica*, 46, pp. 16–34.

Dutt, A.K. (2005), 'Conspicuous consumption, consumer debt and economic growth', in M. Setterfield (ed.), *Interactions in Analytical Political Economy: Theory, Policy and Applications*, Armonk, New York: M.E. Sharpe.

Dutt, A.K. (2006), 'Maturity, stagnation and consumer debt: a Steindlian approach', *Metroeconomica*, 57, pp. 339–64.

Eatwell, J. and Taylor, L. (2000), *Global Finance at Risk*, Cambridge, UK: Polity Press.

Edison, H. and Slok, T. (2001), 'Wealth effects and the new economy', IMF Working Papers 01/77, Washington, DC: International Monetary Fund.

Epstein, G.A. (ed.) (2005), *Financialization and the World Economy*, Cheltenham: Edward Elgar.

Epstein, G.A. and Jayadev, A. (2005), 'The rise of rentier incomes in OECD countries: financialization, central bank policy and labor solidarity', in G.A. Epstein (ed.), *Financialization and the World Economy*, Cheltenham: Edward Elgar.

Epstein, G.A. and Power, D. (2003), 'Rentier incomes and financial crises: an empirical examination of trends and cycles in some OECD countries', Working Paper Series No. 57, Political Economy Research Institute, University of Massachusetts, Amherst.

Godley, W. and Lavoie, M. (2007), *Monetary Economics: An Integrated Approach to Credit, Money, Income, Production and Wealth*, Basingstoke: Palgrave Macmillan.

Graziani, A. (1989), 'The theory of the monetary circuit', Thames Paper in Political Economy, Spring, London.

Graziani, A. (1994), 'Monetary circuits', in P. Arestis and M. Sawyer (eds), *The Elgar Companion to Radical Political Economy*, Aldershot: Edward Elgar.

Hannsgen, G. (2004), 'Gibson's paradox, monetary policy, and the emergence of cycles', Working Paper no. 410, The Levy Economics Institute at Bard College, Annandale-on-Hudson, New York.

Hannsgen, G. (2006a), 'Gibson's paradox II', Working Paper no. 448, The Levy Economics Institute at Bard College, Annandale-on-Hudson, New York.

Hannsgen, G. (2006b), 'The transmission mechanism of monetary policy: a critical review', in P. Arestis and M. Sawyer (eds), *A Handbook of Alternative Monetary Economics*, Cheltenham: Edward Elgar.

Harrod, R.F. (1939), 'An essay in dynamic theory', *The Economic Journal*, 49, pp. 14–33.

Hein, E. (2005), 'Finanzstruktur und Wirtschaftswachstum – theoretische und empirische Aspekte', IMK Studies 1/2005, Macroeconomic Policy Institute (IMK) at Hans Boeckler Foundation, Duesseldorf.

Hein, E. (2007), 'Interest rate, debt, distribution and capital accumulation in a post-Kaleckian model', *Metroeconomica*, 57, pp. 310–39.

Hein, E. (2008a), *Money, Distribution Conflict and Capital Accumulation: Contributions to 'Monetary Analysis'*, Basingstoke: Palgrave Macmillan.

Hein, E. (2008b), 'Rising shareholder power: effects on distribution, capacity utilisation and capital accumulation in Kaleckian/Post-Kaleckian models', in E. Hein, T. Niechoj, P. Spahn and A. Truger (eds), *Finance-led Capitalism? Macroeconomic Effects of Changes in the Financial Sector*, Marburg: Metropolis.

Hein, E. (2009), '"Financialisation", distribution, capital accumulation and productivity growth in a Post-Kaleckian model', Berlin School of Economics and Law, Institute for International Political Economy, Working Paper, 1/2009.

Hein, E. (2010), 'Shareholder value orientation, distribution and growth – short- and medium-run effects in a Kaleckian model', *Metroeconomica*, 61, 302–32.

Hein, E. and Stockhammer, E. (2010), 'Macroeconomic policy mix, employment and inflation in a Post-Keynesian alternative to the New Consensus model', *Review of Political Economy*, forthcoming.

Hein, E. and van Treeck, T. (2010a), '"Financialisation" in Post-Keynesian models of distribution and growth – a systematic review', in M. Setterfield (ed.), *Handbook of Alternative Theories of Economic Growth*, Cheltenham: Edward Elgar, forthcoming.

Hein, E. and van Treeck, T. (2010b), 'Financialisation and rising shareholder power in Kaleckian/Post-Kaleckian models of distribution and growth', *Review of Political Economy*, forthcoming.

Kaldor, N. (1966), 'Marginal productivity and the macro-economic theories of growth and distribution', *Review of Economic Studies*, 33, pp. 309–19.

Kaldor, N. (1970), 'The new monetarism', *Lloyds Bank Review*, 97, pp. 1–17.

Kaldor, N. (1982), *The Scourge of Monetarism*, Oxford: Oxford University Press.

Kaldor, N. (1985), 'How Monetarism failed', *Challenge*, 28(2), pp. 4–13.

Kalecki, M. (1937), 'The principle of increasing risk', *Economica*, 4, pp. 440–7.

Kalecki, M. (1954), *Theory of Economic Dynamics*, London: George Allen and Unwin.

Krippner, G.R. (2005), 'The financialization of the American economy', *Socio-Economic Review*, 3, pp. 173–208.

Lavoie, M. (1984), 'The endogenous flow of credit and the post-Keynesian theory of money', *Journal of Economic Issues*, 18, pp. 771–97.

Lavoie, M. (1992), *Foundations of Post-Keynesian Economic Analysis*, Aldershot: Edward Elgar.

Lavoie, M. (1995): 'Interest rates in post-Keynesian models of growth and distribution', *Metroeconomica*, 46, pp. 146–77.

Lavoie, M. (1996), 'Horizontalism, structuralism, liquidity preference and the principle of increasing risk', *Scottish Journal of Political Economy*, 43, pp. 275–300.

Lavoie, M. (1998), 'The Neo-Pasinetti theorem in Cambridge and Kaleckian models of growth and distribution', *Eastern Economic Journal*, 24, pp. 417–34.

Lavoie, M. (2008), 'Financialisation issues in a Post-Keynesian stock-flow consistent model', *Intervention. European Journal of Economics and Economic Policies*, 5, pp. 331–56.

Lavoie, M. (2009), 'Cadrisme within a Post-Keynesian model of growth and distribution', *Review of Political Economy*, 21, pp. 369–91.

Lavoie, M. and Godley, W. (2001–2), 'Kaleckian models of growth in a coherent stock-flow monetary framework: a Kaldorian view', *Journal of Post Keynesian Economics*, 22, pp. 277–311.

Lazonick, W. and O'Sullivan, M. (2000), 'Maximizing shareholder value: a new ideology for corporate governance', *Economy and Society*, 29(1), pp. 13–35.

Levine, R. (2003), 'More on finance and growth: more finance, more growth?', *Federal Reserve Bank of St. Louis Review*, 85(4), pp. 31–46.

Levine, R. (2005), 'Finance and growth: theory and evidence', in P. Aghion and S. Durlauf (eds), *Handbook of Economic Growth*, Amsterdam: Elsevier.

Lima, G.T. and Setterfield, M. (2008), Pricing behaviour and the cost-push channel of monetary policy, manuscript, http://www.trincoll.edu/~setterfi/mark_setterfield.htm.

Ludvigson, S. and Steindel, C. (1999), 'How important is the stock market effect on consumption?', *Federal Reserve Bank of New York Economic Policy Review*, July, pp. 29–51.

Ludwig, A. and Slok, T. (2001), 'The impact of changes in stock prices and in house prices on consumption', IMF Working Papers 02/1, Washington, DC: International Monetary Fund.

Ludwig, A. and Slok, T. (2004), 'The relationship between stock, house prices and consumption in OECD countries', MEA Discussion Paper Series 04044, Mannheim Research Institute for the Economics of Aging (MEA), University of Mannheim.

Medlen, C. (2003), 'The trouble with Q', *Journal of Post Keynesian Economics*, 25, pp. 693–8.

Mehra, Y.P. (2001), 'The wealth effect in empirical life-cycle aggregate consumption equations', *Federal Reserve Bank of Richmond Economic Quarterly*, 87(2), pp. 45–68.

Moore, B.J. (1988), *Horizontalists and Verticalists: The Macroeconomics of Credit Money*, Cambridge, UK: Cambridge University Press.

Moore, B.J. (1989), 'The endogeneity of credit money', *Review of Political Economy*, 1, pp. 65–93.

Ndikumana, L. (1999), 'Debt service, financing constraints, and fixed investment: evidence from panel data', *Journal of Post Keynesian Economics*, 21, pp. 455–78.

Orhangazi, Ö. (2008), 'Financialisation and capital accumulation in the non-financial corporate sector: a theoretical and empirical investigation on the US economy: 1973–2003', *Cambridge Journal of Economics*, 32, pp. 863–86.

Palley, T. (1994), 'Debt, aggregate demand, and the business cycle: an analysis in the spirit of Kaldor and Minsky', *Journal of Post Keynesian Economics*, 16, pp. 371–90.

Palley, T. (1996), *Post Keynesian Economics. Debt, Distribution and the Macro Economy*, Basingstoke: Macmillan.

Palley, T. (2006), 'Class conflict and the Cambridge theory of income distribution', in E. Hein, A. Heise and A. Truger (eds), *Wages, Employment, Distribution and Growth. International Perspectives*, Basingstoke: Palgrave Macmillan.

Palley, T. (2008), 'Financialisation: what it is and why it matters', in E. Hein, T. Niechoj, P. Spahn and A. Truger (eds), *Finance-led Capitalism? Macroeconomic Effects of Changes in the Financial Sector*, Marburg: Metropolis.

Pasinetti, L.L. (1974), *Growth and Income Distribution*, Cambridge, UK: Cambridge University Press.

Piketty, T. and Saez, E. (2003), 'Income inequality in the United States, 1913–1998', *The Quarterly Journal of Economics*, 143, pp. 1–39.

Piketty, T. and Saez, E. (2006), 'The evolution of top incomes: a historical and international perspective', *American Economic Review: Papers and Proceedings*, 96, pp. 200–5.

Poterba, J.M. (2000), 'Stock market wealth and consumption', *Journal of Economic Perspectives*, 14(2), pp. 99–118.

Rowthorn, R.E. (1995), 'Capital formation and unemployment', *Oxford Review of Economic Policy*, 11(1), pp. 26–39.

Rowthorn, R.E. (1999), 'Unemployment, wage bargaining and capital-labour substitution', *Cambridge Journal of Economics*, 23, pp. 413–25.

Sawyer, M. (2002), 'The NAIRU, aggregate demand and investment', *Metroeconomica*, 53, pp. 66–94.

Seccareccia, M. (1996), 'Post Keynesian fundism and monetary circulation', in G. Deleplace and E. Nell (eds), *Money in Motion*, London: Macmillan.

Seccareccia, M. (2003), 'Pricing, investment and the financing of production within the framework of the monetary circuit: some preliminary evidence', in L.-P. Rochon and S. Rossi (eds), *Modern Theories of Money*, Cheltenham: Edward Elgar.

Skott, P. (1988), 'Finance, saving and accumulation', *Cambridge Journal of Economics*, 12, pp. 339–54.

Skott, P. (1989), *Conflict and Effective Demand in Economic Growth*, Cambridge, UK: Cambridge University Press.

Skott, P. and Ryoo, S. (2008a), 'Macroeconomic implications of financialization', *Cambridge Journal of Economics*, 32, pp. 827–62.

Skott, P. and Ryoo, S. (2008b), 'Financialization in Kaleckian economics with and without labor constraints', *Intervention. European Journal of Economics and Economic Policies*, 5, pp. 357–86.

Steindl, J. (1976), *Maturity and Stagnation in American Capitalism*, 2nd edition, New York and London: Monthly Review Press.

Stockhammer, E. (2004), 'Financialisation and the slowdown of accumulation', *Cambridge Journal of Economics*, 28, pp. 719–41.

Stockhammer, E. (2005–6), 'Shareholder value orientation and the investment-profit puzzle', *Journal of Post Keynesian Economics*, 28, pp. 193–215.

Stockhammer, E. (2008), 'Some stylized facts on the finance-dominated accumulation regime', *Competition and Change*, 12, pp. 189–207.

Taylor, L. (2004), *Reconstructing Macroeconomics: Structuralists Proposals and Critiques of the Mainstream*, Cambridge, Mass.: Harvard University Press.

Tobin, J. (1969), 'A general equilibrium approach to monetary theory', *Journal of Money, Credit and Banking*, 1, pp. 15–29.

Tobin, J. and Brainard, W. (1990), 'On Crotty's critique of Q-theory', *Journal of Post Keynesian Economics*, 12, pp. 543–9.

van Treeck, T. (2008), 'Reconsidering the investment–profit nexus in finance-led economies: an ARDL-based approach', *Metroeconomica*, 59, pp. 371–404.

van Treeck, T. (2009a), 'A synthetic stock-flow consistent macroeconomic model of financialisation', *Cambridge Journal of Economics*, 33, pp. 467–93.

van Treeck, T. (2009b), 'The political economy debate on "financialisation" – a macroeconomic perspective', *Review of International Political Economy*, 16, pp. 907–44.

van Treeck, T., Hein, E. and Dünhaupt, P. (2007), 'Finanzsystem und wirtschaftliche Entwicklung: neuere Tendenzen in den USA und in Deutschland', IMK Studies 5/2007, Macroeconomic Policy Institute (IMK) at Hans Boeckler Foundation, Duesseldorf.

5
Systemic Failure of Private Banking: A Case for Public Banks

Costas Lapavitsas
Department of Economics, SOAS

Abstract

The crisis of 2007–9 represents a systemic failure of private banking. The private nature of banks has created opacity, and exacerbated problems of liquidity, bad assets and capital shortage. Furthermore, private banks have failed in information gathering and risk management, as well as in mediating the acquisition of vital goods by households. It is paradoxical that, confronted with such systemic failure, Keynesian and other heterodox economists have generally made non-systemic reform proposals. This paper draws on Marxist theory to argue that systemic change is necessary, including conversion of failed private into public banks run transparently and with democratic accountability. Public banks could more easily confront the problems of liquidity and solvency; they could also play a long-term role by providing stable flows of credit to households as well as to small and medium-sized enterprises.

JEL Classification Codes: E11, E12, G21, G28

Keywords: Banking, financial crisis, financial regulation, Keynesianism and Marxism

1. Introduction

At the core of the current crisis lies a systemic failure of private banking – both commercial and investment. The failure is systemic because the crisis has been caused by the interaction of several components of the financial system, and, above all, the banks. No single element of finance has been uniquely at fault, and nor has the turbulence been caused by malpractice in a small number of institutions.

The failure is also systemic because several large commercial banks in the USA, the UK and elsewhere were effectively bankrupt during 2008–9.[1] Had governments allowed these to fail, it is probable that there would have been a general banking collapse.

Yet, mere prevention of bankruptcy through extraordinary measures has not resolved the underlying systemic banking problems. As a result there has been persistent disruption of the supply of credit, exacerbating the global recession. It is unlikely that sustained accumulation will be restored without confronting the failure of banking.[2]

In the rest of this essay the systemic failure of private banks is examined in more detail and a case is made in favour of the long-term establishment of public banks. Attention focuses primarily on the USA and the UK but the case holds more generally. The analytical framework is provided by the Marxist theory of finance, particularly recent work on financialization by Lapavitsas (2009, 2010) and Dos Santos (2009), while empirical insights are drawn from Dymski (2009). In sum – and discussed in more detail in section 3 below – financialization represents a structural transformation of mature capitalist economies that has gathered pace since the 1970s and comprises the following three key domestic elements.

First, industrial and commercial enterprises have become adept at obtaining external finance in open markets, thereby lessening their reliance on banks. Enterprises have become financialized in so far as they have acquired financial capabilities, learning to generate profits in open financial markets and through other financial transactions.

Second, and partly as a result of the first, banks have been transformed while developing new fields of profitability. On the one hand, banks have turned to open markets as a source of trading profits as well as profits on own account, fees and commissions. Such profits typically result from investment banking activities, which banks have learnt to pursue in conjunction with commercial banking. The combination of the two has been highly unstable and a fundamental cause of the current crisis. On the other hand, banks have turned to individual income as a source of profit. This typically involves lending for mortgages, consumption and so on, but also charging fees to manage accounts and handle assets of individuals.

Third, the personal income of workers and others has become financialized in terms of both debts and assets. Real wages have been stagnant or growing at low rates during this period, while public provision in housing, health, education and pensions has retreated. Consequently, private finance has emerged as mediator of the acquisition of vital goods that enter the wage basket, such as housing. At the same time, private finance has come increasingly to handle savings and other provision of workers for old age. The emergence of private finance as mediator of workers' consumption and savings has allowed it systematically to extract profits directly out of wages and salaries. This process has elsewhere been characterized as financial expropriation (Lapavitsas 2009).

In this light, the turmoil that commenced in August 2007 and the corresponding failure of private banks represent a crisis of financialization. In the 2000s private finance intensified its turn toward personal income, buttressed by investment banking activities, above all, securitization. The extraction of profits out of wages and salaries was combined with profit making through securities trading, leading to a huge financial bubble in the USA and the UK. The failure of private banking thus also stands for failure of financialization. By the same token, establishment of public banks could help address some of the problematic implications of financialization.

The paper is structured as follows. Section 2 considers heterodox – mostly Keynesian – and mainstream analyses of the crisis, focusing on the systemic aspect of the turmoil. Section 3 examines key empirical aspects of the crisis in detail in order to demonstrate the systemic character of the crisis, and therefore the need for systemic response. Section 4 then turns to financialization and considers the broad underlying structural trends that led to the crisis and thus the failure of private banks. Section 5 broadens the theoretical discussion by recapitulating classical Marxist analysis of finance capital and imperialism, drawing parallels with financialization. Section 6 then considers more closely the likely operation of public banks. Section 7 concludes.

2. A systemic financial crisis requires a systemic response

The systemic nature of the crisis has been highlighted by heterodox economists, in particular by several strands of Keynesians. For a brief period in 2007–8, talk of a 'Minsky moment' even attained global prominence (Whalen 2007). The content of this 'Minsky moment' has never been entirely clear, but the term drew on Minsky's theory of endogenous financial instability (1986, 1992, 1996; and Minsky and Whalen 1996). Minsky claimed that 'money manager capitalism' has emerged in the USA after the Second World War, pivoting on pension and mutual funds, and favouring short-termism. 'Money manager capitalism' has encouraged the systematic migration of capitalist enterprises from 'hedge' to 'speculative' to 'Ponzi' finance. Consequently, financial fragility has increased steadily during the last several decades. Minsky's theory certainly posits financial instability as a systemic aspect of contemporary capitalism. Yet, despite appearances, it does not immediately fit the current turmoil. This, after all, is a crisis induced by mortgage loans to poor households that were subsequently securitized, thus ruining banks and other financial institutions. It has little to do with industrial or commercial enterprises migrating toward Ponzi finance. Indeed, the productive sector has not suffered from excessive leverage throughout the period.

This difficulty has been clear to some Keynesians, including Kregel (2008), who has suggested a compromise. For Kregel, the crisis is Minskyan because adjustable rate subprime borrowers acted as Ponzi units that relied on remortgaging and house price increases to finance past loans.[3] More significantly, the crisis is also Minskyan because, during the bubble, banks exhausted their liquidity cushions, rendering themselves vulnerable to subprime default. Along similar lines, Nesvetailova (2008) claimed that the systemic disappearance of liquidity is a Minskyan process characteristic of the crisis.

Other heterodox economists have used Minsky in a more generic sense, but similarly stressing the systemic aspects of the crisis. Thus, Wray (2007, 2008) put forth detailed analytical descriptions of the US housing market as well as of the process of securitization. The analytical link with Minsky appears to be the Ponzi nature of adjustable rate subprime borrowing as well as the spread of fragility as 'money-manager' capitalism took hold in the USA. More complexly, and relying on a far broader range of analytical and institutional arguments, Crotty (2008, 2009) has claimed that the crisis is due to the New Financial Architecture that has emerged during the last three to four decades. A globally integrated system comprising giant banks and 'shadow banks' gradually took shape encouraging excessive risk taking. For Crotty, relevant insight into risk, and therefore into the inherent instability of this system, are offered by Minsky but also Keynes and Marx.

The emphasis laid by Keynesians on systemic aspects of the crisis has been a major strength of their analysis. This makes it all the more striking, therefore, that the proposed reforms and policy changes have been non-systemic. Thus, Kregel (2009a, 2009b), has suggested that shortages of liquidity should be dealt with by raising wages instead of lowering interest rates to zero. He has also advocated universal banking (combining commercial and investment banking activities) but with a closer matching of maturities and tighter control over the size of loans, emulating German practices.

Similarly, Crotty and Epstein (2008, 2009) have offered a nine-point programme for financial regulation that ranges from reducing asymmetric incentives and moral hazard by regulating bonuses, to extending regulatory oversight over 'shadow banking', to prohibiting the sale of 'too complex' financial securities, to adopting counter-cyclical capital adequacy requirements. These several and partial reforms are in the same spirit as the measures suggested by D'Arista and Griffith-Jones (2008), the list of regulatory changes recommended by Pollin (2009), the brief suggestions by Wray (2009), and the finance section of the radical manifesto issued by Ash et al. (2009).

It is instructive in this respect to note parallels and differences with mainstream analyses of the crisis. Mainstream economics is aware of the systemic nature of the crisis, but lacks systemic theories of financial instability. Nonetheless, it has already put forth concrete empirical accounts of various institutional faults within the financial system that have mutually interacted and presumably led to disaster (Brunnermeier 2009). Not surprising, theoretical emphasis has been laid on the disappearance of liquidity. An influential model has shown that 'funding liquidity' (the ease of borrowing by the trader) and 'market liquidity' (the ease of selling an asset) could be mutually destabilizing, if margins rose due to imperfect information of financiers and rising fundamental volatility (Brunnermeier and Pedersen 2008). Earlier and related work had shown that vicious circles of market liquidity were possible, and if panic appeared, liquidity could disappear down a 'black hole' (Persaud 2002). Furthermore, mainstream theorists are aware of the systemic failure of risk management by banks, describing the underlying cause of the crisis as 'mispricing of risk' (Goodhart 2008).

Remarkably, mainstream economists have been more daring – and even more systemic – in recommending reform than Keynesians. Several partial reforms, including countercyclical regulation of capital adequacy, maturity matching of assets and liabilities, altering banker remuneration, changing the flawed practices of credit rating, and more, have been proposed (Brunnermeier et al. 2009; Dewatripont, et al. 2009). However, other mainstream economists have also recommended outright nationalization of banks (Stiglitz 2009; Posen 2009). To be sure, this was seen as a short-term step allowing for a more efficient handling of the crisis, and banks were eventually to be rendered back into private ownership. Yet, the radical aspect of the proposal, tackling ownership and control relations at the heart of the crisis, cannot be gainsaid.

In comparison, Keynesian reform proposals appear hesitant, something that is probably related to Minsky's own reluctance to advocate public or communal finance. But such timidity is problematic in view of the depth of the current crisis. Private banking has failed in a systemic way, and responses to it should be equally systemic, with the aim of permanently changing the balance between private and public in finance. To be more specific, public banks could be instrumental in effectively confronting the crisis as well as restructuring the financial system and the economy for the long term.

Public banks are a long-standing socialist demand, put forth by Marxist economists (for instance, Hilferding 1981: 368). Examining their potential role in the current crisis, therefore, offers scope for fruitful interaction between Keynesian and Marxist approaches to finance. There is a long record of exchange of ideas between the two currents, the roots of which can be found in the nineteenth-century monetary tradition of the Banking School. The present crisis allows – but also calls – for wider cross-fertilization of heterodox approaches on finance. The severity of the crisis and the complex economic problems it has posed require selective drawing on the full armoury of alternative ideas on finance, theoretical differences notwithstanding.

Keynesian economics has rarely confronted the issue of ownership and control of banks. This is a strange lacuna since, historically, Keynesianism has readily contemplated public ownership of means of production in several areas of the economy, including transport and a variety of public utilities. The prevalent perception as far as finance is concerned appears to be that public control over the central bank plus tight regulation of the operations of financial institutions are sufficient to deliver desired results. However, the systemic failure of 2007–9 has posed directly the issue of ownership and control over banks. Revamped regulation is not an adequate response to the current crisis.

Marxist theory, on the other hand, has considered the ownership and control of banks to be a cause of economic intervention as well as a field of desired transformation. The aim of Marxists is, of course, socialism, while Keynesians generally hope to reform the capitalist economy in order to achieve better results of employment, growth and income distribution. In this respect, the two currents of thought have completely incompatible aims as well as analytical techniques. Nonetheless, in the field of finance there have long been affinities and fruitful exchanges of ideas, as was mentioned above. Analysis of banking from a Marxist perspective offers fresh insights into the failure of contemporary banks and the changes that are socially required. The resulting intellectual interaction could only be beneficial for the development of critical thought in economics, whether Keynesian or Marxist.

3. The crisis of 2007–9 as systemic failure of private commercial banks

3.1. Disappearance of private liquidity and loss of trust

In systemic terms, the disappearance of private liquidity in the course of the crisis is due to commercial banks adopting investment banking functions while expanding loans to individual workers (Lapavitsas 2009). On the liability side, banks increasingly relied on wholesale liquidity to finance securitizations; on the asset side, they securitized loans to generate liquidity at the same time nearly eliminating traditional liquid reserves. When the housing market crashed, the creditworthiness of mortgage-backed securities collapsed, the solvency of banks was put in doubt, and hence liquidity mechanisms seized up generally. Banks hoarded liquidity instead of lending it to each other.

At bottom the disappearance of liquidity reflects loss of trust among banks – as well as of others in banks – primarily due to the poor quality of their assets. Among small savers this became apparent during the run on the Northern Rock building society in the UK in late 2007. Among institutional holders of loanable capital, loss of trust was greatly exacerbated when US authorities allowed Lehman Brothers to collapse in September 2008, while fostering a takeover of Bear Sterns in March 2008. Differential treatment of bank creditors removed the unspoken basis of trust in money markets.

Private banks proved incapable of confronting the loss of trust through their own devices, and were obliged to seek recourse to state intervention. Deposit holders were reassured through strengthened government guarantees, reaching 100 percent of deposit value in the UK. Things were more complicated in wholesale markets, but liquidity policy has basically taken two directions.

First, central banks in the USA, the UK, and even the EU, effectively adopted Zero Interest Rate Policy (ZIRP), originally deployed in Japan in the 1990s. ZIPR amounts to a public subsidy to banks because it drives down the cost of funds, thus widening spreads, including for the acquisition of state paper. Not surprisingly, banks in the USA reported rising profits in early 2009.

Second, central banks directly supplied public liquidity through lending; bank debt was guaranteed; and public securities were made available for banks to use as collateral. Following the Lehman shock,

US and UK central banks adopted 'quantitative easing', another Japanese practice of the early part of the 2000s. This amounts to systematic over-expansion of bank reserves with the central bank, though, unlike Japan, US and UK authorities did not adopt quantitative targets for reserves. 'Quantitative easing' also includes the announcement of the intent to drive down long-term interest rates. Clearly, these policies are also public subsidies to banks since they replace safe public for risky private credit.

The response to the collapse of trust in wholesale markets, in other words, was for central banks (and the state) to substitute themselves for the commercial operation of money markets. The result has inevitably been the tremendous expansion of the balance sheet of the US central bank. Thus, the provision of central bank funds rose from about $0.91 trillion in September 2008 to roughly $2.1 trillion in May 2009. The bulk of the increase was absorbed by the enormous growth of bank reserves (which started to receive interest), rising from about $10bn in September 2008 to about $900bn in May 2009.[4] 'Quantitative easing' is thus another term for banks hoarding liquidity with the central bank. Both the provision of central bank credit and the accumulation of reserves appeared to have declined slightly in June 2009, for the first time since the Lehman shock.

Broadly speaking, liquidity policy has followed Bagehot's traditional advice, namely to lend first and ask questions later. If there is novelty, it lies in the extent to which public mechanisms of liquidity provision have substituted themselves for the market. Nonetheless, mere provision of liquidity through state mechanisms has not been enough to restore trust among banks. Figure 5.1 shows the three month LIBOR–OIS spread, which reflects risk in the interbank market, and stood below 0.1 percent prior to the crisis. In August 2007 the spread rose substantially, but remained below 1 percent; the paroxysm of crisis in September–October 2008 pushed it toward 4 percent, making all business among banks impossible. During the first half of 2009 the spread has declined steadily, though in June 2009 it still stood significantly higher than before August 2007.[5]

The steady shrinking of the spread in the first half of 2009 was partly due to the enormous volume of liquidity supplied by the monetary authorities. It also had to do with the adoption of measures dealing with capital shortages and bad assets, discussed below. Nonetheless, the unprecedented extent of state intervention also lessened the importance of LIBOR-OIS as an indicator of trust among banks. The distinct possibility arose in 2009 that banks continued to mistrust each other in

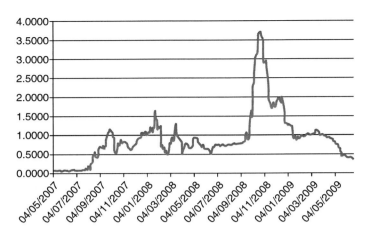

Figure 5.1   Three-month LIBOR–OIS spread (1%–5% on the y axis)
Source: Bloomberg.

the money market but abundant public liquidity disguised reality and rendered LIBOR-OIS less meaningful than before.

In sum, the liquidity policy adopted by central banks – primarily in the USA and the UK but also by the European Central Bank – has ameliorated the worst of the shortages, but this has also been an essentially short-term response. Private banks have been crippled by lending and borrowing decisions, thus destroying trust among them and freezing the money market. The central bank – and the state more generally – has stepped in and engulfed the money market. This situation cannot persist indefinitely, and certainly not in 'free-market' economies. Therefore, there are two broad options for the longer term. One is to remove the underlying causes of collapse of trust among private banks, eventually resuming normal supply of liquidity. The other is to restructure the banking system, including a stronger presence for public banks. Both have major consequences, and raise deeper issues regarding the future of banking.

3.2.   Bad assets

The failure of banks is due, in the first instance, to devalued mortgage- and other asset-backed securities, which put bank solvency in doubt and thus destroyed liquidity. But weakened solvency has also prevented banks from engaging in normal lending. Solvency problems have made banks overcautious, often encouraging them to call back or refuse to roll over loans, while raising the threshold of creditworthiness for new loans.

Tighter bank credit combined with the collapse of securitized loan pools in the USA. Federal Reserve Flow of Funds shows that commercial bank lending declined from $758bn in 2007 to $655bn in 2008, while asset-backed security issues literally vanished, falling from $314bn in 2007 to $–421bn in 2008. Household borrowing took the brunt, collapsing from $849bn in 2007 to $51bn in 2008, with a corresponding impact on aggregate demand and output.

Thus, for regular credit provision to be re-established it is necessary, first, to remove bad assets from bank balance sheets but also, secondly, to ensure either recovery of securitization, or the emergence of alternatives to it. The former is considered immediately below, the latter in section 3.3.

Removing bad assets is a standard requirement for dealing with banking crises. However, the private nature of banks complicates the problem. Banks have been at pains to conceal the extent of bad assets in order to prevent the complete collapse of trust. In a competitive environment, the first to reveal the full extent of the problem suffers disproportionately in terms of access to liquidity, share price, inflow of deposits, and so on. Consequently, state policy toward bad assets has had to be designed amidst relative opacity.

Revelation aside, the deeper problem is assigning prices to bad assets: if set high, buyers face losses, or are driven away; if set low, the banks would be intractably insolvent. The problem is particularly complex in the current crisis because of the nature of the assets involved, particularly in the USA. Collateralized debt obligations typically rest on subprime, Alt-A and prime mortgages, all of which have been continually deteriorating since 2006. Unprecedented rates of non-repayment and general falls in house prices have invalidated historic assumptions built into formal models of asset valuation. Moreover, as was mentioned above, markets in asset-backed securities have collapsed, removing the grounds for establishing prices through repeated and extensive trading. Finally, it is often hard to establish who has ultimate responsibility for payment, who is entitled to returns, and who has legal claim over underlying assets. In market terms, the current value of bad assets on bank balance sheets is probably very low, entailing losses of hundreds of billions of dollars.

Therefore, private banks have found themselves in a quandary. If bad assets were removed rapidly and in market terms, several would become irrevocably bankrupt; but if banks continued to carry bad assets in the hope of obtaining better final prices, their balance sheets would remain illiquid, preventing normal banking functions. The longer that normal banking was interrupted, the more bad assets would probably accumulate in the course of the recession, including commercial property, automobile-related asset-backed securities, and so on.

The political economy of dealing with bad assets, therefore, is transparent, at least in the USA. Private banks have revealed as little as possible of the extent of their bad assets, while trying to shift them off the balance sheet for the highest price. Thus, they have been at pains to create the impression that bad assets have been caused essentially by the drying up of liquidity, rather than by bad credit decisions. As a result they have rendered even more difficult the formation of public policy and the restoration of normal credit supply.

Things became even more complicated when it came to apportioning likely losses from the disposal of bad assets. Small depositors are typically protected by law as well as by the need to maintain monetary stability. But in competitive capitalist markets equity holders are supposed to carry all residual risk, which makes them liable to the full extent of their holdings. In the absence of state support, the value of bank shares would have collapsed completely. Even on capitalist efficiency grounds (moral hazard), therefore, shareholders could have no claim to retrieving value invested. Bondholders and other creditors, on the other hand, have made funds available on the basis of repayment plus interest, while also benefiting from capital gains. But since they have lent to essentially failed enterprises, they should also be in line to take some of the consequences.

The problem is, however, that equity- and bondholders are often pension funds and other institutional investors, who have bought bank securities as portfolio diversification. They are also foreign buyers, frequently from large public and semi-public institutions of developing countries. Thus, the social criteria against which bank stakeholders ought to be ranked are not immediately apparent. On what grounds should the burden of bank failure be shifted onto social layers that have, at most, placed their pension savings in particular funds? And why should bank failure in developed countries impinge upon the savings of people in developing countries? What will be the economic and political implications?

It bears stressing that these issues cannot be tackled through ingenious accounting tricks, but ought to be confronted democratically and in full view of the consequences. But this is hardly possible while private banks are concealing the extent of bad assets, manoeuvring to secure as high a price as possible, and attempting to protect both equity and bondholders. The need for transparency and democratic procedure is particularly acute, if losses are to be borne directly by society in the form of subventions of public funds to banks. Substantial public funds have already been made available to banks, as is discussed below, without direct implications for either shareholders or bondholders. The exclusionary nature of financial policy making (and the privileged access of banks to it) has made democratic decision making more difficult, while protecting bank stakeholders.

Some of these complexities are apparent in the debate that has emerged on aggregating bad assets in a 'bad bank', or equivalently, creating 'good banks'.[6] Thus, Buiter (2009) – who favoured temporary nationalization despite also thinking that it might be politically difficult – proposed the establishment of new public banks that would aggregate the good assets of stricken banks. They would thus be able to resume lending, while leaving failed banks to cope with the rest over time. Bulow and Klemperer (2009), on the other hand, proposed creating 'good' private banks by taking over the whole of the assets, but only the most senior liabilities of stricken banks (including deposits). The remaining liabilities would continue to be held by the failed old banks, which would also hold the equity of the new banks. Ingenious as these proposals are, their cleverness is largely due to attempting to circumvent the political and ideological obstacles posed by the private nature of banks, which created the problem in the first place.

The policy actually adopted by US administrations in late 2008 and early 2009 should be seen in light of the above. Removing bad assets was proclaimed a priority by the Bush administration's Troubled Asset Relief Plan (TARP) in September 2008, and $700bn was committed to it. However, the difficulty of pricing bad assets and the severity of solvency problems in late 2008 and early 2009 forced a change of emphasis toward capital injections, discussed in the next section. Eventually, the Obama administration put forth the Geithner plan in March 2009, in a similar spirit to TARP.

Geithner's plan shared the assumption that bad debts reflect the drying up of liquidity, rather than bad credit decisions (Bebchuk 2009). Its objective, therefore, was to remove these assets by restarting the market for securitized securities, while securing for the banks the highest possible price. Driving the plan was the determination to avoid nationalization (or to appear to do so), while solving the problem by relying on private capital. Thus a mechanism was proposed to auction bad debts to coalitions of private and public funds. Private capital would be allowed to participate by contributing only 1/14 of the funds necessary; the balance would be provided by the public (1/14 equity, 6/7 public debt). The bidding process would therefore favour those who believed that the true value of bad debts was high. Assuming that there would be enough optimists, and as long as banks were prepared to countenance reasonable losses, the auctioning process should result in high prices. For the plan to succeed, therefore, it would be necessary to have enough buyers sharing its underlying assumption that the problem was one of liquidity. But the underlying assumption could well be incorrect and the real problem of banks might be irrecoverable loans, which have led to liquidity shortage. If that turned out to be the case, there would be substantial losses for those who bought the bad assets. This risk would be mostly carried by the public, which would have provided the bulk of the funds, either as capital or debt guarantees.

Despite its stated intentions, the Geithner plan had little in common with a genuine market process. Rather, care was taken to attract private buyers, who were given incentives to drive prices high. Most of the risk, meanwhile, was shifted onto the public. In short, the Geithner plan aimed at assuaging private bank failure by relying on public funds, while allowing private capital to make still more profits despite bearing only a fraction of the risk.[7]

Even worse, however, the Geithner plan would succeed only if banks were prepared to take some losses in to remove bad assets from their balance sheets. But the policy of liquidity provision already succeeded in shoring up bank profits in 2009. Moreover, capital injections were managed fully in the interests of banks, as is shown below. Consequently, banks had little incentive to auction their bad assets even at a small loss. From their perspective it would make more sense to wait to maturity, rather than taking part in the faux-market processes of the Geithner plan. Meanwhile, bank lending continues to stagnate, negatively affecting demand and output.

3.3.   Capital injections

Effective bankruptcy in 2007–9 implied that banks have required additional capital, if they were to continue in operation. By early 2009 US commercial banks and other financial institutions had already received more than \$300bn of capital injections from TARP, typically as preferred stock with guaranteed interest payments. There had also been two bouts of capital injections by the UK government, while several continental European banks also received government funds. Nonetheless, the eventual capital shortfall was likely to be larger, depending on the extent of further losses on bad assets.

Further capital injections, therefore, raised several questions that go to the heart of the banking problem. What would be their likely size? Where would additional capital come from? What would be the implications for managing banks? Dealing with these issues was made considerably more complex because of the private nature of failed banks. Ascertaining the extent of future capital injections requires assessing the performance of bank assets under different economic circumstances. Naturally, the outcome would vary among banks, depending on past decisions and management practices. It seems obvious that independent auditors – preferably public employees – should have taken charge of bank books. But to avoid even the appearance of nationalization, the US and UK governments were chary of such action.

Consequently, in March 2009 the Obama administration introduced the Supervisory Capital Assessment Program – 'stress tests' of 19 banks – to be conducted by US regulatory authorities on the basis of information requested from the banks. Instead of taking charge of the stricken banks, US authorities relied on the banks' own assessment of bad debts under a 'baseline' and a 'more adverse' scenario of the behaviour of the economy as a whole (Federal Reserve 2009a). The authorities subsequently tweaked these assessments, always in close contact with the banks. The quality of the final results, announced in May 2009, was thus in doubt from the beginning. Still, it was estimated that ten out of the 19 banks would need an additional \$185bn to the end of 2010, under the 'more adverse' scenario. The expected losses were due mostly to mortgages and consumer loans. But given that banks had been building up their capital since the end of 2008, particularly as their profitability rose, the actual shortfall was estimated to be only \$75bn (Federal Reserve 2009b).

It should be noted that the 'stress tests' conducted by the US authorities merely assessed the likely losses on loans maturing to 2010. This is a very different exercise from attempting to ascertain the value of the bad assets carried by the banks, and thus the likely magnitude of their losses if they were forced to clean up their balance sheets, as was discussed in the previous section. On this basis, it would be perfectly plausible for banks to have enough (or nearly enough) capital to cover their losses up to 2010, while carrying substantial bad assets that prevented them from engaging in normal lending as well as endangering their solvency after 2010. In short, the 'stress tests' were not only conducted in opaque ways that favoured the banks, but were also of limited value in revealing the underlying state of private banking.

Still, the 'stress tests' helped bolster stock market confidence in banks, allowing them to raise capital through fresh issues of equity. The recovery of market confidence was purely due to the policies adopted by the US state after the Lehman shock. On the one hand, the state effectively insured private banks against bankruptcy through provision of capital, backing for assets, and guarantees on deposits. On the other, the state boosted bank profitability through the disguised subsidies discussed in section 2.1. Thus, around the middle of 2009, the largest US banks were permitted to repay some of the money they had received through TARP earlier in 2008–9. Banks were keen to do so despite having received these funds without significant direct implications for ownership and control. Only relatively minor, and highly contested, conditions were applied, requiring banks to maintain the level of their lending, while limiting the exceptional remuneration of management. But private banks resented even these mild conditions, particularly as there would be competitive advantages for those among them that managed to shake off the restrictions first. Consequently, around the middle of 2009 and barely nine months after the Lehman shock, the largest banks started to repay some of the TARP funds, while taking steps to restore management remuneration to pre-crisis levels. Meanwhile, fresh credit provision by banks remained mediocre, barely maintaining existing levels.

State policies toward private banks, therefore, created deeply problematic outcomes in both the USA and the UK. Large public funds were made available to the managers of failed banks in 2008–9, subsequently to be used to protect shareholders and bondholders from losses arising out of bad lending. Meanwhile, liquidity was supplied in enormous volumes, driving interest rates down and improving bank profitability. Finally, schemes were devised to remove problematic assets in the most painless way for banks. In receipt of this largesse, banks improved their profitability, hoarded liquidity, and avoided the removal of bad assets to escape even modest losses. Not surprisingly, they also avoided expanding loans and providing fresh credit.

In short, public funds and credit were mobilized to create room for banks to wait in the hope that the underlying problems would sort themselves out slowly. Credit creation inevitably suffered, potentially prolonging the recession. In other words, to rescue failed banks the authorities imposed substantial costs on society as a whole, while protecting bank shareholders, bondholders and managers. Society was forced to bear the brunt of the costs because policy makers aimed at protecting the private nature of banks while avoiding assumption of public control.

4. Financialization and the underlying causes of systemic banking failure

The failure of private banking, however, is more deeply systemic than is indicated by the complexities of resolving the crisis alone. For one thing, this is a crisis of the major global banks, not of relatively minor banking systems, particularly those of developing countries, as has often happened during the last three decades. Even the largest of recent banking crises never became truly global, including the US Savings and Loans crisis of the 1980s, the Swedish banking crisis of the 1990s, and the Japanese disaster of the 1990s and 2000s. In this respect, the current crisis is even worse than that of the 1930s since it has hit some of the largest international banks. The core of the global banking system as that has developed in the last three decades has effectively failed. This is unprecedented in the history of industrial capitalism.

Equally unprecedented is that the crisis has originated in mortgage lending in the USA, including to the poorest layers of workers and others. Historically, major banking crises have been typically due to lending to enterprises or states, but not to workers. This extraordinary situation has arisen partly due to financial engineering by banks, above all, the securitization of mortgages. The major banks have failed both in terms of offering financial services to workers and in terms of undertaking financial engineering in open markets.

This failure is related to the transformation of banking in recent years, which has elsewhere been associated with the financialization of contemporary capitalism (Lapavitsas 2009, 2010). In a nutshell, during the last three decades, large corporations (industrial and commercial) have become better able to obtain external finance in open markets. Enhanced ability to issue bonds and commercial paper has lessened corporate reliance on banks, forcing the latter to seek alternative fields of profitability, which have varied from country to country. Two of these have been vital to leading commercial banks: first, mediating transactions in open financial markets (and earning profits through trading) and, second, providing financial services to individuals. Both are instrumental to the current crisis and merit closer consideration in the following sections.

4.1. Banks turn to markets and lose track of risk

Mediating transactions in open financial markets is, in essence, investment banking, profits deriving from fees and commissions from handling securities but, above all, from trading generally as well as on own account. These profits differ in kind from commercial banking profits, which derive primarily from the spread between borrowing and lending rates, as well as from fees and commissions to handle money (foreign exchange, transmission, managing accounts, and so on). Investment banking has some of the character of broking, while also dealing on own account; commercial banking is financial intermediation that also provides money-dealing services. Systematically mixing the two can be profoundly destabilizing. Above all, the solvency and liquidity requirements of investment and commercial banking differ substantially. Investment banks obtain wholesale funds in open markets in order to operate in liquid securities. Commercial banks collect money-like deposits, often protected by law, to invest in both loans and securities. Given the money-like character of deposits, commercial banks must hold substantial liquid assets; they also need significant own capital to support idiosyncratic loans. Investment banks, on the other hand, do not have money-like liabilities to protect, and nor do they make longer-term customer-specific loans. But they need capital to support their borrowing in open markets.

Generalized adoption of off-balance-sheet securitization in the 1990s turned long-term, idiosyncratic debts (mortgages) into securities, thus removing them from the balance sheets of commercial banks. In effect, commercial banks handled these assets in the manner of investment banks (including on own account). The implications for balance sheets were immediate and direct: the reliance on wholesale funds was increased, asset liquidity was reduced, and solvency was weakened. Investment banks in the USA engaged in similar practices, only more extreme as they faced less regulation on capital and liquidity.

Note that the failure of mortgage-backed securitization is not inherent in the technique itself, but rather due to the private and competitive nature of the commercial and investment banks involved. The large state-sponsored organizations of the US housing market (Federal National Mortgage Association and Federal Home Loan Mortgage Corporation) used securitization for decades without comparable problems. Disaster was induced by large-scale entry of commercial and investment banks into mortgage securitization in the early 2000s. This also encouraged the state-sponsored organizations to emulate private bank behaviour, eventually causing their downfall in 2008.

At a deeper level, however, the failure of combining commercial with investment banking is due to banks forfeiting the most elementary functions of banking, namely collecting and assessing information on borrowers, and thus managing risk. Banks delegated the assessment of the creditworthiness of mortgage-backed (and other) securities to credit rating organizations that were typically in the pay of the originator. Risk management of the balance sheet, on the other hand, was entrusted to Value at Risk methods, which rely on arms-length, computationally-intensive mathematical techniques that draw on historical data (Lapavitsas and Dos Santos 2008).

By adopting investment banking functions, commercial banks weakened some of their most fundamental banking skills, including collecting information about borrowers and assessing risk by using banking experience. Thus banks could imagine that they were acting within safe parameters while erecting an enormous superstructure of derivatives on top of US housing loans. The bulk of housing loans, furthermore, were extended to workers whose real wages had been stagnant for years, while subprime loans were often advanced to workers who had no chance at all of repaying. It is a measure of the failure of private banking during the years 2001 to 2007 that it contrived to ignore these blindingly obvious sources of risk.

It is hard to exaggerate the long-term importance of these phenomena. In the 1990s and 2000s private commercial banks reacted to reduced lending opportunities to large corporations by acquiring investment banking functions. But they were unable to deliver these successfully, and in the process forfeited some of their elemental capacity to collect information and assess risk. But then, what is the economic role that private commercial banks deliver in contemporary capitalist economies, which also justifies their enormous profits? This is far from an academic question, as is shown by the collapse of securitized lending since the crisis commenced. If securitization does not recover promptly, and given the limited lending opportunities to large corporations, the long-term lending role of private commercial banks is far from clear.[8]

Note also that the failure of banks is not due to lax regulation. To be sure there has been progressive deregulation of finance during the last three decades, including Big Bang in the UK in 1986 and abolition of the Glass–Steagall Act in the USA in 1999, which formally allowed commercial and investment banking to overlap. But the presumed specialization of banks in collecting information and assessing risk is not conditional on regulation. Rather, it is supposed to be what private banks do inherently. To advocate creation of supervisory bodies in order to induce appropriate behaviour in private banks is to admit that their own inclinations are naturally different.

By the same token, the failure of banks can hardly be dealt with by tougher capital adequacy requirements. There has been much regulation of capital adequacy during the last two decades, and it is fatuous to imagine that the current crisis hinged on whether commercial banks kept 6, or 8, or 10 percent of regulatory capital. Indeed, Basel II regulations arguably exacerbated the crisis in two ways. First, they determined the capital adequacy of large banks by encouraging deployment of in-house computationally-intensive techniques of risk measurement.

Second, they gave an incentive to banks to securitize in order to shift assets off-balance-sheet and thus 'churn' regulatory capital. Such phenomena are associated with 'regulatory arbitrage' and tend to appear under any system of bank regulation. The systemic failure to collect information and assess risk is a far deeper problem, going to the core of what private banks are supposed to do in a capitalist economy.

4.2. Banks turn to individuals

The turn of banks (and the rest of the financial system) toward individual workers is associated with the financialization of personal income. It appears as rising proportions of mortgages and unsecured lending on bank balance sheets, as well as increasing individual indebtedness relative to GDP and to disposable income (Lapavitsas 2009). Furthermore, individual financial assets have also grown relative to GDP, particularly as government policy in the USA, the UK and elsewhere systematically directed savings to capital markets.

For banks, these trends represent the expansion of the field of profitability through lending, but also through mediation of the flow of savings to capital markets as well as of the flow of expenditure via bank accounts. These sources of financial profit are closely related to the retreat of public provision across a range of fields, including housing, health, education, transport, pensions, and so on, during the last three decades. Private capital has been encouraged to meet these social needs, and banks have inserted themselves in these processes, facilitating the accumulation of assets and liabilities by individuals. To a certain extent banks have become social mediators of the acquisition of a range of vital goods by workers.

Financial profit systematically generated by banks that orient themselves toward personal income raises complex theoretical issues. It has no analogue with providing financial services and loans to functioning capitalists, which are remunerated out of future profits. Rather, lending to individuals has an aspect of the old practice of 'trucking' – i.e. the employer providing wage goods at exorbitant prices in tied shops – except that 'trucking' now takes place on a social scale and indirectly. As public provision has retreated in housing, pensions, and so on, workers have had to rely on private finance, on terms favourable to banks and financial institutions.

More specifically, there are systematic disparities in information and social power between banks and individual workers. There are also systematic differences in motivation and purpose, since banks aim for monetary profit, while workers aim for the acquisition of goods.

In this context, it is possible for effectively usurious relations to emerge between banks and individuals, with exploitative aspects. Predatory lending is a part of the mediating role of banks relative to workers, particularly of the weakest layers of workers that were previously subjected to 'redlining' (Dymski 2009). These complex mechanisms that resemble 'trucking' and usury have elsewhere been called financial expropriation (Lapavitsas 2009).

The housing market bubble of 2001–7 in the USA and the subsequent crisis resulted from an escalation of financial expropriation. Financial institutions reached the poorest and most oppressed layers of workers, often black and Latino women. As their traditional skills in 'face to face' credit assessment declined, banks engaged in perfunctory information collection and risk assessment of borrowers. They relied on computationally intensive and arm's-length methods of individual credit scoring, failing to capture the underlying risks. Easy credit unleashed waves of greed among households aiming for capital gains through housing. Throughout this period real wages – the ultimate source of repayment – remained stagnant. Meanwhile, securitization multiplied the claims on the stagnant source of repayment, eventually ruining the banks.

Thus, the true extent of the systemic failure of private banking is not conveyed merely by the effective bankruptcy of large banks due to inadequate information gathering and risk management. Banks have also failed as mediators of the acquisition of vital goods by workers. The housing crisis has left millions homeless in the USA alone, while extreme personal indebtedness in the USA, the UK and elsewhere has forced a retrenchment of consumption. Rising unemployment is likely to exacerbate these phenomena through second order effects. The crisis has shown that private banking is ill suited to mediating demand for housing, pensions and several other goods that enter the wage basket. Alternative mechanisms are necessary, with a clear public character.

5.   Financialization and the Marxist theory of finance capital and imperialism

5.1.   Hilferding's analysis of banks and 'founder's profit'

The analysis of financialization in the previous section echoes the classical Marxist theory of imperialism associated with Hilferding's *Finance Capital* and Lenin's *Imperialism*. It is instructive to take a brief detour at this point examining more closely the parallels between the earlier period and contemporary financialization. This will help place the need for public banks in firmer analytical and historical context.

The obvious point of reference is Hilferding's work, the original source of the concept of finance capital, which provided the foundation for subsequent Marxist analysis of imperialism.

Hilferding's book, published in 1910, aimed to show that an epochal transformation of capitalism had taken place in the preceding decades: from competitive markets comprising generally small-scale units of productive capital, to controlled markets dominated by huge monopolies in close relations with banks. To this purpose, Hilferding paid particular attention to credit, banks, stock markets, the emergence of finance capital, and the economic policy of finance capital, i.e. imperialism.

Hilferding's (1981, pp. 83–96) analysis of banks started with a discussion of trade (or commercial) credit that is advanced spontaneously between capitalist enterprises in the form of bills of exchange. This is 'circulation credit', i.e. credit supplied in order to finance mostly enterprise needs for circulating capital. Banks intervene and centralize the flows of trade credit by replacing bills with their own credit, i.e. with banknotes which circulate as a more advanced form of credit money. Banks also collect idle money hoards generated in the circuits of industrial capital, which they turn into loanable money capital and make available to functioning capitalists through lending. This is 'capital or investment credit' that earns the rate of interest.

These analytical distinctions drew heavily on Marx's analysis of credit in *Capital*.[9] But Hilferding broke new ground by associating the supply of investment credit with the formation of fixed capital by industrial enterprises. He also observed that investment credit necessarily generates a close link between banks and enterprises since it finances fixed capital investment and its repayment takes a long time. Consequently, banks are obliged to collect information and monitor enterprise operations. This penetrating insight was advanced decades before neoclassical banking theory started to appreciate the importance of monitoring and 'commitment' relations between banks and enterprises. Unlike contemporary mainstream theory, moreover, Hilferding was alive to the implications of investment credit for the power balance between industrial and bank capital. Thus, the monitoring activities of banks allow them to control industrial capital, a development that is fundamental to the subsequent emergence of finance capital.

However, Hilferding went too far by asserting that industrial enterprises are increasingly forced to rely on investment credit because the scale of capitalist production and the need for fixed investment grow over time. For Hilferding, this led to enterprises finding themselves under the tutelage of banks, a putative tendency of mature capitalism that ultimately led to the emergence of finance capital. This part of Hilferding's argument is incorrect, as Sweezy (1942, p. 267) noted several decades ago. There is no secular tendency toward greater reliance of industrial enterprises on bank loans to finance their investment.

This constitutes a fundamental point of difference between Hilferding's analysis of finance capital and the discussion of contemporary financialization in the previous section. During the last three decades, large enterprises have tended to rely on retained profits to finance investment. Furthermore, enterprises have systematically tapped open financial markets to obtain external finance, also acquiring skills in extracting financial profits. In short, contemporary monopoly capital is not dominated by banks, while becoming financialized itself. In this connection, Hilferding drew unsound conclusions from the financial operations of German (and Austrian) corporations and banks at the end of the nineteenth century, which he mistakenly interpreted as characteristic of all advanced capitalism.

Hilferding then turned his attention to joint-stock capital and the stock market, as well as to banks as capitalist enterprises. Hilferding's discussion of joint-stock capital lays emphasis on the separation of ownership from the control of capital, and hence on the character of the shareholder as capitalist, including the differences with the classical capitalist entrepreneur. Following Marx, Hilferding (1981, pp. 108–9) treated investment in shares as akin to money lending. Funds invested in shares come from society's great pool of loanable money, given that shares can be easily sold and the shareholder could secure return of capital without much trouble.

Thus, for Hilferding, separation of ownership from control turns the shareholder into someone who advances money capital expecting to earn interest-like returns while maintaining liquidity, that is, effectively, a rentier. Always with an eye on power relations, Hilferding (1981, pp. 118–20) stressed that the main beneficiaries of the separation of ownership from control are the large shareholders, who end up controlling huge enterprises with a relatively small capital outlay.

The transformation of active capitalist into shareholder, moreover, has implications for profits and financial asset prices. Hilferding (1981, pp. 110–16) offered the first thorough Marxist analysis of share price determination as a process of discounting future profits. This is an innovative part of his book and includes the concept of 'promoter's profit' (*Gründergewinn*), better translated as 'founder's profit', which is not to be found in Marx's work.

Founder's profit arises because the expected return on shares tends to be equal to the rate of interest (plus a risk premium), given that shareholders are in a similar position to lenders of money. Marx's (1981, p. 482) claimed that the average rate of interest tends normally to be below the average rate of profit, a postulate that Hilferding accepted. The price of shares is the discounted value of the expected profits from an enterprise's productive activities (share prices being a form of fictitious capital). Meanwhile, the total amount of capital actually invested in the enterprise is also equivalent to the discounted value of the expected profits. But the rate of discount for the share prices is the rate of interest (plus risk premium) while that for the actual capital is the (higher) rate of profit. Consequently, the total value raised through a share issue (the total share price) is greater than the amount of capital actually invested in the enterprise. The difference is founder's profit.

For Hilferding, founder's profit amounts to capitalized future profit of enterprise, that is, profit that remains to the functioning capitalist after payment of interest. The issuers of shares, but also banks that are closely linked with enterprises and manage the issuing of shares, can obtain the future profit of enterprise in one fell swoop. Founder's profit is a further element contributing to the emergence of finance capital and thus the transformation of mature capitalism.

Hilferding's concept has the merit of drawing theoretical attention to the profits made by original owners whose companies are floated on the stock market, say, through Initial Public Offerings. These profits can be gigantic, as has been demonstrated repeatedly in financialized capitalism since the early 1980s. Exceptional profits might also be made by existing public enterprises that issue fresh batches of shares. Founder's profit, finally, invites attention to the profit made by banks that mediate share issuing, which frequently, but not exclusively, appears as underwriter's profit. All these types of profit are of considerable relevance to financialized capitalism, particularly in view of the turn of banks toward open markets in order to generate profits.

Nonetheless, applying Hilferding's concept to contemporary financial markets requires considerable caution. For one thing, the notion that founder's profit corresponds to future profit of enterprise – received by the share issuers as a lump sum, while the shareholders receive interest – requires further elaboration. It commonly happens, for instance, that the original owners retain substantial tranches of shares even after the enterprise has gone public. What happens to the putative profit of enterprise that corresponds to the retained shares?

Even less clear in Hilferding's account is the reason why, in a competitive capital market, banks should be able systematically to appropriate large parts of founder's profit. What would be the economic reason for buyers and sellers of shares to tolerate banks acquiring potentially enormous sums of money capital on the basis of mere differences in rates of discounting? Hilferding (1981, pp. 127–9) claimed that banks could do so because they committed money capital to share transactions while maintaining the confidence of society in the stock market. But this argument is uncharacteristically weak, particularly under contemporary conditions when the buyers of shares are typically other financial institutions, including pension funds and insurance companies. It is not immediately obvious why these buyers would provide mediating banks with founder's profit – effectively, rents – that derived simply from a process of discounting at two different rates of discount. And that is without even mentioning the profits that banks make through trading on own account as well as by mediating in derivatives markets.

What is at issue here is explaining the financial profits made through Initial Public Offerings and other shares transactions (as well as the profits of banks from trading in open financial markets) in ways that are compatible with value and profit creation in the sphere of production. These profits are evidently fundamental to contemporary financialized capitalism. The strength of Hilferding's concept of founder's profit is that it connects these to share price determination and creation of value in production. However, the analytical path that he opened is in need of urgent development if it is to account for contemporary phenomena.

5.2. Finance capital

Hilferding (1981, p. 225) then introduced the pivotal concept of finance capital, and took it as characteristic of the era of imperialism. This new form of capital emerged partly due to advancing concentration and centralization of industrial and banking capital. Large banks and industrial corporations were drawn together because corporations borrowed to finance fixed capital formation, and because banks took a leading role in floating shares in the stock market. Banks became closely involved with the running of enterprises and made large gains in the form of founder's profit, while retaining much of their own capital in liquid, money form. Consequently, banks had a significant power advantage over industrial capital – they were the senior partners in finance capital dictating its actions and behaviour.

Hilferding's concept of finance capital played a tremendously important role in the development of Marxist thought after Marx. It was widely accepted by his contemporaries, most notably by Lenin in his analysis of imperialism. In the course of the twentieth century finance capital often became synonymous with monopoly capital in Marxist literature, mostly due to Lenin's influence. Its relevance was sometimes asserted in conditions that barely resembled those of Hilferding's day – such as the post-war boom of the 1950s and 1960s – and even by writers who adopted a critical perspective on Lenin's theory of imperialism.[10]

Hilferding's concept should be treated with great caution in the analysis of financialization. The tendency toward monopolistic competition has been present throughout the twentieth century, to be sure. Since the 1970s large multinational enterprises have come to dominate the world economy. But a range of relations actually exists between contemporary industry and finance, often with national characteristics. Moreover, there is no universal long-term tendency for industrial capital to rely on bank loans to finance fixed capital formation. Thus, during the post-World-War-II period, industrial capital in the USA has not become increasingly reliant on banks, while banks and industry have not tended to amalgamate. On the other hand, during the same period in Japan, industrial capital has indeed relied heavily on bank finance. Connections between the two types of capital have been strong, but it would be wrong to think that banks have dictated terms to Japanese industry. Similarly varied observations can be made about other large capitalist countries, including Germany, France and Britain.

In short, finance capital does not adequately capture the complexity and range of relations between industrial and banking capital in the course of the twentieth century, and even less during the period of financialization. Nevertheless, the concept is still important because it focuses attention on the organic and institutional links between these two types of capital. Such links were not present when Marx wrote *Capital*, but they have been characteristic of capitalism since the end of the nineteenth century, notwithstanding the variety of forms across particular countries. Large banks today, for instance, systematically collect and assess information on enterprises (large and small), often hold company shares, and might place their personnel on company boards. The point is, however, that in financialized capitalism, banks are not necessarily the dominant partners in bank–industry relations. Even in the realm of provision of external finance to industry, they are often matched by other financial institutions, including pension funds, money trusts and insurance companies.

Finally, and as was mentioned above, large industrial enterprises have engaged in substantial financial activities on own account throughout the period of financialization. Such activities have included independent issuing of debt in open markets (commercial paper, bonds, warrants, and so on), supplying consumer and trade credit, engaging in foreign exchange markets as well as transacting in forward, futures and derivatives markets. These phenomena are vital to the financialization of capital in the modern era. In this light, the value of Hilferding's concept lies less in capturing key aspects of modern capitalism and more in pointing out the growing importance of financial transactions for all forms of capital in mature capitalism.

5.3. Imperialism

Drawing on his economic analysis, Hilferding finally proposed a theory of imperialism. His views proved a cornerstone of the classical Marxist debates on imperialism largely because of their influence on Lenin. These debates were concerned with the sudden surge of European imperial expansion during the last quarter of the 19th century, rather than with imperialism as a general historical phenomenon. By and large, classical Marxist theories avoided bland historical generalizations and related imperialism to well-defined economic processes of their era. They typically sought to account for phenomena such as the 'scramble for Africa' and the rise of militarism among European powers at the end of the 19th century. These were shockingly novel events for societies that had not known a major European war since 1815 while being pervaded by the ideological belief that capitalism meant rational progress in human affairs. Needless to say, the wars and political upheavals that have accompanied the last two decades of financialization have lent fresh relevance to the old Marxist theories.

Hilferding treated imperialism partly as policy of the capitalist class. However, the deeper strength of his theory – and its appeal for Lenin – came from its focus on the historical inevitability of imperialism, particularly for Germany in which capitalism developed late. Hilferding's analysis started with the aggressive tariff policies generally adopted in the last quarter of the 19th century. This phenomenon had been examined earlier by the brilliant Austro-Marxist Otto Bauer (2000, pp. 370–81), who related imperialism to the shift from the protective tariffs of early capitalism (seeking to shield domestic industry) to the aggressive tariffs of mature capitalism (seeking to destroy foreign industry).

For Hilferding (1981, ch. 21), monopolistic cartels advocated aggressive tariffs in order to create an exclusive territory that shored up profitability and stabilized domestic combinations of enterprises. Consequently, finance capital sought to compete by expanding its own exclusive, tariff-protected territory, rather than by merely selling commodities. But since an exclusive territory weakened other cartels' potential for commodity export, aggressive tariffs also encouraged the export of capital. The latter referred to capital invested abroad which remained under domestic control and whose profits were repatriated – in other words, a type of foreign direct investment. Hilferding evidently thought that export of capital took place toward less developed countries that offered lower wages and other advantages to corporations.

Thus, the imperialist policy of finance capital represented a major rupture with the laissez-faire policies that characterized mid-19th-century Britain. The model countries of finance capital were Germany and the USA. Given that Germany was a late developer, joint-stock capital in association with banks made possible the mobilization of the country's scattered resources. Late development also meant weaker social opposition to advanced technology. As Germany overtook Britain, its finance capital came to rely on the state, particularly on the military to sustain the creation of exclusive territories. Imperialism inevitably led to competition in armaments, constant threat of war among the imperialist countries, and racism toward the dominated.

In short, Hilferding's theory related imperialism to the epochal transformation of capitalism that was represented by finance capital. Imperialism sprang from the transformation of the mechanisms of capitalist competition and accumulation. Hilferding gave specific economic content to imperialism by relating it to phenomena that were novel at the time, including the emergence of giant cartels, giant banks, aggressive tariffs, and export of capital. His theory was able to account for key political phenomena, such as militarism and the threat of war, while insisting that the working class must oppose imperialism. It is not surprising that Hilferding's theory appealed to Lenin, who adopted much of it, while adding to it a stronger emphasis on monopoly as well as the view that imperialist countries are parasitical and contain a 'labour aristocracy'.

What remains of Hilferding's theory of imperialism in the current period of financialized capitalism? His emphasis on the centralization of capital seems valid, given the mergers and acquisitions that have been a salient feature of the world economy since the 1970s. His stress on the export of capital is also relevant, as the world economy has witnessed several enormous waves of capital export since the mid-1970s. Above all, Hilferding's focus on finance as a pivotal mechanism in the transformation of capitalism is prescient given the gigantic growth of the financial system in the course of financialization.

But there are also aspects of Hilferding's theory that are irrelevant, or highly specific to his own historical period. Thus, while contemporary imperialism seeks territorial control, there is no tendency toward aggressive tariffs or exclusive territorial rights, much less toward formal colonial empires. Similarly, despite the resurgence of militarism and successive military interventions across the world since the early 1990s, there is no arms competition among the leading capitalist countries and no prospect of war among them for the foreseeable future. The military and political dominance of the USA precludes such developments.

More significantly, Hilferding's view that finance capital represents the highest point in the evolution of private capital is simply incorrect. Related to this is his notion that British finance (what would now be called market-based or Anglo-Saxon finance) is 'backward' and stands to be replaced by German finance (bank-based or German-Japanese finance). Things have turned out differently in the course of the 20th century. For one thing, the USA currently offers a paradigmatic type of market-based finance, together with Britain. For another, market-based finance has established international ascendancy since the 1980s, partly due to political support by the leading imperialist country, the USA.

These observations point to an underlying weakness in Hilferding's overall analysis of capitalist transformation and imperialism. Hilferding sought to establish structural, 'endogenous' reasons for the emergence of finance capital, while implicitly focusing on Germany. Yet, the structure of the capitalist financial system and the connection between banking and industrial capital do not easily admit of 'endogenous' theorization, as is obvious with a century's hindsight. Relations between production and finance tend to be historically specific, and subject to institutional and political factors that shape the financial system. The USA became paradigmatic of market-based finance when it emerged as the dominant economy in the 20th century. In contrast, Japan was paradigmatic of bank-based finance in the course of catching up with more developed countries, but has partly shifted direction after it became the second largest capitalist economy.

6.   Establishing public banks – a rational and desirable step

The preceding discussion helps place the proposal for public banks in its appropriate context. It was shown earlier that the crisis represents failure of private banking and requires a systemic response, including a permanent shift away from private and individual toward public and collective interests in finance. Thus, establishment of public banks should not be merely a temporary measure to deal with the crisis but a first step in a broader policy of restructuring finance. Public banks would help redefine the relationship between finance and the rest of the economy under conditions of financialization. Put differently, public banks would make it easier to confront the immediate pressures of banking crisis as well as influencing the long-term role of banks. Establishing them could be an important step in introducing broader policies to tackle financialization and its implications.

A point to note at the outset, however, is that the proposal for public banks is not (and could not be) a blueprint for how such banks ought to work. Prescriptive proposals made by Marxist political economy are quite general in character, including that for public banks. The reason is that radical economic proposals ought to be shaped in part by the social groups that are affected by them. It is not for economists or other social scientists to devise theoretical plans for the detailed functioning of public banks. Rather, the actual shape of public banks ought to reflect the democratic expression of interest by the social groups that are involved in the issue, including bank workers, homeowners, indebted workers, small business owners, and so on. Unfortunately, the public voice of such groups is currently weak. The most that can be done at this stage, therefore, is to contribute to public debate by putting forth a general prescriptive argument in favour of public banks.

6.1. Public banks to deal with the crisis

Establishing public banks would make it easier to deal with the crisis by lifting the obstacles placed by private banks. This is apparent for liquidity, which has dried up because of the collapse of trust in banks. Public banks would immediately command trust since they would be backed by society's guarantees, resources, and money-creating powers. With trust restored, liquidity would become more easily available, including re-strengthened flows of deposits. This would lessen bank reliance on central banks, possibly lifting the need for quantitative easing, and thus limiting the extraordinary expansion of central bank balance sheets. Monetary policy would be immediately placed on a sounder footing.

Public banks would also have social authority to deal with the problem of solvency transparently and democratically. For one thing, public banks would have no reason to conceal bad debts incurred by private banks, and nor would they need to maintain the fiction that problematic assets are due to liquidity shortages. Even more strongly, there would be no need to engage in the complex interactions and evasions of 'stress tests'. Public supervisors would take charge of bank books throwing light on bad credit decisions, including irrecoverable housing loans to workers on low and stagnant incomes, speculative loans to commercial real estate, purchases of mortgage-backed securities without assessment of risk, and so on. With full revelation, it would become possible to apportion resultant losses using social and democratic criteria, including income inequality and job security. Public banks would be instrumental to society deciding which social classes would carry the burden domestically, and what would be done with foreign bondholders. Equity owners have in practice already been expropriated by the failed actions of private banks. Bondholders and other lenders could be ranked on social criteria to determine the incidence of loss. The full cost of not honouring debts incurred by private banks to foreign lenders would also become clear to society as a whole, providing the basis for collective decision making.

It is apparent, however, that these are not technical matters to be decided by experts behind closed doors. They ought to be tackled in ways that favour the many rather than the few, which makes it necessary to rely on free and organized expression of popular will. In this light, establishing public banks ought to be more than mere nationalization, and certainly not the simple replacement of failed private managers by state bureaucrats. Rather, public banks ought to be democratically run and fully accountable to society as a whole. The boards of public banks ought to have full representation of popular interests, including trades unions and civil society organizations. Their remit ought to be set socially and collectively, their decision making ought to be transparent, and their activities ought to be accountable to elected bodies.

This is not to imply that public ownership and control over banks is a simple matter that does not run risks of corruption and inefficiency. But note that the systemic failure of private banking has cast fresh light on these issues too. As for other listed corporations in recent years, bank 'governance' has been based on 'shareholder value' (Lazonick and O'Sullivan 2000). This has ultimately drawn on the efficient market hypothesis, which asserts the merits of stock markets in assessing information about corporations and the economy. Corporations have engaged in a search for short-term returns with no clear effects on efficiency (Erturk et al. 2004). For banks, meanwhile, the search for short-term returns has encouraged financial engineering in open markets that has ruined solvency and liquidity.

'Shareholder value' has also encouraged remuneration schemes for traders and managers that have fostered recklessness. Enormous bonuses have been systematically paid on the basis of short-term performance, with little concern for long-term implications. Losses have been borne primarily by equity holders, while managers have not suffered commensurately. The institutional mechanisms of ownership and control of the last three decades seem to have allowed managers (and simple functionaries) of finance to earn huge incomes, while jeopardizing the existence of banks. Private owners made significantly profits while the bubble lasted, only to be wiped put as the crisis struck.

Public ownership and control would ameliorate and – with full transparency and accountability to elected bodies – even eliminate the principal–agent problem that bedevils private banks. This is something that mere public regulation of private banks could not achieve. But further analysis of this issue requires going beyond the problem of dealing with the banking crisis to consider broader aspects of systemic bank failure.

6.2. Long-term functioning of public banks

It is clear from the above that establishing public banks ought to be more than a short-term measure, aiming to restore failed banks to health before rendering them to private ownership. It has already been suggested that long-term public banks be established to provide credit as a public utility (Erturk et al. 2009), while in the UK there is trade union support for a Post Bank. Several long-term aims of public banks ought to be considered in the light of the above.

For large enterprises in developed capitalist economies public banks are unlikely to be a decisive source of credit, given that the former have easy access to open financial markets. But for small and medium-sized enterprises, as well as for individuals, public banks would be indispensable providers of finance. Bank borrowing by small and medium-sized enterprises (including bank-mediated trade credit) is typically necessary for fixed and circulating capital. Borrowing by individuals, on the other hand, allows for smoothing of consumption profiles, even if it has expropriating aspects under present conditions. Mature capitalist economies rely on such credit for the completion of countless small capital circuits, which sustain aggregate demand. In effect, future output and personal income are anticipated by large numbers of small decision-making units, which obtain funds in advance, and proceed to organize current investment and consumption accordingly.

Since these economic units correspond to a significant part of social reproduction, it is possible that aggregate returns for banks would be stable, provided that the flow of credit remained steady and avoided speculative excesses. If, on the other hand, the flow of credit was disrupted, capital circuits and individual consumption would be disturbed, possibly leading to rising unemployment. There is reason to think of the provision of such credit as a public utility – in the sense of a universal provision requirement rather than natural monopoly – akin to transport, electricity, water, and so on.

Naturally, the analogy should not be stretched too far as credit is not a normal commodity, but rather a set of economic relations based on trust and the anticipation of future returns. The point is, however, that in contemporary capitalist societies broad layers of small enterprises but also workers have come to depend on the steady reproduction of such relations. Credit to individuals and to small enterprises already has a social aspect, as is manifested by its constant manipulation through regulations and central bank policy. Public banks could strengthen its social character by providing institutional and organizational mechanisms to regulate its flow as well as deploying elements of aggregate forecasting and planning.

The social nature of such credit is perhaps clearer in relation to worker and other households. Public banks would find a ready field of activity in advancing credit for housing, education, health, and consumption in general. Supplying such credit could be undertaken with reasonable stability, if based on reliable information about income, employment, and personal conditions. The credit scoring techniques that private banks have used so badly in recent years would find a natural home in public banks. The predatory and exploitative practices of financial expropriation would also come to an end.

Needless to say, such social credit would be an adjunct to restoring public provision across a range of wage goods, which ought to be a mainstay of public policy. In this respect, establishing public banks would be part of a general reversal of the financialization of personal income during the last three decades. Public banks would offer greater flexibility in public provision, including more choice for households in housing, education and elsewhere. Naturally, public provision of wage goods and availability of social credit would themselves be adjuncts to a policy of raising real wages.

More than that, however, public banks could also take upon themselves aspects of development banking since they would have both social authority and the requisite information about borrowers and the economy. Public banks could thus be part of a general policy to deal with financialization by supporting a revival of production and moving economies away from finance. They would be natural institutions to guide aggregate investment and promote new fields of activity, including 'green' industries in which mature capitalist economies appear to have a comparative advantage.

Provision of development credit by public banks would necessarily take place within a broad institutional framework that would direct aggregate investment toward socially selected fields. As part of this framework, public banks would be shorn of investment banking functions, thus enhancing the stability of finance. Moreover, provision of finance for development by public banks could also include large enterprises that would seek to develop productive capacity. Such a step would naturally pose the problem of coordinating the activities of public banks with those of open markets in finance. Public banks could then act as levers for the broader restructuring of finance, imposing social regulation on financial markets, including prices and trading volumes. A permanent shift in favour of social and collective as opposed to private and individual interests could be brought about in capitalist economies. This would strengthen the forces favouring a more radical transformation of capitalist society and, dare one say it, socialism.

Public banks would not, of course, be free of problems. Corruption linked to political manipulation of lending would be a danger. But it is plain ideology to assume that private automatically perform better than public banks with regard to corruption. Public interests, when fully articulated, represented and organized, can prevent corruption more successfully than the various ineffectual mechanisms of regulation that have proliferated in financialized capitalism.

Finally, there is the issue of the technical capacity of state and society to run banks. On this it is enough to observe that the growth of finance in recent years has produced hundreds of thousands of finance specialists many of whom are currently unemployed or live in extreme uncertainty. There is no shortage of technical expertise that could be hired by public banks. What is lacking is political will but also pressure from below demanding radical transformation. As the systemic failure of private banking becomes clearer in the years to come, that could well change.

7. Summary and conclusions

The crisis of 2007–9 is an event with major repercussions for the financial system as well as for production and income. It was shown in this paper that the crisis represents a systemic failure of private banking in respect of liquidity shortage, credit decisions and capital adequacy. More fundamentally, the crisis represents a systemic failure of private banking to collect information about borrowers and to assess risk. The latter are supposed to be defining functions of banking, but contemporary banks have failed to deliver them. Finally, private banking has proven problematic in mediating the acquisition of consumer goods by working people, including housing.

In broader terms the crisis is the result of the transformation of mature capitalist economies, analysed here in terms of financialization. This is structural change that includes less reliance of corporations on bank lending, a corresponding turn of banks toward investment banking and lending to individuals, and increasing reliance of workers on the financial system for consumption and provision for old age. The systemic failure of private banking has occurred within this framework.

The theoretical framework necessary to analyse the crisis poses corresponding difficulties. Keynesian economics has relied primarily on the work of Minsky, which has offered insights regarding the systemic nature of the crisis, but has not allowed for equally systemic conclusions regarding policy. The typical response has been to call for stronger and broader regulation. In contrast, this paper drew on Marxist political economy and thus stressed the importance of the private nature of banks in causing and prolonging the crisis. More generally, the focus of Marxist economics on property – and therefore class – relations is important when considering the relationship between finance and the economy. Marxist analysis of finance could have a fruitful interaction with Keynesian economics as the 21st century unfolds.

In this light, it was argued that the establishment of public banks would be an appropriate response to the crisis. Public banks could confront the crisis, particularly liquidity and solvency, more easily and with fewer costs for society than private banks. But public banks could also be a longer-term response to the systemic failure of private banking. They could provide long-term credit with some aspects of public utility to both households and small and medium-sized enterprises. Such credit would sustain employment and output in the medium term. Public banks could also provide long-term credit to large corporations encouraging a shift of mature economies away from financialization and towards more socially desirable directions.

Notes

1. It is, of course, impossible to tell exactly which banks were effectively bankrupt, opacity being part of the systemic failure of private banking. But all US investment banks have ceased to exist in an independent form since late 2008. Moreover, it is probable that Citibank and Bank of America in the USA,

Royal Bank of Scotland and Lloyds/HBOS in the UK, and UBS in Switzerland would have succumbed to the turmoil had it not been for overt and covert government support.
2. Throughout the rest of this paper 'bank' refers to commercial banks. When necessary, investment banks are specified.
3. Needless to say, lumping households and enterprises together as borrowing 'units' is problematic since it obfuscates qualitative differences in behaviour.
4. The inflationary implications of this expansion, and of the tacit abandonment of inflation targeting, remain to be seen.
5. Providing relevant data for this article is very much a case of hitting a moving target, particularly as important policy decisions have changed frequently. May–June 2009 is an arbitrary cut-off point, but does not affect the gist of the analysis.
6. Other technical ways of ring-fencing bad assets are also available from the long experience of bank failures during the last three decades (Caprio and Klingebiel 1996).
7. For further, if brief, analysis of the plan see the Appendix at the end of the paper.
8. For mainstream economics, incidentally, the systemic failure of banks to collect information and manage risk thoroughly undermines the 'new economics of finance', that is, the dominant theoretical analysis of banking during the last three decades. This approach justifies the existence of banks in terms of skills in information collection and risk management (Freixas and Rochet 1997). If this is why banks are supposed to exist, modern private banks are redundant.
9. See Marx (1976, ch. 3, and 1981, sec. V).
10. For instance, Barratt-Brown (1970).

References

Ash, M., Balakrishnan R., Campbell A., Crotty J., Dickens E., Epstein G., Ferguson T., Ghilarducci T., Greisgraber J.M., Griffith-Jones S., Guttman R., Jayadev A., Kapadia A., Kotz D., Meerepol M., Milberg W., Moseley F., Ocampo J.A., Pollin R., Sawyer M. and M. Wolfson. 2009. 'A progressive program for economic recovery and financial reconstruction', http://www.peri.umass.edu/fileadmin/pdf/other_publication_types/PERI_SCEPAstatementJan27.pdf.
Barratt-Brown, M. (1970), *After Imperialism*, 2nd edn, New York: Humanities Press.
Bauer, O. (2000), *The Question of Nationalities and Social Democracy*, Minneapolis and London: University of Minnesota Press.
Bebchuk, L. (2009), 'How to make TARP II work', Discussion Paper No 626, Cambridge, Mass.: Harvard Law School.
Brunnermeier, M. (2009), 'Deciphering the liquidity and credit crunch 2007–2008', *Journal of Economic Perspectives*, 23(1), pp. 77–100.
Brunnermeier, M. and Pedersen, L.H. (2008), 'Market liquidity and funding liquidity', *Review of Financial Studies*, advance publication, doi:10.1093/rfs/hhno98.
Brunnermeier, M., Crockett, A., Goodhart, C., Persaud, A., and Shin, H. (2009), *The Fundamental Principles of Financial Regulation*, Geneva Reports on the World

Economy 11, Preliminary Conference Draft, International Center for Monetary and Banking Studies.

Buiter, W. (2009), 'The "good bank" solution', Maverecon, http://blogs.ft.com/maverecon/2009/01/the-good-bank-solution/.

Bulow, J. and Klemperer, P. (2009), 'Reorganising the banks: Focus on the liabilities, not the assets', VOX, http://www.voxeu.org/index.php?q=node/3320.

Caprio, G. and Klingebiel, D. (1996), 'Bank Insolvencies: Cross-country Experience', Policy Research Working Paper 1620, Washington, DC: World Bank.

Crotty, J. (2008), 'Structural Causes of the Global Financial Crisis: A Critical Assessment of the "New Financial Architecture"', Political Economy Research Institute, Working Paper 180.

Crotty, J. (2009), 'Profound structural flaws in the US financial system that helped cause the financial crisis', *Economic and Political Weekly*, 44(13), pp. 127–35.

Crotty, J. and Epstein, G. (2008), 'Proposals for Effectively Regulating the US Financial System to Avoid yet Another Meltdown', Political Economy Research Institute, Working Paper 181.

Crotty J. and Epstein, G. (2009), 'Regulating the US financial system to avoid another meltdown', *Economic and Political Weekly*, 44(13), pp. 87–93.

D'Arista, J. and Griffith-Jones, S. (2008), 'Agenda and Criteria for Financial Regulatory Reform', FONDAD, http://www.fondad.org/uploaded/Arista-Griffith-JonesonFinancialRegulatoryReform.pdf.

Dewatripont, M., Freixas, X. and Portes, R. (2009), *Macroeconomic Stability: Key Issues for the G20*, London: CEPR.

Dos Santos, P. 2009. 'On the content of banking in contemporary capitalism', *Historical Materialism*, 17(2), pp. 180–213.

Dymski, G. (2009), 'Racial exclusion and the political economy of the sub-prime crisis', *Historical Materialism*, 17(2), 149–79.

Erturk, I., Froud, J., Johal, S. and Williams, K. (2004), 'Corporate governance and disappointment', *Review of International Political Economy*, 11(4), pp. 677–713.

Erturk, I., Froud, J., Johal, S., Leaver, A and Williams, K. (2009), Memorandum to the House of Commons – Treasury, http://209.85.229.132/search?q=cache:eN9HSiTRwusJ:www.publications.parliament.uk/.

Federal Reserve Bank (2009a), 'The Supervisory Capital Assessment Program: Design and Implementation', April 24, http://www.federalreserve.gov/newsevents/press/bcreg/bcreg20090424a1.pdf.

Federal Reserve Bank (2009b), 'The Supervisory Capital Assessment Program: Overview of Results', May 7, http://www.federalreserve.gov/newsevents/press/bcreg/bcreg20090507a1.pdf.

Freixas, J. and Rochet, J.C. (1997), *Microeconomics of Banking*, Cambridge, Mass.: MIT Press.

Goodhart, C.A.E. (2008), 'The background to the 2007 financial crisis', *International Economics and Economic Policy*, 4, 331–46.

Hilferding, Rudolf (1981 [1910]), *Finance Capital*, London: Routledge & Kegan Paul.

Kregel, J. (2008), 'Using Minsky's cushion of safety to analyze the crisis in the US subprime mortgage market', *International Journal of Political Economy*, 37(1) (Spring), 3–23.

Kregel, J. (2009a), 'It's that "vision" thing', Public Policy Brief 100, Annandale-on-Hudson, NY: The Levy Economics Institute of Bard College.

Kregel, J. (2009b), 'Background considerations to a regulation of the US financial system: third time a charm? Or strike three?', Working Paper 557, Annandale-on-Hudson, NY: The Levy Economics Institute of Bard College.

Lapavitsas, C. (2009), 'Financialized capitalism: crisis and financial expropriation', *Historical Materialism*, 17(2), pp. 114–48.

Lapavitsas, C. (2010), 'Financialization, or the search for profits in the sphere of circulation', *Economiaz*, forthcoming.

Lapavitsas, C and Dos Santos, P.L. (2008), 'Globalization and contemporary banking: On the impact of new technology', *Contributions to Political Economy*, 27, pp. 31–56.

Lazonick, W. and O'Sullivan, M. (2000), 'Maximizing shareholder value: a new ideology for corporate governance', *Economy and Society*, 29(1), 13–35.

Lenin, V. (1964), *Imperialism, the Highest Stage of Capitalism*, vol. 22, *Collected Works*, Moscow: Progress.

Marx, K. (1976), *Capital*, vol. I, London: Penguin/NLR.

Marx, K. (1981), *Capital*, vol. III, London: Penguin/NLR.

Minsky, H. (1986), *Stabilizing an Unstable Economy*, New Haven: Yale University Press.

Minsky, H. (1992), 'The Financial Instability Hypothesis', Working Paper 74, Annandale-on-Hudson, NY: The Levy Economics Institute of Bard College.

Minsky, H. (1996), 'Uncertainty and the Institutional Structure of Capitalist Economies'. Working Paper 155, The Levy Economics Institute of Bard College.

Minsky, H. and Whalen, C. (1996), 'Economic Insecurity and the Institutional Prerequisites for Successful Capitalism', Working Paper 165, The Levy Economics Institute of Bard College.

Nesvetailova, A. (2008), 'The End of a Great Illusion: Credit Crunch and Liquidity Meltdown', Danish Institute for International Studies Working Paper 2008/23.

Persaud, A. (2002), 'Liquidity Black Holes', WIDER Discussion Paper No 2002/31, http://62.237.131.23/publications/dps/dps2002/dps2002–31.pdf.

Pollin, R. (2009), 'Tools for a new economy', *Boston Review*, January/February, http://bostonreview.net/BR34.1/pollinphp.

Posen, A. (2009), 'A proven framework to end the US banking crisis including some temporary nationalizations', Testimony Before the Joint Committee of the US Congress Hearing on "Restoring the Economy: Strategies for Short-term and Long-term Change"', February 26, http://www.iie.com/publications/papers/posen0209.pdf.

Stiglitz, J. (2009), 'A Bank Bailout That Works', *The Nation*, March 4, http://www.thenation.com/doc/20090323/stiglitz/print?rel=nofollow.

Sweezy, P. (1942), *The Theory of Capitalist Development*, New York and London: Monthly Review.

Whalen, C. (2007), 'The US Credit Crunch of 2007: A Minsky Moment', Public Policy Brief 92, The Levy Economics Institute of Bard College.

Wray, L.R. (2007), 'Lessons from the Subprime Meltdown', Working Paper 522, Annandale-on-Hudson, NY: The Levy Economics Institute of Bard College.

Wray, L.R. (2008), 'Financial Markets Meltdown: What Can We Learn from Minsky?', Public Policy Brief 94, Annandale-on-Hudson, NY: The Levy Economics Institute of Bard College.

Wray, L.R. (2009), 'The Return of Big Government', Public Policy Brief 99, Annandale-on-Hudson, NY: The Levy Economics Institute of Bard College.

Appendix

Aspects of the Geithner plan

The plan invites public–private coalitions to bid at auction for the bad assets of banks. Bids are to be funded at 1/7 equity (half by private capital, half by the state) and 6/7 debt guaranteed by FDIC, i.e. effectively public debt. The coalitions will have responsibility for managing and collecting on the assets.

Assume that the nominal value of the assets is Z, the price paid at auction is X and the value eventually collected is Y. The profit function for private capital (ignoring interest paid on borrowings) is:

$$\Pi = 1/2(Y-X) - 1/14X \tag{1}$$

Hence,

$$E(\Pi) = 1/2E(Y) - 8/14X \tag{2}$$

Thus,

$$\max E(\Pi) = 1/2E(Y) \tag{3}$$

Breakeven is at:

$$E(\Pi) = 0, \text{ hence } X_{br} = 7/8E(Y) \tag{4}$$

Finally, maximum price is at:

$$X_{max} = 7/8Z \tag{5}$$

The price paid will depend on E(Y). Since prices are determined at auction, it is likely that there will be several views on E(Y). Take bidders who believe that Y is distributed normally over 0 and Z, with mean $E(Y)_1$. In $(E(\Pi),X)$ space the expected profit function will be a straight line running from maximum profit, $1/2E(Y)_1$, on the $E(\Pi)$ axis, to breakeven, $7/8E(Y)_1$, on the X axis, and stopping at the vertical on X_{max}. Bidders are in-the-money to the left of $7/8E(Y)_1$, while out-of-the-money to the right and until X_{max}. The ratio of the former to the latter area is a measure of the potential profitability of the scheme.

Now take bidders who believe that the distribution of Y is skewed to the right, hence $E(Y)_2 > E(Y)_1$ and thus $X_{br2} > X_{br1}$. It follows trivially that the expected profit function is shifted in parallel and to the right. Hence the ratio of the in-the-money to the out-of the-money areas rises.

Thus the scheme favours bidders who believe that problematic assets have a high expected value, i.e. they are not truly bad. This is consistent with the underlying assumption that the problem is really one of liquidity, not of bad credit decisions by banks. Optimistic bidders are likely to drive prices up at auction, ultimately pushing X toward X_{max}. Consequently, the scheme benefits the banks, while shifting most of the risk onto the public which has provided the bulk of the funding.

6
Endogenous Money in 21st Century Keynesian Economics*

Terry Barker
Cambridge Trust for New Thinking in Economics

The use of money, like other human institutions, grew or evolved.
'The mystery of money', Allyn Abbott Young
(1924; revised 1929), p. 265[1]

Abstract

This chapter provides a theoretical treatment of money and its role in 21st century Keynesian economics and in the 21st century economy, e.g. with some reference to the credit crisis of 2007 onwards. To start, the treatment of money in 20th century Keynesian economics is reviewed, including that provided by Keynes. Then the current theory of endogenous money is briefly summarised as it developed towards the end of the century and into the current century. The chapter continues by elaborating the extensions to the consensus Post Keynesian theory in the literature. Money is defined in terms of seven characteristics: 1. trust, 2. divisibility, 3. "invariance" in value over space and time, 4. limitation in supply, 5. acceptance as a unit of account, 6. convenience and 7. attractiveness. The chapter goes on to elucidate the concept of economic invariance. The role of money in spatial and temporal economics is briefly addressed, so that the

*Thanks to the editors Philip Arestis and Malcolm Sawyer for extensive and helpful discussions on theory and to contributors to the 2009 Bilbao conference of Post Keynesian Economics, as well as Martin Sewell, David Taylor, Serban Scrieciu and Paul Ekins for comments and Martin Sewell and Mairéad Curran for editorial assistance. Thanks are also due to The Three Guineas Trust, one of the Sainsbury Family Trusts, and to Cambridge Econometrics Ltd, for the financial and other support to the University of Cambridge allowing the research underlying this chapter to go ahead.

202

essential symmetry between exchange rates (exchange rates for different moneys at a point in time) and interest rates (costs of or return to holding one money over time) is highlighted. There is a brief discussion of the role of money in the current crisis. The chapter concludes with a discussion of one more attribute of money: money as magic.

JEL Classification Code: E40

Keywords: Money, endogenous money, Keynesian, Post Keynesian, 21st c. economics

1. Introduction[2]

Money is a resource at the heart of the economic system. It is the blood of the system, diffusing ever more thinly throughout the body politic, bringing energy and supporting economic life. Money reaches extremities such as the hidden and criminal economies that few other resources can touch. Interestingly, money is also like blood in that there is a mystery about it, and something strangely indecent: talk of money is exciting and often replete with plans and dreams of getting it and spending it. Finally, it appears that humans have *evolved* such that their primary proximate goal is social and sexual activity; and that wealth, among other attributes, may be considered by many as a proxy for the value of human family, friendship, and mating; so it becomes clear that humans are or might be strongly motivated to accumulate money. Money is therefore a human tool, like the energy system or an emission trading scheme, to be used to make more money and satisfy human desires for society and sex by hopefully accumulating wealth.

The discovery of money is one of the great achievements of human society, comparable to the discovery of fire. The use of some form of money – closer to a commonly accepted product used in barter than to a credit card in a modern economy – appears to have been present in human societies for a very long time. Modern money was invented as coin and paper notes in ancient Chinese civilization and its use has become pervasive in economies throughout the world, with global currencies such as the dollar, the euro and the yen being almost universally recognized.[3]

'Money' is given many meanings in economic literature and discourse, ranging from its identification with notes and coin in circulation, to its definition as a set of monetary assets with particular characteristics, and to wealth in general as when we say 'she has money'. At its most general, money is, in Simmel's words, 'the symbol of the spirit, forms and thought of modern civilization' (quoted by Frankel, 1987). Money is a resource created by human society. It is a social construct, being used and accorded value by human society. One social group, namely the banking community, has as its main function the creation and management of money in the economy.

This chapter provides a theoretical treatment of money and its role in *21st-century Keynesian economics* and in the *21st-century economy*, e.g. with some reference to the credit crisis of 2007 onwards. The objective is to explain what money is, why money as a concept is so elusive, why it is difficult to measure at the best of times and impossible to measure in a financial crisis, how the concept has evolved and matured in Post Keynesian analysis, and what are the implications of the new theory of money, expounded here, for understanding and resolving the global economic crisis. The new theory is placed in the context of Keynesian economics and, more widely, the classical, neoclassical and so-called heterodox traditions of economics.

Section 2 contains a review of the treatment of money in 20th-century Keynesian economics, including the approach taken by Keynes. Then in section 3 the current theory of endogenous money is briefly summarised as it developed towards the end of the century and into the current century. Section 4 elaborates the extensions proposed to the "consensus" Post Keynesian theory in the literature as synthesised by Fontana (2009). In the chapter that follows, money is defined initially in terms of seven characteristics: 1. trust, 2. divisibility, 3. "invariance" in value over space and time, 4. limitation in supply, 5. acceptance as a unit of account, 6. convenience and 7. attractiveness. The chapter goes on in section 5 to elucidate the concept of economic invariance. The role of money in spatial and temporal economics is briefly addressed, so that the essential symmetry between exchange rates (exchange rates for different moneys at a point in time) and interest rates (costs of or return to holding one money over time) is highlighted. Section 6 is a brief discussion of the role of money and monetary policy in the current crisis. Finally in section 7, the chapter concludes with a discussion of one more characteristic of money: 8. money as magic.

2. 20th-century neoclassical, monetarist and Keynes's treatment of money

Money in general equilibrium theory (*neoclassical*) is treated as a means of exchange, essentially, although not properly, as a means of making the indivisible divisible. As the New School discussion puts it 'Walras's story [about the role of money] is full of holes'[4] and ever since Walras's work was recognised, neoclassical writers have been trying to sort out the inconsistencies and contradictions. Walras himself thought that money was a kind of capital needed for future payments (it is an asset after all, but so is human education, a forest ecosystem and expert-system software) whose services entered the consumers' utility function. If so, money can be treated with the same mathematical apparatus as all other products – that is, there is a marginal utility of monetary services. The problem with this treatment (as stressed by Patinkin, 1956) is that money is also *required* for transactions. How is money to be treated both as an asset with desired services and as a requirement for exchange? An even greater problem with the Walrasian treatment is that if money is needed solely in order to make future payments, and the agents holding it have perfect foresight, why do they need to hold it at all, because as an alternative they could hold an interest-bearing asset? Hahn writes: 'The most serious challenge that the existence of money poses is this: the best developed model of the economy cannot find room for it. The best developed model is, of course, the Arrow–Debreu version of Walrasian general equilibrium' (1983, p. 1). The Post Keynesian critique (Arestis, 2009) is that the equilibrium models used by the central banks (following the New Keynesian tradition) do not have, surprisingly, the banking sector in them, and so are intrinsically incapable of modelling any banking crisis, despite the fact that there are many such past crises for empirical modelling (Reinhart and Rogoff, 2008).

The *monetarist* school does not normally distinguish the characteristics of money and the monetary assets that embody these characteristics. Friedman (1987) states that money has three properties: a means of exchange, a store of value, and a unit of account. In monetarism, put simply, in the long run the growth of the money supply determines inflation, so that if the money supply is exogenous and if it can be controlled, the rate of inflation can be managed by controlling the money supply. Friedman has since partially repudiated his reworking of the classical and neoclassical quantity theory of money (2003).

Keynes (1921, 1937) paid great attention to the role of money, and developed a theory of the speculative demand for money. Weatherson[5] (2002, pp. 47–62) contains a summary of Keynes' views on money:

> Keynes distinguishes four motives for holding money (General Theory (GT) [Keynes (1936)]: Ch. 13; Keynes 1937: 215–23). Two of these, the transactions motive and the finance motive, need not detain us. They just relate to the need to make payments in money and on time. The third, the speculative motive, is often linked to uncertainty, and

indeed Keynes does so (GT: 201). But 'uncertainty' here is just used to mean absence of certainty, that is the existence of risk, which as noted above is not how I am using 'uncertainty'. As Runde (1994) points out, an agent who is certain as to future movements in interest rates may still hold money for speculative reasons, as long as other agents who are not so certain have made mistaken judgements. The fourth motive will hold most of my attention. Keynes argues that we may hold money for purely precautionary reasons.

Importantly, Keynes accepted *equilibrium* as an organising concept (Johnson et al., 2004) and largely, as many of his predecessors and successors, treated the macro economy in terms of *aggregated* variables such as land, labour and capital, e.g. the concept of the 'marginal efficiency of capital' (Johnson et al., 2004, p. 224). His theory also implied the endogeneity of money, despite him also arguing that money can be treated as exogenous (Foster, 1986).

However, all these authors and schools accept equilibrium as an organising concept in economics. A more productive line of reasoning regards equilibrium as a misleading if not worthless concept in economics (and empirically unverifiable).[6]

3.   Endogenous money in 21st-century Keynesian economics

3.1.   21st century Keynesian and Post Keynesian economics

Keynesian economics also generally accepts equilibrium as a useful concept, but Post Keynesians (e.g. Philip Arestis, Cardim de Carvalho, Paul Davidson, Sheila Dow, Giuseppe Fontana, Nicholas Kaldor, Hyman Minsky and Malcolm Sawyer) do not. Critical realists (e.g. Tony Lawson), who refer to post-Keynesian economics, appear to be more philosophers than economists, and some realists discount the usefulness of econometrics, or dispute whether average representations of economic behaviour can be included usefully in models, or whether economic events, such as the outcome of the 2007–2009 crisis, can be predicted. Some Post Keynesians (see Cardim de Carvalho, 2009) have recognized the problem of aggregation that can be resolved by distinguishing the many forms, which monetary assets take, from the characteristics of money (see below), where the common feature of monetary assets is that their nominal price is fixed. However, all Post Keynesians stress the importance of uncertainty and expectations in understanding economic behaviour.

3.2. The Post Keynesian Horizontalist-Structuralist theory of endogenous money

Moore (1978, 1879, 1981), Kaldor (1981), S. Weintraub (1982), Arestis (1987, 1988), Arestis and Biefang-Frisancho Mariscal (1995) and Sawyer (2009a) explain why money is endogenous. Fontana (2009, chapter 8) presents the main sides of the debate between those who favour the Horizontalist and those that favour the Structuralist analysis of endogenous money (see Lavoie, 2006, and Dow, 2006, for the Horizontalist and Structuralist analyses respectively). Money is endogenous because its demand is derived from the desire of holders of money in all its forms for liquidity. Banks provide liquidity in exchange for returns from bank lending for financial or real investment, or speculation (if they are acting as "casino banks"), so the desire for loans then leads to the banks supplying loans. The loans thereby create money as a property of the banking system. And the degree to which the money created remains in existence depends on the willingness of social groups to hold money (the 'demand for money') and the reserve requirements of the regulator (a 'supply-side' restriction).[7] In other words, the creation of money by the banking system is a systemic property in that social groups taking out bank loans then deposit the money in banks, so that the banks can lend it out again, all subject to reserve requirements. In short, the supply of money becomes derived from the demand, and money is endogenous.

Fontana reconciles the Horizontalist and Structuralist analyses through the use of a diagram showing the interconnectedness of interest rates, bank loans, bank deposits and bank reserves and by making a distinction between a single-period and a continuous or series of sequential, dynamic adjustments, relying on Hicks' development of monetary theory (Fontana, 2009, chapter 6).

The assumptions underlying the theory set out by Fontana (op. cit.) are: 1. we know what "money" or "liquidity" is, although whether this means "perfect money" (as defined below), or a monetary aggregate, is unclear; 2. we can reasonably restrict the analysis to a producer–consumer–banks economy in multiple time periods, in the context of general uncertainty and inability to convert all risks to certainty equivalents; 3. non-ergodicity, "history has effects"; and 4. institutions matter and can change. And the key results are: 1. the formation of expectations is critical to the system; 2. money is normally demand-led via creation of bank liabilities; 3. banks create money subject to central banks' reserve requirements and interest-rate policies (in normal times, namely away from the "zero-bound") as expounded by Robinson (1943); 4. portfolio choices by wage earners, commercial banks and central banks are critical and inconsistencies can lead to collapse of the financial system 5. monetary and fiscal policies should be inter-related and flexible to accommodate "events".

3.3. Structuralist theory of endogenous money: a critique aimed towards an extension

The Structuralist theory represents the more complex and more realistic view of the role of money, so a critique starts with the realism of the assumptions required in the theory. Taking these one by one as listed above.

1 Structuralists know what money is. However, Barker (1996, p. 95) argues, in contrast to the structuralists (Sawyer, 2003) that we do *not* know what money is, collectively, since it is subjective and any aggregation depends on a definition that, in turn, is specific to a specific currency-region and period-of-time where and when expectations are stable, i.e. in well-behaving economies in normal times.
2 The analysis should include at least the aggregate social groups of national economies, governments, investment banks, and non-bank financial companies dealing in assets, so as to be able to explain financial crises and the Big Crunch of September 15, 2008, and their consequences.
3 If history has effects, then the treatment of endogenous money should be seen in the context of the *irreversible and asymmetric* history of money creation and destruction, e.g. the Big Crunch is a catastrophic non-linear event.
4 And if institutions matter and can change, then monetary theory can be developed to explain monetary evolutions via institutional change and destruction.

3.4. Extensions to the theory of endogenous money

The critique above suggests some extensions to the theory. First, the treatment of monetary assets as forms of money with money having many characteristics is critical to an understanding of the nature of money (Barker, 1996, elaborated below). Second, there is space-time symmetry in the price of money (exchange rates and interest rates). Third, it is worth embedding the monetary institutions such as banks (central, investment or wholesale, and retail) in the wider economic system. Fourth, it is also worth distinguishing well-behaving economies from ill-behaving ones. This distinction is critical in understanding the behaviour of the world economy since the collapse of the world money supply became apparent in September 2008. And fifth, expectations themselves can be asymmetrical, leading to Keynesian liquidity traps and the current global crisis emerging with the collapse of various banks starting in 2007. These five extensions are set out in the following sections of the chapter.

4. Properties of money

For the purpose of the analysis that follows, money will be defined precisely as a 'resource with a set of characteristics that are embodied in different combinations in monetary assets'; examples of such assets are notes and coin, bank deposits, credit and debit cards, bank loans and various government-backed, short-term bills of exchange. The important distinction between the characteristics of money or its 'essence' on the one hand, and the forms of money or monetary assets on the other, was clearly set out by Simmel in 1900 (1978 translation, pp. 119–20), who also emphasized the innumerable errors that arise if this basic distinction is not made.[8] For Young (1929, Mehrling and Sandilands, 1999, p. 266) the crucial characteristic of money is its exchangeability, whilst money itself can take many forms. He counts ten forms of money (Mehrling and Sandilands, 1999, p. xviii), and what (he argues) they have in common is that they 'are all elastically "interchangeable" with the standard money, gold.'

Key concepts in 21st century Keynesian economics are 'banks' and 'liquidity preference'. Banks are social groups whose primary function is to create and manage forms of money, such as notes and coin, debit and credit cards, and (until the crisis of 2007 onwards) collateralized debt obligations (CDOs). Liquidity preference is the demand for money (effective or not) by social groups such as governments, banks, companies and households. Banks and liquidity preference are discussed later in the chapter. Good banks in well-behaving economies do not need to be modelled because they are by definition trusted, so that the role of banks and money becomes hidden and it is not necessary to model them whilst bad banks in ill-behaving economies, e.g. the investment banks from 2007 onwards, are not trusted and their demise or any collapse in the money supply must be modelled to understand the dynamics of the system.

The characteristics that form the set that describe 'perfect money' include the following seven distinct items:[9]

1. Complete trustworthiness

If money is to be accepted as a means of exchange, then those who are to receive it will be willing to do so only to the extent that they trust that it will have effective value in future exchange.

2. Perfect divisibility

Money has to be divisible in order to allow exchange with integral goods and services of any value. Perfect money has the characteristic of complete non-integrality.[10]

3. Complete invariance over space and time

Money is most useful if its value remains constant over space and time. This can be seen as an aspect of the trustworthiness of money.

4. Complete limitation of supply

A freely available asset is no use as money. Only those assets that are scarce by nature (e.g. gold or silver) or by design (e.g. government-printed notes) can be used as money, unless social conventions or taboos are sufficiently strong. If supply is not limited and managed by a public (e.g. nationalized central bank) or a private regulator, then the value of money (in terms of its purchasing power) will not be completely invariant over space and time.

5. Complete acceptance as a unit of account or numeraire

Money is used in pricing as a measure of value, and in accounting as a unit of account.

6 Perfect convenience as a means of exchange

Since it is to be used in both everyday transactions and multimillion dollar deals, money has to be available in a convenient form, facilitating those transactions of very low value as well as those of very high value. This is a practical aspect of the divisibility property of money.

7. Attractiveness as a physical object, or as an immaterial form of money, e.g. credit cards

Since money is used by everyone in an economy, perfect money is also physically alluring and attractive.

It may be difficult to find some way in which all these characteristics are combined. Some of these characteristics are mutually exclusive, for example, a perfectly divisible and attractive asset such as mercury is no use as perfect money because it is inconvenient to carry about or to divide, apart from being poisonous. And some characteristics imply others, for example, invariance if experienced for long enough yields trustworthiness. And some are much more important than others, with divisibility, invariance and convenience being key properties. Simmel

(1978, p. 137) has an amusing 'recorded fact' concerning Russian silver coins of several centuries ago of such minute size that they could not be picked up by hand. Following an exchange, the purchaser had to tip the coins out of the purse on to a surface, and divide them, and both the purchaser and the seller had to pick up their own coins with their tongues and spit them into their respective purses. Convenience and hygiene were sacrificed for exchange and divisibility.

Although we think of money in physical terms – gold, silver, notes and coins – it is the services that monetary assets offer that are important, rather than their physical form. Most of these services are yielded when money is exchanged, but one of these services (money as a unit of account) is a general service yielded through time, allowing the valuation of all goods and all other services in an economy. The services are attached to certain assets, usually financial (pieces of paper and certificates, promises to pay or contracts), i.e. monetary assets.

There is no single asset that embodies all the characteristics of money. Various monetary assets, such as US dollar bills, come close, but with the following qualifications. They are not limited in supply, being under the control of the US Treasury; they are not convenient for very high value transactions, because one would need suitcases full of notes; they are not *perfectly* divisible, but are practically divided into quarters, nickels, dimes and cents; and they are not invariant over time, since the average price of the basket of goods and services bought by the dollar-bill user is liable to rise – a feature also known as price inflation.

Monetary assets, whether created by central banks or created by banks, are subject to regulation by the central bank (or similar) with the central bank acting as lender of last resort. Such assets are in fact the principal means of exchange throughout the world today. Governments and central banks create and regulate money on behalf of their citizens and have done so for hundreds of years. Often, several different monies (e.g. gold and silver, dollars and roubles) may be in circulation at the same time (e.g. when their citizens opt to use another country's money), but governments and central banks are usually in the position to manage only one of these monies. Since there is no perfect money, it is impossible to give an unambiguous and precise definition to key concepts in the management of money. For example, changes in the 'money supply' have to be defined in terms of changes in the total of a set of monetary assets. If notes and coins are added to bank deposits, different combinations of monetary characteristics are added together, rather like adding apples to oranges in the definition of the 'fruit supply'. In obtaining an index of the value, supply or price of fruit, each type of fruit is weighted together using some conventional procedure. Only in the case of measuring the total value of fruit at a particular time, would the values of the different fruits be simply summed. In order to compare the stock of fruit at two different times, it is usual to distinguish quantity and price (unit-value) changes. Similarly with the money supply: if the change in the stock of money is interesting, then some procedure allowing for the different unit-values of the different kinds of money is useful.

The rest of this section is concerned with a more detailed discussion of seven properties of money, starting with trust and continuing with the role of money as a means of making the indivisible divisible. It goes on to elucidate the concept of economic invariance (with its opposite, economic variance) an essential and measurable characteristic of perfect money as well as being a measurable characteristic of other resources.

4.1.   Trustworthiness as a property of money

The importance of money and the trust in the quality of goods and services that money can buy, and the reputations of the bankers who create money and of other market players, leads on to the concept of trust. Trust, by definition, cannot be bought and sold. Rather, trust is a central feature of social relations, a moral resource. Trust is similar to, but not the same as, compassion, love, altruism, and care for others. Trust can no more be bought and sold than compassion can be bought and sold. It is quite obvious that the purchase of compassion is meaningless, because compassion is, by definition, expressed without the expectation of reward; trust is in the same category.

Trust is closely related to reputation. Trustfulness is an inherent characteristic of people; it is instinctively assessed when people meet and is revealed by experience; it represents consistency in behaviour and has the connotation of integrity in behaviour. Some individuals may be very charming, but also very untrustworthy, or some firms may seem to offer a very good bargain in the goods and services they sell but be untrustworthy in that they are liable to sell goods and services with negative characteristics that only emerge when the goods are in use.

This suggests that the treatment of trust as a commodity, whatever that means, is one of what Boulding calls 'errors of taxonomy'. Clearly, trust is not a characteristic of goods and services but an inalienable characteristic of people and social groups, although there is a sense in which the quality of replicated goods corresponds to the trust in the group, usually the company that produces these replicated goods is fully aware of this fact.

Goodwill, however, *is* sold when, for example, companies go bankrupt: their reputation is assessed, a value is put on it, and then it can be put on the market and sold; many companies go bankrupt without any goodwill whatsoever. Normally goodwill is exchanged in private deals before the bankruptcies are arranged. The goodwill that is associated with reputation and the quality of life of the employees, and the general social standing of the firm, can be very valuable, especially for service providers where there is no physical good to be measured. Goodwill is an important part of the value of a firm, for example when a company is bought or sold.

4.2. The divisibility characteristic of money

Simmel explains the divisibility of money as one of its most important properties as a means of exchange. In the development of a barter economy the

> value of both objects of exchange ... becomes more easily commensurable if one object is divisible; ... The most developed form of divisibility is attained with exchange against money. Money is that divisible object of exchange, the unit of which is commensurable with the value of every indivisible object. (1900, quote from 1978 translation, pp. 127–8)

Or, again more recently, in his attempt to introduce 'indivisible commodities' or integralities (see note 10) into Walrasian general equilibrium theory, Broome declares 'One of the essential characteristics of money is that it is divisible within anyone's perception, and thus permits easy trade' (1972, p. 227).

The veil of money is so transparent yet so effective in hiding the divisibility of money, that this function can easily be overlooked. People come to believe that goods and services are, to all intents and purposes, perfectly divisible, simply because their possession can be shared and their value distributed by using money. The exchange of money in a transaction is a sleight of hand whereby the characteristic of divisibility is imputed to the good or service bought, and not recognized in the money itself.

4.2.1. The divisibility of monetary assets

Gold and silver, used as money, have the property of being divisible as much as necessary, although the actual division is costly and inconvenient. Minted and printed money is divisible by design, with the smallest unit being the smallest unit of value seen to be useful in the economy. Thus in general, economies with low incomes tend to have lower-value coin and notes than economies with high incomes.

The divisibility of money is distinct from its role as a medium of exchange. In parts of East Africa, cattle have been used as a means of exchange, but the cattle are not divisible, at least if they are to survive as cattle (and money) rather than being reduced to meat. But then cattle become more likely the unit of account, and the exchange of goods can be measured in terms of sub-units of cattle with some form of ledger to record the transactions. One of the important developments in the history of money has been the increasing ease with which it can be divided, firstly by the use of coins, then by that of coins *and* paper money, and, most recently, by the addition of credit and debit cards.

4.2.2. *Money's role in sharing integral resources*

The divisibility of money also allows it to be used as a means of allocating integral resources. The ownership of economic organizations can be divided such that they can be separately owned by any finite number of individuals and other social groups. For example, commercial companies can be partly owned through the equity shareholding of banks, other companies or individual people. The consumption of an integral good or service can be divided between several people by using money. If a few friends, for example, want to go on a car journey together, they can share the cost between them by using money. (The car and the journey are both indivisible, the car by its function, and the journey because it has to be complete.)

4.2.3. *The integrality (illiquidity) of some monetary assets*

Although one of the primary attributes of money is its divisibility in space and time, some monetary assets are, paradoxically, integral (or indivisible) in time because they are defined for time periods, e.g. a 60-day time deposit account with a bank, whose value falls if this period is divided, usually through incurring a penalty cost, agreed in advance, for transferring value out of the 60-day account before the 60 days have elapsed. This integrality over time is illiquidity. In general most assets, whether physical, monetary, or other financial, can be made liquid (i.e. turned into a monetary asset such as notes and coin or a current account balance) at the risk of a cost penalty. The difference between a monetary asset, such as a 60-day account, and most other assets, is that the account is managed by a bank and expected to be a close substitute for other monetary assets; it automatically becomes another monetary asset (a current balance) at a fixed date in the future, and its value, excluding interest rate receipts, fluctuates with that of other monetary assets.

4.3. Money as invariant[11] over space and time

Perfect money should retain its value over space and time. Economic variance is the tendency for resources, including individuals, social groups, institutions, money, goods and services, their characteristics and their values, to change over space and time (Barker, 1996, p. 83). Perfect invariance is the persistence of the resource characteristics completely unchanged over space and time. On the time-scale of the human race, the daily cycle of sunrise and sunset is perfectly invariant.

4.3.1. *Invariance and people*

The invariance of the human mind and body is essential for trade over economic space-time. It allows for the separation of production and consumption across space, with products made for the domestic market also being suitable for the foreign market, and for their separation in time, with production having to come first.

One particular characteristic of a person is an invariance through time in personality and mental facilities, and in physical attributes on maturity. The same relative invariance can be observed over time in social groups, neighbourhoods, villages, cities, regions, nations and supranational groups. This allows the development of continuing, tailored, personal services such as medical, dental or beauty-care provision at one extreme, and at the other, the ability to recruit new employees, and the reasonable assurance of employers that their existing employees will continue to be skilled and experienced; it allows workers to choose new employers and to be confident of what sort of conditions they are likely to experience; and it allows for the collection of reasonably consistent economic statistics.

Some aspects of the individual do change in time. People 'learn by doing' and 'learn by consuming'; indeed, they learn by experience in all the economic roles they act out, and modify their behaviour accordingly. Formal education and training also change the characteristics of individuals so that they cannot be assumed to be invariant over time in certain key abilities and skills.

4.3.2. *The invariance of replicated units*

Many, if not most, replicated units (goods and services) have the property of almost perfect invariance over economic space-time, that is, they retain their combination of characteristics in different locations *and* over time. For example, a tin of Heinz baked beans, or a Walls Magnum 'stick product' (an 'ice lolly') are recognizably similar, if not identical, in different countries and cities, and from one year to the next. In fact, manufacturers go to great lengths to maintain this invariance as much as possible, and the commercial rights associated with it are topics of great importance to many multinational corporations. Recipes and ingredients are commercial secrets and the subject of extensive legislation regarding their ownership and use.

Economic invariance is not, however, complete and perfect for any resource. Some allowance usually has to be made for local conditions and changes over time, partly because of the high costs of maintaining the invariance and partly because of local differences in taste. For example, European continental taste allows – and even encourages – flecks of vanilla pod as a visible constituent of a vanilla Magnum; in the UK until recently this was unacceptable, being regarded as alien to ice-cream. Correspondingly the appearance of a Magnum and its packaging may be modified slightly from one year to the next, but not so much that the consumer would notice.

4.3.3.   Branding and invariance

The power of branding, the term used by the advertising trade for the creation of a product, its maintenance in the consumer vision, and its relationship to economic invariance is illustrated by the experience of the Coca-Cola Company when it slightly modified the formula for the Coca-Cola drink. The episode, recounted by Schulz (2000), is revealing about the importance of branding to the producer and the consumer. Branding creates an image of a product or service whose quality characteristics can be relied upon, irrespective of location or date of purchase; branding helps to identify and safeguard the characteristic of invariance over economic space-time. The consumer wants some guarantee of what he or she will eventually receive when a product is purchased for subsequent consumption. The producer wants to retain consumer satisfaction and a continuing (through time) and expanding (through space) market for the product.

The value of the branded replicated unit is so great that it can, and is, readily extended to related products. Associated with Magnum ice-cream is a whole collection of quality stick products aimed at the adult luxury ice-cream market. Indeed, the value of a brand can extend to apparently wholly unrelated products, e.g. the application of the Caterpillar tractor brand to a type of boot. However, the replicated unit does not need to be branded. It may be just an internationally recognized standard, e.g. a quality of crude petroleum with characteristics similar to those of Brent crude oil.

The property of economic invariance extends far beyond replicated units. One central invariance for human biology and the social sciences is that of the human mind and body. By and large, the human body retains the same shape and abilities over space-time. People have become heavier, taller and stronger and they live longer (although not in all societies), but these changes are rather slow in economic terms, and relatively smooth and predictable. This relative invariance is relied upon in the design and manufacture of many economic products, either because these products are made for the human body – to eat, to sit in or on, to live, work or sleep in or on, or to use – or because they require human attendance for their operation, so they have to be safe and unthreatening, as well as designed for human attention in case they go wrong.

4.3.4. *The invariance of money*

The economic invariance of money over space means that at any given moment large numbers of almost simultaneous, identical transactions can take place over a monetary area. Millions of people can buy National Lottery tickets across a country, paying the same price, and each person can be sure that every other person has the same chance (per unit of stake) through the fact that money has the same value throughout the monetary area. Similarly, it may be important that all the people in a profession, say primary school teachers, are paid on the same salary scale on the same day, for the same work, throughout the country. The invariance property of money over space allows such transactions to happen as a normal feature of an economy.

However, it is also the case that many replicated goods and services have different prices in different locations in the same monetary area at the same time; in some real way they are location-specific. The invariance-over-space property of money and the fact that these goods and services are replicated (i.e. they are exactly the same in all characteristics other than location) allows us to know that they have different economic values depending entirely on location, and hence to deduce the favourable and unfavourable locations in particular markets. Since the attributes of locations normally change relatively slowly over time, a comparison of the prices of replicated units in different monetary areas, allows for the measurement of international comparisons of purchasing power.

4.4. Perfect money should be limited in supply

Invariance is a fundamental concept in economics, especially for money, allowing plans to be made and helping to make predictions easier, both for producers in designing their goods and services with the expectation of a market, and for consumers in feeling confident that their purchases will give satisfaction when eventually consumed. Perfect money should be limited in supply, so that its value is maintained over time.

4.5.   Money as a numeraire

The characteristic of money as a *numeraire* is different from that of money as a means of dividing integralities. In a world where all goods and services are perfectly divisible, money would still have several other functions including those of a means of convenient exchange and of a *numeraire*. This aspect of money (its use in converting every other resource into one special resource, money, using monetary units) if taken to extremes ('economism'), leads the world around us to become homogenised through common monetary valuation. There are other valid valuations, such as those associated with aesthetics, love and compassion, and ethics or 'right' behaviour, that can contradict or negate the monetary valuation. In other words, intrinsic values should be distinguished from monetary values (Barker, 2008, section 4).

4.6.   Convenient money

Clearly this is a useful property as money is used as medium of exchange and that process of exchange will be facilitated by money being available in convenient forms. For example, money in the form of a debit or credit card is easy to carry around for use in buying goods and services, but perhaps surprisingly, not necessarily equally of use in buying monetary services.[12]

4.7.   Attractive money

And money might as well be attractive, as gold, silver, notes and coin.

5.   Symmetry in the spatial and temporal roles of money

5.1.   Money in space-time economics

The spatial and temporal variance of money is critical in understanding the relationship between interest rate and exchange rate policy. The next section provides an analysis of the demand for monetary assets and an explanation for Goodhart's Law: 'any observed statistical regularity [in the growth of monetary assets] will tend to collapse once pressure is placed upon it for control purposes'. The effects of exchange and interest rate changes are then explored, and the relationship between the two rates is discussed: exchange rates allow exchange of monetary assets over space; and interest rates allow the exchange of monetary assets over time. Finally the asymmetrical expectations regarding interest and exchange rate changes as interest rates approach zero are discussed. These imply the potential ineffectiveness of reflationary monetary policy, with the likelihood of unstable rates over space and time, as the economic system falls into a Keynesian liquidity trap. In a modern economy, with innovations such as telecommunications and the internet, the role of money becomes even more important simply because at any instant of time, e.g. when using a telephone or a fax, individuals or groups can transact at a distance purchases and sales with confidence in the stated monetary value in the different parts of the economy, in the different parts of economic space. For example, if I wish to send flowers to someone in another part of the country, I can effectively negotiate with a distant florist the exact value of the flowers, using the function of money as a means of exchange over economic space.

Money allows for the separation of production and consumption. Without money, the producer of a particular good or service must first seek out those who wish to use that particular good or service and is then limited to barter trade. Money widens the scope of barter exchange, for it is then enough for the producers to accept money in exchange for their goods and services. On the consuming side of the transaction, the consumers no longer need to seek out particular producers in order to conduct trade, or indeed offer something else immediately useful for exchange. Instead, the consumers can use money to go to the market and buy the goods and services as and when they wish.

The existence of money allows the separation of production and consumption not only across time but also across space: 'The extent and intensity of the role that money plays...is...manifested as the conquest of distance. ... [It] makes possible those associations of interests in which the spatial distance of the interested parties is absolutely negligible' (Simmel, 1978, p. 476).

5.2. The role of money in continuous pricing

The lowest value coin, that is to say the smallest indivisible unit of money, is a unit of almost negligible value in the economy; thus money is as divisible as required. The divisibility of money is much enhanced in a credit money system where potentially the smallest unit of money becomes limited by the number of decimal places people are willing to employ. The divisibility function of money allows prices to be virtually continuous for individual goods and services so that a replicated good can have one price in one location, and a different price in another.

The possibility of almost continuous changes in price across economic space may be illustrated by the prices of a replicated good sold at various stations along a railway line running across the US, from New York on the Atlantic to San Francisco on the Pacific. Assume that time can be ignored, that there is a certain amount of competition between the suppliers of the good, that normal profits are made, and that there is a market at each station along the route. The price of the replicated good can and will vary according to the distance from its origin, say New York, along a continuum according to the transport costs. Assuming rational behaviour, and allowing for overhead costs, it would be expected that the gradation of price-change would be more-or-less in proportion to the distance.

A similar phenomenon can be observed in the price of a fixed quantity of petrol that varies according to the distance from the refinery. This is a more complicated example because there are many refineries, many companies, many petrol stations, and different degrees of competition within the different markets. However, by and large the further the distance of the sale of petrol from the refinery, the greater the increase in price of the replicated good compared with its price at the point of production.

5.3. The temporal role of money

> Rhythm may be defined as symmetry in time, just as symmetry is rhythm in space... Rhythm is for the ear what symmetry is for the eye... The development of money ...exhibits certain rhythmic phenomena... (Simmel, 1978, pp. 488–93)

Money is a convenient, and indeed, efficient, means of exchange over time. This is particularly obvious over short periods (days, weeks and months) in economies with low inflation, when monetary assets are treated as invariant over time. In these periods, the temporal invariance of money allows wages to be paid once a week or once a month, invoices to be raised and subsequently paid, credit of all sorts to be issued, and contracts to be made including payment at future dates.

Perfect money can allow the separation of activities over time; it can allow specialisation at an early stage of production by one social group, and at a later stage by another; it can allow the separation of production and consumption, of investment and saving. One of Keynes' achievements was to explore and analyze the invariance-over-time property of money, i.e. money as a store of value. Keynes' insight (1936, pp. 233–4) was that, in some circumstances, the benefit of holding wealth in the form of current account balances to take advantage of money as a store of value, might well completely outweigh the benefit of holding the wealth in the form of interest-bearing assets. If individuals and social groups become extremely concerned about the future and the value of non-monetary assets, or if interest rates approach zero (the liquidity trap), they may well be prepared to forego all interest and other receipts and hold all their wealth in non-interest-bearing monetary assets in order to take advantage of the invariant value of money over time.

5.4. The demand for aggregate money

The total demand for money cannot be directly observed, except by introspection, since it includes many forms of money although it may be measurable by the technique of hedonic functions, when the most important characteristics of the forms of money in the aggregate are measured and allowed for in the estimation of the function. However, the demand for different monetary assets is measurable and is widely measured and, through understanding the nature of this demand, the roles of the rate of exchange and the rate of interest rate can be explained.

The markets for monetary assets have the following features. Each monetary asset combines different characteristics of money. All are divisible in space but with varying degrees of divisibility or liquidity over time. To illustrate, take three characteristics of monetary assets, namely convenience, return and risk that are important for an analysis. *Convenience* refers to divisibility and use in exchange; *return* is the monetary benefit or cost of holding the asset, including the foreign exchange conversion, interest or other return; and the *risk* is that of monetary gain or loss in the case of illiquid assets. A tentative allocation of different characteristics of money to different forms of money is shown in Table 6.1.

Table 6.1   Characteristics of money and monetary assets

Characteristic	Notes & coin	Debit cards	Bank current accounts	Savings & loans	Time deposits	Index linked loans	Foreign exchange
trustworthiness	•••	•••	•••	••	••	•••	••
divisibility	••	••	•••	••	•	•	•
invariance	••	••	••	•	•	•••	•
supply limitation	•••	•	••	•	••	•••	•
numeraire							
convenience	••	••	•••	••	•	•	•
attractiveness	•••	•••					

Note(s)
••• denotes: almost perfect
•• denotes: viable
• denotes: not very good

As a result of economies of specialization and scale, these assets are available only in a finite number (i.e. there is no continuous spectrum of assets), each with a different combination of characteristics. The following seven assets, rated in domestic currency (£), are chosen for the purpose of this analysis: notes and coin or 'cash'; debit cards, current account balances in commercial banks; balances in saving and loan accounts; time-deposits in banks; balances in a fictitious current account index-linked to inflation which holds its value in spite of inflation by means of a rate of return *guaranteed* at the rate of inflation; and foreign exchange values in the domestic currency. The last asset, a current account in dollars, is included to show how exchange rates enter into decisions.

The assets are desired for their characteristics, not for themselves. For ease of understanding, all characteristics are expressed as positive ones, which the holder is assumed to desire: more convenience, higher return and lower risk. The holdings and the market are in a state of flux in time with cash being spent, cards being used, cheques being written, balances being run down and replenished, and time-deposit accounts maturing. There is a cost in collecting information and making transactions in the rebalancing of the portfolio of assets to satisfy some criterion, such as a legal requirement, or the need to avoid an overdraft, or the accumulation of liquid assets to permit a house purchase. Because of economies of scale and indivisibilities, the rebalancing is not continual, but periodic; and in many organizations the rebalancing is done regularly by specialized departments. To offset the costs of rebalancing, there are monetary gains from shifting the portfolio towards assets with higher returns and away from the accumulation of losses.

Figures 6.1 and 6.2 show a notional individual's and a nation's holdings of monetary assets on 1 January to illustrate the theory. The figures are each divided into three graphs. The top right-hand graph shows the convenience of the asset along the horizontal axis, plotted against its nominal return on the vertical axis. In general, the more convenient is the asset, the lower is the return. The lower right-hand graph shows convenience plotted against risk, with certainty shown along the lower horizontal axis. The top left-hand graph shows the current nominal value of the holdings of each asset on 1 January, plotted against the return. The positions of the assets in the figures are schematic, since it is not easy to obtain or estimate returns, or risks, let alone 'convenience'.

If the markets have the features set out as shown above, and assuming that exchange rates and interest rates are fixed and the economy is growing at say 2 percent p.a. with a similar rate of average price inflation, the positions of the assets in the figures will follow a pattern as follows.

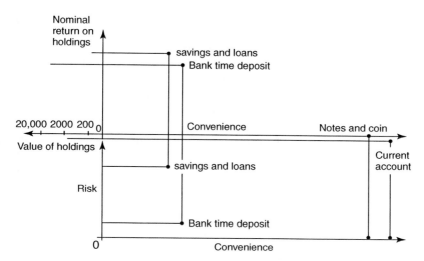

Figure 6.1 One person's holdings of monetary assets, 1 January

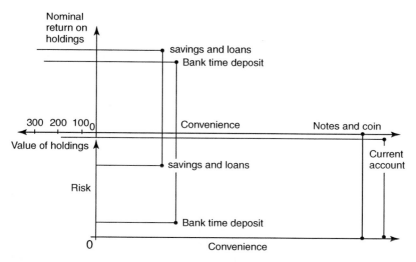

Figure 6.2 National holdings of monetary assets, 1 January

1 All the assets will be efficient ones in the sense that none will be dominated by any other in the combination of characteristics they possess, i.e. none will be inferior in every characteristic compared with another asset. Note, however, that only the three characteristics

are shown in the figures. There are other characteristics that may also be important.

2 The figures also show that there is plenty of room for new assets to emerge with new combinations of characteristics which will find a ready market, although probably at the expense of existing assets that are close to the new one in its combination of characteristics.

3 Trade-offs between convenience, return and risk suggest the following relationships: the higher the convenience, the lower the return, assuming that the risk of the assets in question is equal; the lower the risk, the lower the return, assuming that the convenience is equal; and the higher the convenience, the higher the risk, assuming that the return is equal.

4 Since perceptions and expectations of convenience, returns and risk are changing all the time, there is likely to be a rather poor relationship between a simple addition of these assets and the measure of activity in the economy, such as the sum of monetary flow transactions for production, i.e. gross output. The idea that managing the money supply of money will in turn manage the level of activity appears to be far-fetched, but it has had great influence in the conduct of economic policy.

5 The attempted control of the growth of one or a combination of monetary assets as a means of controlling the 'supply of money' or even as a means of controlling the rate of inflation, is liable to become increasingly ineffective as the financial system switches to existing or new monetary assets that are not controlled. This is Goodhart's Law, named after Charles Goodhart, a former Chief Adviser to the Bank of England, and a member of the Bank of England Monetary Policy Committee.

5.5. The explanation for Goodhart's Law[13]

The law is defined as 'Any observed statistical regularity will tend to collapse once pressure is placed upon it for control purposes' (Chrystal and Mizon, 2003, p. 223).[14] The purpose of controlling the "money supply" was ultimately to control the rate of inflation, following the acceptance of the monetarist analysis of the causes of inflation in the 1980s, e.g. by the UK government under Prime Minister Margaret Thatcher.[15] One of the best examples of the law in action relates to the attempt by the UK government to control the rate of inflation by controlling the measure of broad money £M4 in the late 1970s. £M4 appeared to be a good leading indicator of inflation, so it was controlled without imposing any other measures to control aggregate demand (Chrystal and Mizon, 2003, pp. 225–6). The attempt failed and inflation rose sharply in 1979 and 1980, following the second world oil price shock.

The problem is that any particular monetary asset only imperfectly supplies the services of money, and the financial system may be adept at creating new assets to perform particular functions of money. In other words, different monetary assets may be highly substitutable in terms of the monetary services they provide, and indeed these services are largely unmeasurable. This in turn implies that attempts to control a specific set of monetary assets (the target), for example by controlling interest rates (the instrument), may well fail, because the financial system is sufficiently flexible in providing the underlying monetary services demanded by social groups. This will be especially true if the financial system is being deregulated and new financial services and institutions are being created and tested as in the UK in the 1980s.

The analysis implies further that if a control variable, or instrument of policy, such as a tax rate on a product, for example, a carbon tax on fossil fuels, cannot be substituted by other tax rates, because all are subject to the legal control of the governments, then as long as the product being taxed cannot be replaced easily by untaxed products, the generalized Law will not become operative.

5.6.   The supply of monetary assets and the level of economic activity

One of the principal services required of monetary assets is their use as a means of exchange, e.g. as a way of buying and selling goods and services. It seems reasonable that the stock of assets required for this purpose should be related to the total value of the transactions involved. However, this value includes not only transactions in the current flow of goods and services as might be measured by gross output, but also those involving transfers between people (such as gambling), the exchange of houses and other second-hand physical assets, and the exchange of financial assets, such as stocks and shares and foreign currencies. This total value will be very much larger than gross output, and in countries such as the UK and the US, changes in its price level are likely to be dominated by changes in prices of financial assets. If the economy is growing smoothly so that the value of gross output is closely correlated with the total of monetary transactions, then a relationship between the value of some monetary aggregate and the value of gross output might appear for a short period in an economy, but it is unlikely to be stable. It seems even less likely that the effect of reducing the supply of some monetary asset will of itself reduce the general price level for the flow of new goods and services.

5.7.   Exchange rates and interest rates

Exchange rates and interest rates are closely linked, one being the rate for transferring money over space and the other the rate for transferring money over time. However, space and time in economics are not symmetrical, and the demand for money is derived from the demand for goods and services for consumption. Consumption requires production; and production, in the long term, requires investment. The rate of interest provides an incentive for those holding monetary assets to agree to abstain from the use of those assets; one function of the banks and the financial system is to allow investment to be financed from the savings of those receiving the interest on monetary assets.

5.8.   A change in the exchange rate

What will happen if, after a long period of fixed rates, the authorities reduce the exchange rate, and this change is both unexpected and generally seen as unlikely to be repeated? There will be a rebalancing of portfolios in favour of assets with a higher return, in this case favouring $-assets, whose return will be higher in terms of £s; the value (in £s) of the asset will rise. The holdings of $-assets will rise as a higher return is sought at the expense of risk and convenience. If devaluation leads to an expectation that the domestic currency is less stable, then the risk of $-assets will fall, providing a second incentive to move holdings into them.

5.9.   A change in the rate of interest

What will happen if, after a long period of fixed rates, the authorities *raise the rate of interest*, and this change is both unexpected and generally seen as unlikely to be repeated? Again there will be a rebalancing of portfolios in favour of assets with a higher return – the interest-bearing assets. This may take some time, since asset-holders have to wait until some assets reach maturity before rebalancing their portfolios, unless the penalty cost is less than the potential gain in extra interest.

5.10.   Changes in both the rate of interest and the exchange rate

When both rates change together, the situation is much more complex and the outcome less predictable. The various expectations of all those affected come into play, each group affecting other groups.

Small, apparently inconsequential, events can change the public mood and lead to large swings in market sentiment.

5.11. A whole-system approach

The institutions that create and destroy money should be embedded in any model of the wider economic system and the system extended to include government and trade, e.g. to include national economies, governments, investment banks, and non-bank financial companies dealing in assets. It should also be extended to allow for systemic risk, and the international-investment banks being unregulated compared to the national-retail banks regulated by the central banks. The institutions should be refined in their definitions to distinguish well-behaving economies versus ill-behaving ones and to include many diverse consumers, producers, governments, prices, wage rates, monetary assets and interest rates. Finally, the system approach should allow for space-time symmetry in the prices of money (exchange rates and interest rates) and asymmetrical expectations and the Keynesian liquidity trap. These features are discussed in section 6.

6. Implications for understanding money and monetary policy in the current crisis

Neoclassical, New Keynesian and monetarist theory all tend to be limited in scope so limiting analysis of key features of the Big Crunch, i.e. that the investment banks creating loans and financial assets have been unregulated, without central bank control, that the rapidly changing dynamics of monetary collapse have not been well understood or measured. The evidence here is that few empirical measures of trust or uncertainty in the system (volatility over time of various market rates – stock prices, exchange rates, commodity prices, interest rates) have been widely agreed or published. In addition, the debate has had weak or no emphasis on (or expected fitting to) macroeconomic or indeed any data and has been much more oriented to debate, education and learning. Since the theory has not developed sufficiently to allow for competing governments (governments make laws, tax activities and spend to provide public goods) it has not been able to explain "light-touch regulation" or the emergence of a massive unregulated supply of money that eventually turned toxic.

6.1. Well- and ill-behaving economies

Well-behaving economies should exhibit full employment, have no severe structural imbalances (e.g. urban–rural), with inflation not expected to arise at full employment, social partners content with distribution of income, stable expectations about the future, key signals to manage markets "working", i.e. the central banks being in control of interest rates via banks' base rates or exchange rates and finally the rule of law being generally observed, e.g. bankruptcy when a bank becomes insolvent. The role of money in well-behaving economies is that, given stable expectations, all social groups can plan their use of money in an orderly way, and respond to signals appropriately. This means that the finance ministry and central bank can manage the economy via signals and incentives, such that credit is created in response to the demand for credit, which is linked with real investment.

The analysis so far suggests some testable postulates: first, those monetary aggregates may provide information on, for example, intentions to spend, but they do not affect behaviour: people do not spend because they have money, but possession of money may signify intention to spend. Second, the volume of money in existence can be ignored in an analysis of the real economic system without affecting the explanatory power of the analysis, provided that banks provide credit on demand (to creditworthy customers). When banks apply credit rationing, then the workings of banks do have a (possible substantial) impact on ability to spend and hence on the real economy. Third, that when an economy becomes ill-behaving, the policy rules become misguiding and perverse and money matters again.

The analysis also suggests a theory to explain the Big Crunch. The banks should be divided into international investment banks that are unregulated and national retail banks that are regulated by the central banks. The governments should be included in the theory to make laws, to tax and spend and to provide public goods. The theory is that effective money supply collapsed to an unknown extent when the Lehman Brothers bank went bankrupt on 15 September 2008. Effective money demand fell in a vortex of distrust, increasing debt, collapsing output and increasing unemployment. The rate of fall of global output and trade has been similar to that of the Great Depression (Eichengreen and O'Rourke, 2009) suggesting that the collapse is governed by the inertia in the system rather than the extent of the mistrust. Interest rates, exchange rates, prices and wage rates become unstable; prices flutter. The outlook may continue to deteriorate until trust is re-established via the bad banks being made bankrupt. When trust in banks is damaged, non-banks move deposits from more to less risky banks and to bank notes. In the specific period September 2008 to September 2009, trust was partly restored after March 2009, when President Obama adopted a consensus approach to the banks while injecting substantial liquidity into the system. However the crisis appeared far from being resolved in September 2009.

6.2. Asymmetric expectations when the rate of interest approaches zero (the liquidity trap)

When interest rates are well above zero, say above 3 percent ('interest rates', as other prices in this paper, are always taken to be defined as *nominal* interest rates) then expectations will normally be such that social groups will be divided as to whether the next movement for whatever reason will be up or down. These expectations can be managed by the banks to reflate or deflate the economy. However, when interest rates approach zero, and since zero is regarded as a floor, expectations become increasingly deflationary: at zero, any interest rate change can only be upwards, therefore deflationary and this will have potentially catastrophic effects on the holding on monetary assets for speculative purposes, a situation identified by Keynes as a liquidity trap. When interest rates can only rise, bond prices can only fall, so all bonds will be potentially converted into money at unpredictable rates. Expectations themselves become unstable because the monetary regime is in uncharted territory as reflationary monetary policy becomes increasingly ineffective, and all social groups do not know how the banks and the governments will respond. Command-and-control policies become the main means by which the authorities can manage the system, giving a pronounced advantage to systems, such as the Chinese one, which can respond quickly and effectively to restore effective demand.

6.3. The Japanese liquidity trap, 1995–2002

The Japanese economy fell into a liquidity trap in the early 1990s, so there is recent experience of how it will affect the global economy in 2009. Figure 6.3 shows the outcome of a set of stochastic simulations of an econometric model of the global monetary system operated by researchers at the European Central Bank (Coenen and Wieland, 2003). The figure shows the chance of Japan falling into a liquidity trap (the zero bind) at various 'equilibrium' rates of interest, with equilibrium defined as the long-run solution for interest rates. The chance is about 20 percent for a 2 percent rate of interest.

The US had interest rates at around 2 percent in mid-2003, so that if the US monetary system is at all similar to the Japanese one, there was already an appreciable chance of the US falling into the trap before the financial crisis took hold, with the risk increasing by any chance series

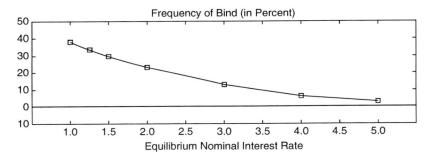

Figure 6.3   ECB Analysis of risks of a liquidity trap
Source: Coenen and Wieland (2003).

of deflationary shocks. Monetary and fiscal policy proved ineffectual to push or pull Japan out of the trap over the eight years since 1995. With the US, Japan, and the UK all with near-zero interest rates, there is now a serious risk of the global economy repeating the Japanese experience in a global liquidity crisis that could, on past evidence, last for years.

6.4. The risks of falling into a global liquidity trap in 2009 and 2010

The risk of a liquidity trap has now become substantial at the global level in 2009 and 2010, a far more serious situation than Japan in the 1990s since there are no external sources of reflation and optimism to help pull the different world economies into strongly positive expectations and growth rates. Any economy that seeks to reflate strongly alone, e.g. China in 2009, will see an appreciable proportion of any extra effective demand leaking to imports, making the policy more difficult to succeed. The full theoretical and quantitative analysis of the global liquidity trap requires the understanding, firstly, of how the economic system in particular fixed investments, responds to interest rates and changes in stocks of monetary assets, and, secondly, of how economic policy, both monetary and fiscal, operates in small and large open economies and in the world economy. Here the main reasons for concern are listed.

6.5. Reasons for concern for the world economy after 2008

Under the policies being promoted by many governments and bankers in late 2008, the risks of a liquidity trap have increased as various central banks have reduced interest rates towards zero. Individual private banks benefit from the liquidity trap because they can borrow at near zero interest rates and lend at higher rates and hence restore their balance sheets and restore profitability. However, it is not in the interests of the banking system as a whole because once in the trap, it becomes very difficult for policies to provide sufficient traction to pull economies out of the trap, certainly at a country level.

There are several reasons to suggest that the global liquidity trap closed in early 2009:

1 The private banks have slowed their own investing. Typically social groups facing bankruptcy will not invest as much as before for the future, which has become much more uncertain. Since the banking and finance sector's investments world-wide are substantially larger than those of, for example, the electricity sector, the global economy will experience a recession if the banks behave as if they are bankrupt.

2 The private banks are encouraging savers to save and not consume (a reversal of their earlier money creation). It is now in their interests to promote saving rather than consumption as in the pre-crisis periods.

3 The banks are cutting their lending and forcing real-economy companies and households into bankruptcy. In their efforts to restore their own balance sheet profitability, they are withdrawing loans and adding stricter conditions for new lending, so actively reducing growth investment throughout the global economy.

4 Investors are in despair, prices are unpredictable, and carbon prices tend to zero, hence real investment is in "free fall". This is despair in the 'animal spirits' of investors in Joan Robinson's vivid language.

5 Householders are also very concerned and are seeking to restore their own saving rates, after they have fallen in the US and UK to near zero. The recovery of these rates to normal levels of about 7 percent or higher over the next two or three years will alone bring about a global depression.

6 Governments are also concerned about their long-term balance sheets, and some are seeking to cut future spending to reduce potential deficits. However, in order to get out of a liquidity trap, governments must take radical action: print money, spend aggressively, and hopefully restore the system to stable growth.

7 Globalization accelerates and spreads the reductions in national effective demand in a "classical" multiplier process. The equipment exporters (e.g. construction, vehicles, Japan, Germany) suffer first and most. This is perhaps the most serious deflationary force of all.

In 2009 world governments appear not to understand the depth and scale of the financial crisis. The situation remains unresolved beyond the governments taking over the risks to the banking system and meeting to decide new rules on transparency and integrity, much needed but too late. The key fact is that the co-ordinated actions over 10–12 October 2008 to the time of writing have not yet restored LIBOR and OIS rates to "normality". One solution after another has so far failed to calm the markets for more than a day or two since the scale of the problem was revealed by the bankruptcy of Lehman Brothers on 15 September 2008. There is a risk that the crisis will continue to get worse, that the partial nationalisations will reveal debts toxic even at the scale of government debt. It may be that in order to restore trust in markets, to get the global economy back on an even keel, and to lance the political animosity building up against the banks, something even more radical needs to be done. This section briefly summarises the cause of the crisis as discussed above, but mainly focuses on a global plan to solve it.

6.6.   The LIBOR rates

The LIBOR and OIS rates are obvious indicators of mistrust between the banks and this mistrust will end only when the toxic debt is identified and somehow removed from the system. The proposed solution of flooding the banks with good money (government-backed liquidity) will not help because the good money is being added to untold amounts of the bad money, which has accumulated nearly everywhere with access to the investment banks' toxic debt.[16] (There are no major investment banks left at this stage in the crisis, because the stock markets have valued them as worthless, or they have been turned into retail banks and given access to liquidity and the retail banks' small depositors' cash.)

Therefore the governments' guarantees on commercial terms will not restore trust. The bad banks will remain bad and the bad money will remain diffused through the system. The state is flooding the system with good money in the hope that this will drive out the bad money, but it is the bad money that appears to be keeping the ex-investment banks afloat. The end result of adding good money to all this bad money may be a dollar crash and global hyperinflation. The extra liquidity is therefore potentially catastrophic for the real economy.

6.7.   The scale of the financial catastrophe

Those managing the money supply understand that we are living through and observing a non-linear catastrophic event in the global monetary system that requires fundamental changes in the system to restore trust. However, many bankers are in denial: they think their banks are "really" solvent; "the markets have gone haywire and are not to be trusted"; "the herd is panicking"; and we should as soon as possible return to "normal". However, a wider assessment of the policy events of the last year suggests that the bankers themselves have been seeking to support their banks, via interference by central banks and governments in the operation of the financial markets to change the rules and take on the private risks.

There is probably a temptation to close the markets, as has been done in Russia several times since the big crunch. Another temptation may be to suspend bank shares, to avoid market valuations in a switch from mark-to-market valuation to "fair" valuation.[17] Again, these solutions will not work because the fundamental problem of the bad money diffused through the system is not being addressed.

6.8. Fundamental reform of the system

No one knows what will work to stop the collapse and restore order. We are in uncharted territory. A crisis of this magnitude is unprecedented in scale, although not in relation to previous bank failures and their effects on economies. The problem is global, a systemic market failure whose correction must involve all the major parties including at least the main OECD economies and Brazil, India, Russia and China. Without global coordinated action to restore the market system, e.g. by forcing the banks that would otherwise be bankrupt except for state support into bankruptcy, or at least simulated bankruptcy, it seems very likely that the crisis will be repeated or continue to deepen and develop into a twenty-first century Greater Depression (Barker, 2009).

7. Conclusion: money as magic

This chapter has briefly summarized the treatment of money in 20th century and 21st century Keynesian economics. It has then explored in more detail the treatment in Post Keynesian economics, relying on Fontana (2009) for a review, then developed the theory by suggesting extensions and expounding the analysis in (Barker, 1996) to explain seven properties of perfect money, as distinct from the properties of monetary assets, the monetarist approach to money. The essential symmetry of money over space and in time is then discussed, and this leads into the use of the theory to understand the credit crisis of 2007 onwards and propose (briefly) a plan for resolving the crisis including the bankruptcy of the bad banks.

The analysis also suggests a further property of money that becomes apparent when it goes bad: money as magic. Money is a mystery (Young, 1929; Kalecki, 1940). "Money is also a very vague concept and can only be defined arbitrarily" (Boulding, 1992, p. 67). In English culture, children are asked "Does money grow on trees?" "Does money come out of a "hole in the wall"?" At a certain age, about 8 to 10 years old, children treat money as "growing on trees". Children believe that banks create and destroy money.[18] For children, money is magical in that there is a provider with complete discretion and the money buys what children want. And there seems no limit to the supply, because it is not "real", just attractive coin and note or a credit/debit card. When the system of money creation collapses, money disappears like magic, and the world economy collapses.

Notes

1 *The Book of Popular Science.* New York: The Grolier Society. Group IX Ch. 31: 4231–40. Reprinted in Mehrling and Sandilands (1999).
2 This chapter draws heavily on the text and ideas in Chapter 3 of Barker (1996). This introductory section treats money in general, not necessarily as it is treated in Keynesian economics. It is impossible to treat all the Post Keynesian texts properly in the word limit of the chapter, so I have relied heavily on King (1995) and referred to the first major publication by authors and later critical references. Finally, 'money' and 'liquidity' are treated for the purposes of the chapter as synonymous, although there are differences in that liquidity could be treated as a particular form of money associated with the social groups that provide credit, e.g. as in Weintraub's (1982) list of the characteristics of liquidity, which are different from the list of properties of money given below.
3 Paper money first came into use in China, in the Ninth Century AD, according to Needham and Tsuen-Hsuin (1959). Temple (1986) remarks that its original name was 'flying money' because it was so light it could blow out of one's hand. As 'exchange certificates' used by merchants, paper money was quickly adopted by the government for forwarding tax payments. Real paper money, used as a medium of exchange and backed by deposited cash (a Chinese term for metal coins) apparently came into use in the tenth century. The first Western money was issued in Sweden in 1661. America followed in 1690, Scotland in 1695, France in 1720, England in 1797, and Germany not until 1806. http://www.asiasociety.org/education-learning/resources-schools/elementary-lesson-plans/chinese-inventions.
4 http://homepage.newschool.edu/het//essays/money/encaisse.htm.
5 http://www.brown.edu/Departments/Philosophy/homepages/weatherson/interest.pdf.
6 In addition the uses of aggregated variables and assumptions (e.g. the representative agent) in these and other schools of economic thought ignore the individuality of people and social groups (Barker, 1996: chapter 2, 1998,

2008: section 4) and the probability of evolution when a species knowingly faces possible extinction.

7 Sawyer (2009b) argues that the demand and supply analysis of money should be discarded. However it does seem useful to allow for money having a demand derived from its proxy value as a resource to achieve social and sexual well-being, and as constrained by supply, e.g. the available quantity of gold in an entirely gold-based economy.

8 The neoclassical approach to money, based on the quantity theory of money, does not make this distinction and seems rather confused.

9 Weintraub (1982) has seven motives for liquidity.

10 Economic indivisibility or integrality is defined as 'that property of resources which gives them economic value such that if they are divided they lose value to some significant extent.' Alternatively and more concisely a good or service is defined as integral if its economic value falls if and when it is divided.

11 I am indebted to Michael E. McIntyre for suggesting the name for this property. The term invariance is used in mathematics and physics, e.g. in the term automorphism invariance, meaning a special type of transformation which leaves a relation unchanged (Narens and Luce, 1987). Faden (1977, p. 56) uses the term isomer, borrowed from chemistry, to indicate a resource not tied down to a specific region or time instant, i.e. invariant over space and time; the word invariance has more appeal and is used here with a less precise meaning than that given to isomer.

12 In the UK in 2009, it is more time-consuming to transfer money between banks than to buy other goods and services from retailers via cards.

13 McIntyre (2000) adds 'Professor Marilyn Strathern FBA, following Hoskin (1996), has re-stated Goodhart's Law more succinctly and more generally [Strathern, 1997]: "When a measure becomes a target, it ceases to be a good measure." Goodhart's law is a sociological analogue of Heisenberg's uncertainty principle in quantum mechanics [but with crucial differences relating to the observed and the observer in the social sciences]. Measuring a system usually disturbs it. The more precise the measurement, and the shorter its timescale, the greater the energy of the disturbance and the greater the unpredictability of the outcome. See also the extended discussion by Hoskin (1996). Hoskin's article illustrates the wide applicability of Goodhart's law, and provides an illuminating historical discussion of what 'accountability' has come to mean today.'

14 Chrystal and Mizon (2003, pp. 222–6) give an excellent assessment of the law and point out that it was first formulated and demonstrated in relation to the control of monetary aggregates by means of interest rates.

15 The theory was developed by Friedman and the Chicago School. It has since been partially repudiated by Friedman (2003).

16 An extended analogy of the situation is as follows. In the global village, the bankers are in charge of the well of clean water needed for health and growth in the global economy and the governments are in charge of the springs of clean water that all flow into the well. When the banks report that the well and indeed the ground water are full of toxic debt, that poisons the economy, the governments provide a tanker of clean water. However, when poured down the well, this proves ineffective and the water remains poisoned.

The bankers request a second tanker, but this time after they have received it, they refuse to pour it down the well, saying that they need it for themselves; otherwise they too will be poisoned or bankrupted. The rest of the economy is starved of funding and forced into lower growth and potential bankruptcy.

17 Such a move would signal the end of the capitalist system, since market valuations would be replaced by the banks' valuations of their worth, rather like the Marxist theory of value in which goods and services are to be valued by their labour content, not their market values.

18 They do, but not in the obvious way of printing and destroying bank notes.

References

Arestis, Philip (1987–1988), 'The credit segment of a UK Post Keynesian model', *Journal of Post Keynesian Economics*, 10(2), pp. 250–69.

Arestis, Philip (2009), 'The New Consensus in Macroeconomics: A Critical Appraisal', in G. Fontana and M. Setterfield (eds), *Macroeconomic Theory and Macroeconomic Pedagogy*, Basingstoke: Palgrave Macmillan, pp. 100–17.

Arestis, Philip and Iris Biefang-Frisanscho Mariscal (1995), 'The endogenous money stock: empirical observations from the United Kingdom', *Journal of Post Keynesian Economics*, 17(4), pp. 545–60.

Barker, Terry (1996), *Space-Time Economics*, Cambridge: Cambridge Econometrics.

Barker, Terry (1998), 'Use of Energy Environment-Economy Models to Inform Greenhouse Gas Mitigation Policy', *Impact Assessment and Project Appraisal*, 16(2), pp. 123–31.

Barker, Terry (2008), 'The economics of avoiding dangerous climate change. An editorial essay on The Stern Review', *Climatic Change*, 89: 173–94. doi: 10.1007/s10584-008-9433-x.

Barker, Terry (2009), 'Understanding and resolving the "Big Crunch"', Cambridge, www.neweconomicthinking.com.

Boulding, K.E. (1992), *Towards a New Economics*, London: Edward Elgar.

Broome, John (1972), 'Approximate equilibrium in economies with indivisible commodities', *Journal of Economic Theory*, 5, pp. 224–49.

Cardim de Carvalho, Fernando (2009), 'Uncertainty and money: Keynes, Tobin and Kahn and the disappearance of the precautionary demand for money from liquidity preference theory', *Cambridge Journal of Economics*, doi 10.1093/cje/bep020.

Chrystal, Alec and Paul Mizen (2003), 'Goodhart's Law: Its origins, meaning and implications for monetary policy', in Paul Mizen (ed.), *Central Banking, Monetary Theory and Practice: Essays in Honour of Charles Goodhart, Volume One*, Cheltenham: Edward Elgar, pp. 221–43.

Coenen, Günter and Volker Wieland (2003), 'The zero-interest-rate bound and the role of the exchange rate for monetary policy in Japan', *Journal of Monetary Economics*, 50(5), pp. 1071–101.

Dow, S.C. (2006) 'Endogenous money: structuralist', in P. Arestis and M. Sawyer (eds) *A Handbook of Alternative Monetary Economics*, Cheltenham, Edward Elgar, pp. 35–51.

Eichengreen, Barry and Kevin H. O'Rourke (2009), 'A tale of two depressions', *Vox*, 1 September.

Ergungor, O. Emre (2007), 'On the resolution of financial crises: The Swedish experience', Federal Reserve Bank of Cleveland, Policy Discussion Paper, Number 21.

Ergungor, O. Emre and James B. Thomson (2006), 'Systemic banking crises' in Andrew H. Chen (ed.), *Research in Finance*, vol. 23, Bingley: Emerald, pp. 279–310.

Faden, Arnold M. (1977), *Economics of Space and Time: The Measure-Theoretic Foundations of Social Science*, Ames, Iowa: Iowa State University Press.

Fontana, Giuseppe (2009), *Money, Uncertainty and Time*, Abingdon, Oxon: Routledge.

Foster, Gladys Parker (1986), 'Endogeneity of money and Keynes's General Theory', *Journal of Economic Issues*, 20(4), pp. 953–68.

Frankel, Jeffrey (1987), Georg Simmel, *New Palgrave*, vol. 4, p. 333.

Friedman, Milton (1987), 'Quantity theory of money', *The New Palgrave: A Dictionary of Economics*, vol. 4, pp. 3–20.

Friedman, Milton (2003), 'Fed rate cut is no panacea for equities' by Vince Heaney, *Financial Times*, 24 June.

Granger, C. W. J. (1980), 'Testing for causality: A personal viewpoint', *Journal of Economic Dynamics and Control*, vol. 2, pp. 329–52.

Hahn, Frank (1983), *Money and Inflation*, Cambridge, Mass.: MIT Press.

Hoskin, Keith (1996), The 'awful idea of accountability': Inscribing people into the measurement of objects', in Rolland Munro and Jan Mouritsen (eds), *Accountability: Power, Ethos and the Technologies of Managing*, London: International Thomson Business Press, pp. 265–82.

Hutton, Will (1996), *The State We're In*, revised edition, London: Vintage Books.

Johnson, L. E., Robert D. Ley and Thomas Cate (2004), 'The Concept of Equilibrium: A Key Theoretical Element in Keynes' Revolution', *Atlantic Economic Journal*, 32(3), pp. 222–32.

Kaldor, N. (1972), 'The irrelevance of equilibrium economics. *The Economic Journal* 52, pp. 1237–55.

Kaldor, N. (1981), 'Fallacies of monetarism.' *Kredit und kapital*, 14(4), pp.451–62.

Kaldor, N. (1985), *Economics without Equilibrium*. UK: Cardiff Press.

Kalecki, M. (1940) "The 'mysteries' of the money market", *Oxford University Institute of Statistics Bulletin* 2(8) October, pp. 2–5.

Kenway, P. (1994), *From Keynesianism to Monetarism, the Evolution of UK Macroeconometric Models*, London: Routledge.

Keynes, J. M. (1936), *The General Theory of Employment, Interest and Money*, London: Macmillan Press (1973).

Keynes, J. M. (1937), 'The "ex-ante" theory of the rate of interest', *The Economic Journal*, 47(188), pp. 663–9.

Keynes, J. M. (1971–89), *The Collected Writings of John Maynard Keynes*, ed. D.E. Moggridge, vols I–XXX, London: Macmillan.

Keynes, John Maynard (1921), *Treatise on Probability*, London: Macmillan.

King, J. E. (1995), *Post Keynesian Economics: An Annotated Bibliography*, Aldershot: Edward Elgar.

Kirman, Alan P. (1992), 'Whom or what does the representative individual represent?', *Journal of Economic Perspectives*, 6(2), pp. 117–36.

Lancaster, Kelvin (1971), *Consumer Demand: A New Approach*, New York: Columbia University Press.

Lavoie, M. (2007) 'Endogenous money: accommodationist', in P. Arestis and M. Sawyer (eds), *A Handbook of Alternative Monetary Economics*, Cheltenham, Edward Elgar, pp. 17–34.

Llewellyn, John (1995), 'Empirical analysis as an underpinning to policy', paper presented to a conference held to celebrate the 50th Anniversary of the Department of Applied Economics, University of Cambridge, Queens' College, Cambridge, December.

Loomes, Graham (1991), 'Evidence of a new violation of the independence axiom', *Journal of Risk and Uncertainty*, 4(1), pp. 91–108.

Loomes, Graham, Chris Starmer and Robert Sugden (1991), 'Observing violations of transitivity by experimental methods', *Econometrica*, 59(2), pp. 425–39.

Loomes, Graham, Chris Starmer and Robert Sugden (1992), 'Are preferences monotonic? Testing some predictions of regret theory', *Economica*, 59(233), pp. 17–33.

McIntyre, Michael (2000). Goodhart's law. http://www.atm.damtp.cam.ac.uk/people/mem/papers/LHCE/goodhart.html.

Mehrling, Perry G. and Roger J. Sandilands (eds) (1999), *Money and Growth: Selected Papers of Allyn Abbott Young*, London: Routledge.

Miller, D. (1995), 'Commodities and consumption', *Annual Review of Anthropology*, 24, pp. 141–61.

Moore, B.J. (1978), 'A post Keynesian approach to monetary theory', *Challenge* 21(4) September–October, pp. 44–52.

Moore, B. J. (1979), 'The endogenous monetary stock', *Journal of post Keynesian Economics*, 2(1), 49–70.

Moore, B. J. (1981), 'The difficulty of controlling the money stock'. *Journal of Portfolio Management*, 7(4), Summer, pp. 1–14.

Narens, Louis and R. Duncan Luce (1987), 'Meaningfulness and invariance'. In J. Eatwell, M. Milgate, and P. Newman (eds), *The New Palgrave: A Dictionary of Economic Theory and Doctrine*, New York: Macmillan Press, pp. 417–21.

Needham, Joseph and Tsien Tsuen-Hsuin (1959), *Science and Civilization in China. Volume 5, Chemistry and Chemical Technology. Part 1, Paper and Printing*, Cambridge: Cambridge University Press, p. 48.

Patinkin, Don (1956), *Money, Interest, and Prices*, Evanston, Ill.: Row, Peterson.

Reinhart, Carmen M., and Kenneth S. Rogoff (2008), "Is the 2007 U.S. subprime crisis so different? an international historical comparison," *American Economic Review*, 98(2), pp. 339–44.

Robinson, J. (1943), 'Creating money', *Accountancy*, 54(1), pp. 64–5.

Runde, Jochen (1990), 'Keynesian uncertainty and the weight of arguments', *Economics and Philosophy*, 6(2), pp. 275–92.

Runde, Jochen (1994), 'Keynesian uncertainty and liquidity preference', *Cambridge Journal of Economics*, 18(2), pp. 129–44.

Sawyer, Malcolm (2003). 'Kalecki, Keynes and the post Keynesian analysis of money' published as 'Kalecki, Keynes et l'analyse post-keynesienne de la monnaie' in Pierre Piegay and Louis-Philippe Rochon (eds) *Théories Monétaires Post Keynésiennes*, Economica ISBN 2–7178–4614-X pp. 83–98.

Sawyer, Malcolm (2009), 'Teaching macroeconomics when the endogeneity of money is taken seriously', in G. Fontana and M. Setterfield (eds), *Macroeconomic Theory and Macroeconomic Pedagogy*, London: Routledge, pp. 131–43.

Sawyer, Malcolm (forthcoming), 'Endogenous money and the tyranny of demand and supply', in Louis-Philippe Rochon (ed.), *Post-Keynesian Monetary Theory Horizontalism and Structuralism Revisited: Reflections and Development*, London: Edward Elgar.

Samuelson, Paul Antony (1947), *Foundations of Economic Analysis*, Cambridge, Mass.: Harvard University Press.

Scarf, Herbert E (1981a), 'Production sets with indivisibilities, Part I: generalities', *Econometrica*, 49(1), pp. 1–32.

Scarf, Herbert E (1981b), 'Production sets with indivisibilities, Part 2: the case of two activities', *Econometrica*, 49(2), pp. 395–423.

Scarf, Herbert E (1986), 'Neighbourhood systems for production sets with indivisibilities', *Econometrica*, 54(3), pp. 507–32.

Scarf, Herbert E (1994), 'The allocation of resources in the presence of indivisibilities', *The Journal of Economic Perspectives*, 8(4), pp. 111–28.

Schulz, Eric (2000), *The Marketing Game: How the Best Companies Play to Win*, London: Kogan Page.

Simmel, Georg (1900, second edition 1907), *The Philosophy of Money*, translation by Tom Bottomore and David Frisby (1978), London: Routledge and Kegan Paul.

Simon, Herbert A (1978), 'Rationality as process and as product of thought', *The American Economic Review*, 68(2), pp. 1–16.

Simon, Herbert A. (1982), *Models of Bounded Rationality*, vols 1 & 2, Cambridge, Mass.: MIT Press.

Smith, Adam (1776) *The Wealth of Nations*, London: Everyman (1910).

Strathern, Marilyn (1997), '"Improving ratings": Audit in the British University system', *European Review*, 5(3), pp. 305–21.

Temple, Robert (1986), *The Genius of China*, New York: Simon and Schuster.

Von Mises, Ludwig (1949, 1996), *Human Action*, Fourth edition copyright 1996 by Bettina B. Greaves (Irvington: Foundation for Economic Education) (first published 1949).

Weatherson, Brian (2002), 'Keynes, uncertainty and interest rates', *Cambridge Journal of Economics*, 26(1), pp. 47–62.

Weintraub S. (1982). 'Money-demand motives: a reconsideration', *Économique Appliquée*, 35(3), pp. 361–76.

Wicksell, J.G.K. (1901), *Lectures on Political Economy, Volume 1*, (translation by E. Classon, published by Routledge, Kegan and Paul, 1934).

Williamson, Philip (1984), 'A "bankers' ramp"? Financiers and the British political crisis of August 1931', *English Historical Review*, 99(393), pp. 770–806.

Young, Allyn Abbot (1929) 'The mystery of money', *The Book of Popular Science*. New York: The Grolier Society. Group IX Ch. 31: 4231–40. Reprinted in Mehrling and Sandilands (1999).

Zelizer, Viviana, (2006), 'Money, Power, and Sex', *Yale Journal of Law and Feminism*, vol. 18, p. 303, 2006; Princeton Law and Public Affairs Working Paper No. 06–009. Available at SSRN: http://ssrn.com/abstract=944055.

Index